**Illinois Central College
Learning Resources Center**

Frontier Women

FRONTIER WOMEN

The Trans-Mississippi West
1840–1880

JULIE ROY JEFFREY

CONSULTING EDITOR

Eric Foner

American Century Series

🕮 HILL AND WANG NEW YORK

A division of Farrar, Straus and Giroux

Library of Congress Cataloging in Publication Data
Jeffrey, Julie Roy. Frontier women.
(American century series)
Bibliography: p. Includes index.
1. Women—The West—History. 2. Frontier and pioneer
life—The West. I. Title.
HQ1438.W45J43 1979 301.41'2'0978 79–12279
ISBN 0–8090–4803–5 ISBN 0–8090–0141–1 pbk.

FOR

———————————

Chris, Michael, and Sophia

Acknowledgments

During the years of working on this book, I accumulated more than my fair share of scholarly debts, and it is now time to thank those who so generously helped me. Both David William Cohen and John Walton provided me, at different times, with a quiet place to work; without these hideaways, the book would have taken much longer than it did. Many of my early research questions were answered by Douglas Martin, who also assisted me in planning research trips. I appreciate the help over the early hurdles. Judy and Richard de Neufville, Tom and Dorothy Haskell, and Peg and Bob Peters were hospitable and patient during extended research visits. Without them, doing the research would have been far less enjoyable than it was. Maureen Ursenbach Beecher, historian of The Church of the Latter-day Saints, came forward to help an unknown scholar and assisted me with the chapter on Mormon women. I thank her for her good advice and support. My colleague, Jean Baker, and my friends Peter Frederick, Bob Peters, and Peter Stearns all read the manuscript and gave helpful and direct criticism. The book is far better than it would have been without their comments. Finally, Ron Walters helped me along at every stage of the project, and as he knows, I owe much to him.

My publisher, Arthur Wang, and my editor, Eric Foner, were patient, critical, and encouraging. It has been a pleasure to work with them. Over the last years, Goucher College both understood my preoccupation with pioneer women and generously supported my work.

My greatest thanks are reserved for my husband, Chris, who coped at home during my many research trips and days at the library, and for my children, Michael and Sophia, who were interested in the project and understanding of the pressures a book can cause. It is because of their understanding and support that I have dedicated my book to them.

Contents

INTRODUCTION

From the earliest years of this country's history, Americans turned their backs on their homes and headed for the frontier. The frontier's location crept west toward the Mississippi as pioneers slowly cleared the wilderness and tamed it. By the 1840's, pioneers had pushed their way across the Mississippi to claim areas just west of the river; half the continent still lay before them. In the next four decades, the tempo of the westward movement quickened. Waves of emigration swept over the prairies and plains to the West Coast, then rolled back and began to trickle into the unsettled areas between the Mississippi and the Pacific. Between 1841 and 1867, the years of heaviest traffic on the overland trails, 350,000 traveled by wagon to California and Oregon. Many more went part of the way, to destinations like Salt Lake City and Colorado. With the completion of the transcontinental railroad in 1869, the journey west became easier and the frontier ever more alluring. By 1880, that half of the continent which forty years earlier had contained less than 1 percent of the nation's people boasted over 20 percent of the population. Finally, during the decade of the eighties, eager pioneers pushed out beyond the hundredth meridian into some of the most inhospitable and unpromising of the unclaimed lands which stretched from the Dakotas to Texas. Many of them would retreat, defeated by the hostile and arid plains frontier. By 1893, though uninhabited areas in the trans-Mississippi West remained, most agreed with historian Frederick Jackson Turner that the era of the frontier had finally come to an end.

The frontier fascinated Americans from the beginning with its promise of adventure and the opportunities it seemed to offer to acquire land, to find health or gold, and to enjoy religious freedom. Historians, sharing the nation's interest in the frontier, tried to explain its importance for American character, culture, and institutions. It was the historian who had proclaimed the end of the frontier, Frederick Jackson Turner, who provided the most compelling and influential interpretation of the frontier's significance. As Americans moved from east to west, Turner argued, the new environment gradually weakened inherited culture and forced them to create new institutions and new values appropriate for a new country. Democracy, nationalism, and individualism all took their distinctive form on the frontier and contributed to the development of a unique American character.

Although Turner's hypothesis came under heated attack in the 1930's, those who attempted to prove or disprove parts or all of his interpretation in the following decades gave little thought to Turner's focus. When Turner wrote of pioneers and speculated on the interaction between pioneers and the wilderness, the pioneers he had in mind were men: fur traders, miners, cattlemen, and farmers. The historians who reexamined Turner's thesis by and large retained this male perspective. Some noted, in passing, that the frontier produced the new democratic woman as it had fostered the new democratic man and pointed to victories for female suffrage there. A handful briefly contrasted the adventurous male pioneer with his presumably passive and long-suffering wife. Few paid much attention to the records left by the women themselves. Indeed, most historians overlooked the women altogether, never stopping to consider that their work omitted the experiences of almost half the pioneers crossing the Mississippi.

This book seeks to remedy the neglect. Migration was a family affair, and one cannot understand the frontier without considering the experience of the young married women who made up the bulk of adult female emigrants, or of their daughters. Nor can one approach the study of pioneer women without considering their cultural perspective. The nineteenth-century frontier differed in many ways from earlier frontiers; for women some of the most significant differences stemmed from new ideas and expectations about their sex's role. Nineteenth-century society sharpl‚ distinguished between the world of men and the world of women, and defined women as agents of civilization and keepers of morals. It also created new standards for female behavior, standards which the twentieth century has often seen as restrictive or Victorian. How these views of woman's role and new social norms affected women's experience in the wilderness becomes a central question for the historian who seeks to remedy the general neglect of women in the West.

If (as Turner believed) the move to the frontier meant the abandonment of civilization by frontiersmen, what did it mean for their wives and daughters, who presumably thought themselves responsible for civilizing the wilderness? Although this book is not bound by Turner's interpretation, the examination of pioneer women obviously provides an opportunity to test his and others' hypotheses about the West, to refine and expand them. Did the West, for example, offer women any special economic or political opportunities as Turner and others have argued it did for men? Did living on the frontier result in the shattering of familiar norms or in the strengthening of them? Did women play a part in the process of mediating between culture and environment and in building new communities on the frontier? And what did the Western experience mean for them?

These are some of the questions which this book addresses. But there are other specific concerns as well. Women's participation in the westward movement provided a test for the power of nineteenth-century beliefs about woman's place. Although these conceptions seemed farfetched on the frontier, even counterproductive, they lost little potency, for they helped women hold on to their sexual identity and offered them hope of an ever-improving life. Ideology proved to be as pervasive as it was powerful. Pioneer women's records suggest the extent to which ideology seems to have crossed class and regional lines. Historians of the nineteenth century have concluded that urban middle-class women in the East readily accepted the new definitions of woman's place emerging in the first decades of the century but have been uncertain about how far down the social scale these ideas penetrated. The many primary sources used for this work reflect the views of literate American women from different regions and backgrounds. Pioneer women most recently from the Midwest and upper South and often from rural or small-town backgrounds left the most records. They rarely belonged to the lowest social class; those on the bottom of society could not afford to emigrate. Many came from the middle class. But internal evidence suggests the lower-class origins of at least some of the women and almost all of the Mormon pioneers. Their records show wide acceptance of domestic ideology and support for new standards of female behavior. Why this ideology was so attractive to this mixed group merits exploration.

A few words should be said about what the book is not. The book is not about the many immigrant women who went west, nor does it cover the experiences of native American women, black women, or Spanish American women in the West. Although historians have neglected all of these, the scope of this work necessitated focusing on the thousands of white American women going to the trans-Mississippi West in the decades of heavy migration between 1840 and 1880. Nor does the book give equal space to these women's husbands, brothers, and fathers, although it illuminates some of their experiences. Once again, the constraints of this work prevented a more comprehensive treatment of the men going alone or with their families to the frontier.

Nor does the book try to cover all the frontiers west of the Mississippi. The terms "frontier" and "West" are vague ones and rightly so, since one generation's western frontier was not the next's. Therefore, the focus is first on the agricultural frontier, which was located primarily in the Far West in the eighteen-forties, fifties, and sixties and then, in the seventies, in parts of the Dakotas, Nebraska, and Kansas. The focus then moves on to the mining frontier, which opened in California with the gold rush of 1849 and erratically jumped to Colorado, to the Pacific Northwest, and to the Black Hills of South Dakota. Finally, the urban frontier is examined. In addition, one chapter explores the Mormon frontier in Utah.

Evidence for the book thus comes from different places and different time periods but focuses on the two main stages of frontier development. During the first phase of frontier settlement, lasting anywhere from two or three years to perhaps ten, conditions were primitive and population scattered. All too often, accounts of frontier life suggest that this relatively brief period was the norm for an extended period of time. In fact, settlers came to the frontier quite rapidly, and during the second stage, social and economic conditions markedly improved. This period of community building eventually ended without fanfare as the community came more and more to resemble those to the east. The pioneer generation lived through both periods. It is their records which I have used, paying careful attention to the sequential nature of frontier life.

The evidence upon which this study draws varies. Over two hundred women's journals, reminiscences, and collections of letters, as well as a number of interviews, provide the basis for much of this work. Some of these are published. Most are not and may be found either in the Western collections of a few major libraries or in state historical societies. These repositories are listed in the bibliography. Clearly, the sources were written by only a few of the women going west. Most pioneer women were too busy to write much, while others probably agreed with Rachel Haskell, who thought the events of her life "so slight it is hard to keep the sum." It is, of course, the slight events which interest the historian who wishes to examine the experiences and feelings of ordinary women leading ordinary lives on the frontier. Although the number of sources are limited, they are varied in content and style. Together, I believe they give a good picture of the frontier experience for ordinary women. In addition to women's records, I have consulted men's accounts, legal records, scattered educational and church records, as well as some material on women's organizations. The quotations in the book retain the spelling and punctuation of the originals. A wide range of secondary sources also proved useful.

During the course of doing the research for this book and writing it, my attitude toward my subject shifted, and I think it is important to explain this shift. My original perspective was feminist; I hoped to find that pioneer women used the frontier as a means of liberating themselves from stereotypes and behaviors which I found constricting and sexist. I discovered that they did not. More important, I discovered why they did not. Though my own ideological commitment remains the same, I now have great sympathy for the choices these women made and admiration for their strength and courage. I have continually wondered whether any of us would have done as well.

Frontier Women

1

"Glimpses
of Western Life"

The March 1835 issue of the popular *Western Monthly Magazine* contained a poem entitled "The Emigrant Bride." Although "The Emigrant Bride" hardly lived up to the Cincinnati journal's literary aspirations, its awkward verses spoke directly and meaningfully to many of the magazine's female readers. For the poem described a familiar situation, one which captured some of the positive and negative aspects of women's participation in the westward movement. The first verse pictured a bride, joyously poised to accompany her new husband to the "far-off west." Her eager enthusiasm and willingness to start a new life on the frontier, however, gave way to grief as she realized that she was to leave her mother's grave, perhaps forever. Going west, then, meant leaving loved ones and familiar places, and these thoughts overcame the young woman, rushing "o'er her breast,/ In a heavy, whelming tide." Yet her anguish passed, as her dear friend and bridesmaid took on the daughter's duty and promised to care for the sacred gravesite. At the poem's end, the bride followed her husband with a clear conscience to her new home in the West.

Although the poem neatly resolved the conflicts between duty to mother and duty to husband, love for the old home, desire for the new (mother is, after all, dead and not inconsolably weeping on the threshold of the family homestead), it suggests the contrary emotions of joy and anguish which many women felt as they participated

3

in the national adventure of moving west. The emotional stress of departure on which the poem focused was, of course, only one of the experiences with which women would wrestle and which would influence the accommodation they would ultimately make to the frontier. Obviously, external factors, related to the new environment, played a part in shaping the response of women to pioneer life. Primitive living conditions, unaccustomed duties, all affected pioneer women in a variety of ways which were often just as obvious to themselves as to later commentators. But as "The Emigrant Bride" suggests, internal cultural factors were as crucial, if not so evident, in coloring women's adjustments to the frontier as the primitive environment and its hardships. New standards for female behavior emerging during the early nineteenth century and women's own expectations about their role in society helped to shape their reactions to the frontier. So, too, did the debate on the frontier's significance for American culture, which generated competing views of women's place in the westward movement.

The intellectual and cultural setting, then, distinguished the nineteenth-century female pioneering experience, for women now came to the frontier with a cultural perspective which clashed with the realities of the frontier. Pioneer life forced women into "unfeminine" activities and undermined new concepts of womanhood. In the most fundamental way, as Western scholars have often pointed out in their analysis of the male pioneering experience, the frontier brought culture into conflict with environment. The resolution of women's particular conflict could take one of several forms. Women might modify or even reject ideas of their place or, alternatively, inflate them to the point where they claimed for themselves the mission of civilizing the frontier. Or, despite adverse circumstances, women might cling to familiar ideas hoping for a time when they might reassert them and give them meaning once more.

An analysis of nineteenth-century women's pioneering experience, then, begins with the ideas of "womanhood" that emerged in the early decades of the century. Economic changes triggered intellectual ones. The development of a market economy and the beginning of industrialization in the Northeast late in the eighteenth century separated the sexes by transforming the place and nature of work. Put more simply, economic changes ended a home system of production involving the whole family and began one involving men and a few single women working away from home. The new workplace of factories, shops, and businesses increasingly emphasized disciplined work styles and valued production, rationality, time, money. At home, however, women continued to labor in an unstructured, loose, and sociable manner. Home became more and more distinct from the male workplace.

As the approaches to work changed, and as the places where men and women labored diverged, the value and significance of women's work decreased. Though often toiling long and hard, middle-class women no longer performed tasks which were economically central to their families; they rarely produced vital goods or earned much money. As women's activities became less important to their family's financial position, female prestige suffered. The initial impact of a market economy and industrialization on the position of women, then, was to make it marginal.

Although these changes (which here have been schematized) were most obvious among the urban middle classes in the industrializing Northeast in the early decades of the century, farm women, still the majority of American women, were also affected. The increasing availability of manufactured goods after 1810 reduced the importance of female home manufacturing, even though the farm family continued to work as a unit. Moreover, as farmers began to produce cash crops for regional markets, the proportional value of women's labor in the family declined. By 1820 the recognition of the new situation was embodied in the language and thus suggested its general applicability. The female world was more and more often described as "woman's sphere," to reinforce the notion of the distinction between a superior male world and a subsidiary female world.

To compensate for women's shrinking economic role, Sarah Hale, editor of *Godey's Lady's Book*, popular writer and lecturer Catherine Beecher, and numerous others developed and publicized a sexual analysis which claimed women had significant cultural and social responsibilities.

Accepting the sexual polarization triggered by economic changes, the publicists defined the competitive public world of men as dangerous and destructive. Home, woman's sphere, was described as a place of "retirement" and "retreat," as a private spot where women provided men with the peace and quiet missing in the public world.

But women did more than provide domestic tranquillity for harassed men; publicists claimed women were responsible for communicating moral and cultural values, too often forgotten in the workplace, to their families. Husbands, exposed as they were to the hazards of the public world, were, of course, a major focus of feminine concern. "Who, like a guardian angel, watches over his interests, warns him against dangers, comforts him under trial; and by . . . pious, assiduous, and attractive deportment, constantly endeavors to render him more virtuous, more useful, more honourable, and more happy?" asked one popular preacher. Who else but a woman? And who else but women were to shape and mold the young, who would, in turn, determine the ultimate nature of society? A mother's failure to train her children to value restraint and to honor the moral virtues was the republic's loss. The proponents of domesticity insisted that women had the responsibility of maintaining values and ensuring social stability in a time of rapid change; women were ultimately responsible for the national welfare.

Characteristics unique to women helped them carry out their social mission. Unlike acquisitive and materialistic men, women were said to be "disinterested." Sheltered from the business world, possessing few material goods (the earnings and property of married women belonged to their husbands), women lacked resources and the reasons for pursuing selfish goals. They naturally devoted themselves to others. As feeling, rather than thinking, creatures, lacking egotism and pride, women were uniquely able to perceive and act upon moral truth. Their physical charms and affectionate nature provided them with useful advantages in their encounters with husbands and children.

Rather than being socially marginal, as economic changes suggested, women were responsible for the nation's moral health, the publicists insisted. But how could the claim of women's moral superiority be reconciled with the actual subordination of women in American society? Acknowledging the legal and social reality of male power, proponents argued that female submission was actually the symbol of female superiority and the mark of moral leadership. Women, like Christ, humbled themselves so they could be exalted. In any case, moral superiority depended on innocence, not knowledge; women had to be shielded from the corruptions of the world. Husbands were entitled, if not obliged, to guard women's purity so that they could fulfill their moral obligations to society.

Although the cult of domesticity evolved in the East and applied specifically to urban middle-class women there, its influence ranged beyond the confines of New England and the middle class. The ideas about women's nature which were gradually applicable to women of different classes and backgrounds were vigorously espoused by the middle and upper classes in all regions, who worried not only about the transformations stemming from industrialization and the growth of a market economy but about the dislocations caused by the westward movement, geographic mobility, and eventually immigration. Domesticity met these fears by isolating a source of social and cultural stability and glorifying it. Between 1830 and 1860, the new ideology became the standard, though it often bore slight resemblance to the actuality of individual women's lives.

In the rural South, for example, the new ideas about woman's sphere circulated by journals, sermons, novels, and speeches flourished. That well-born Southern women, at least, attempted to live up to the new cultural norms is clearly evident in their diaries and other writings. "To repress a harsh answer, to confess a fault, and to stop (right or wrong) in the midst of self-defence, in gentle submission, sometimes requires a struggle—like life and death; but these *three* efforts are the golden threads with which domestic happiness is woven; once begin the fabric with this woof, and trials shall not break or sorrow tarnish it," testified one woman.

In the South, it was not the new industrial order which explained the currency of domestic ideals but slavery. Domesticity was clearly relevant in a number of different settings. The clear demarcation of woman's sphere as separate and subsidiary was a necessary part of a social analysis which gave white males total authority over all others, especially over all blacks. Not surprisingly, some of the most avid exponents of slavery were also staunch publicists for the cult of domesticity. George Fitzhugh, defender of the peculiar institution, explained: "Woman naturally shrinks from public gaze, and from the struggle and competition of life." Thus, each woman should have "a husband, a lord and master, whom she should love, honor and obey." "In truth," Fitzhugh concluded, "woman, like children, has but one right and that is the right to protection. The right to protection involves the obligation to obey."

Although Southern women were thought to be "most deeply interested in the success of every scheme which curbs the passion and enforces a true morality," and although their task included restraining "man's natural vice and immorality," the emphasis on obedience suggests that women's social role was severely restricted by the presence of slavery and the need for conformity. The Southern version of domesticity ran the risk of becoming nothing more than a glorification of female charm and gentility, leaving woman as merely "the most fascinating being in creation . . . the delight and charm of every circle she moves in." Many Southern novels of the pre-Civil War period portrayed women as marginal ornaments, suggesting that at least a segment of Southern society understood domesticity in this way.

Of course, a similar interpretation of women's role existed in the North. Even though domestic propagandists stressed the significance of the female sphere and described women's duties as essential to the health and moral well-being of society, the catalogue of approved female characteristics could be translated into a model of female behavior that could become an end in itself. The image of feminine conduct could easily become the most meaningful message for those women who, in truth, found little productive work to do in their homes or opportunity for transforming either their families or society. An examination of the popular *Godey's Lady's Book* shows that, despite editor Sarah Hale's dedication to the goal of carrying "onward and upward the spirit of moral and intellectual excellence in our own sex, till their influence shall bless as well as beautify civilized society," there was a growing emphasis on fashion, manners, and romanticism to which women responded by buying the magazine. Gentility, which many of the women's magazines espoused, could become a mask for fashionable idleness and superficiality.

Women's magazines, which carried these messages to female readers all over the country, had, by the 1830's and '40's, become prime vehicles through which the ideology of domesticity spread. The development of inexpensive printing techniques during the early nineteenth century had enabled magazines to become an important medium of cultural communication. New presentations of female behavior were easily and cheaply available in magazines even in rural and frontier areas. Significantly enough, the pioneer thrust into the Midwest was accompanied by a rash of periodicals for women, originating not in the East but in the Midwest itself. Magazines for the general public, speeches, and printed sermons also agreed upon woman's mission, her nature, and her most desirable characteristics. Although one can never be sure how far down the social order these views extended, it seems likely they were widely accepted at different social levels. Those who never came into contact with middle-class literature, for example, could find woman's sphere clearly described in their schoolbooks. After the Bible, more Americans read textbooks than any other kind of printed material. In 1840, 40 percent of all white children between the ages of five and nineteen were in school. By 1850, the percentage had risen to over 50 percent. Their school texts portrayed self-sacrificing domesticated women and described suitable female behavior in detail. A woman's "voice is gentle; her pronunciation is delicate; her passions are never suffered to be boisterous . . . she never foams with anger; she is seldom seen in any *masculine* amusement." Female scholars discovered their destiny would be the care of a husband "with tenderness . . . to recompense his care with soft endearments." For those who could read, and by 1860 the white literacy rate was 90 percent, the messages were consistent, clear, and available in a number of forms.

Geographic mobility, aided by improved transportation in the first decades of the century, also facilitated the spread of ideas.

Pioneer families, often moving three or four times, were, in fact, carriers of domestic ideology. Existing diaries, letters, and reminiscences of pioneer women, generally married, from differing economic strata but usually coming most recently from small-town and rural areas in the Midwest, show remarkable acceptance of domesticity.

Of course, assenting to ideas was not the same as living up to their prescriptions. Domesticity described the norms and not the actual conduct of American women. There was considerably more variety in the behavior of women than ideology would suggest. Still, norms were important because they established the behavioral context for those who tried to reject them as much as for those who attempted to realize them. They shaped personality and colored expectations. For many women the cult of domesticity provided a psychologically compelling meaning for their lives.

Some of the psychological gratification which domesticity provided stemmed from the claim of woman's moral superiority. But other satisfactions existed as well. As women were increasingly seen to have duties and qualities different from men's, and as woman's sphere was portrayed as equal if not, perhaps, superior to man's, female friendships took on a special meaning. Theory suggested that men were driven by base carnal passions and unsuited to be women's companions. Women were the best companions for one another. The reality of many women's lives supported theory. The separation of the male and female worlds and the shift in women's status often gave women more in common with each other than with men. Shared experiences and shared perspectives made female friendships more central for many women than their relations with their husbands, even though domesticity suggested that women were to devote their lives to the well-being of husband and children. There is evidence to suggest that many women found security and well-being through their relationships with other women.

If female companionship took on added importance in the structure of women's lives, so, too, did female association on a wider scale. The logic and reality making individual women friends brought them together in voluntary female associations, which mushroomed between 1800 and 1830. Within the female benevolent society, women found a congenial peer group and tasks especially suited to their moral nature. Protestant clergymen supported these female associations, with their religious and charitable goals, and fostered women's special ties with Protestantism. Although voluntary associations were, in one sense, a natural outgrowth of domesticity and American religious life, they had far-reaching implications, by proclaiming that women had some public duties and religious responsibilities outside the family circle. Moreover, no matter what the organization's purpose was, the mutual association of women helped to establish a sense of collectivity and the belief that women as a group had distinct interests which men might not share. As women in the 1830's added specific moral concerns like the abolition of slavery and prostitution to their interest in missionary and benevolent work, the possibility of conflict with the male world and a sharpened sense of sexual identification increased.

Whatever individual women understood by domesticity and whatever they did to realize it in their own lives, the new ideology provided them with a comprehensible place in a changing world. But emigration to the West seemed to threaten it. As families moved into the wilderness, they moved into a world bearing little resemblance to the one they had left. Far from the city marketplaces and factories, far from the country peddler with his pack of manufactured goods, the pioneer family had to become self-sufficient. Much of the model of appropriate female behavior had to disregarded. As all family members worked to feed, clothe, and protect themselves, pioneer women regained the economic importance which most women in settled areas had lost. And although the sex division of work generally remained, necessity could cause a blurring of sexual boundaries. Pioneer women's lives were less rigidly circumscribed than domesticity allowed and their activities suggested the flaws in its analysis of woman's nature. Yet, if their ability to work alongside men suggested developing a new understanding of woman's place, there were potential losses, one being that "delicacy in woman . . . the most powerful enemy to the barbarism of man" which nineteenth-century society defined as necessary for progress.

On the one hand, the reality of frontier life suggested problems in the cult of domesticity. A more flexible definition of woman's place, however, threatened to rob women of their claim to moral superiority, which resulted from the rigid separation of the spheres. On the other hand, the cult of domesticity, with its insistence on female service, could be stretched to expand women's moral and cultural responsibilities. If women served families and society by maintaining social values, molding behavior, and preserving culture (tasks men had abandoned by entering the marketplace), the necessity of creating a new society in the West could be seen logically as theirs, not men's. Rather than being guardians of culture and morality, women might become creators.

That some women, at least, anticipated that the West would provide just such an opportunity for maximizing their social and cultural responsibilities is clear. As emigration to the West was recognized as one of the nation's greatest challenges, there was a conscious attempt to capture the teaching profession. The schoolroom was of paramount importance, many believed, in the attempt to civilize the West. Catherine Beecher, a prominent figure in the movement, propagandized tirelessly both for increasing the support for Western education and for restructuring the teaching profession to favor women. Backed by the American Lyceum, in 1835 Beecher began her campaign to send groups of women teachers to the West. In the following years, Beecher made a convincing case, warning that Western children were growing up without the benefit of either a practical or a moral education. As many as 90,000 teachers were needed, she suggested, if the tides of barbarism were to be pushed back. From a practical point of view, few teachers would be men. For, "it is chimerical to hope," said Beecher, that men would respond to the call "when there are multitudes of other employments that will . . . lead to wealth." Teaching did not pay enough for men, but it did for "disinterested" women. Thus, Beecher concluded, "it is woman who is fitted by disposition and habits and circumstances, for such duties, who to a very wide extent must aid in educating the childhood and youth of this nation."

Theoretically, Beecher's proposal was a logical, economical extension of the cult of domesticity. The teacher was a kind of mother;

teaching represented "the road to honourable independence and extensive usefulness," because a woman would never find it necessary to "outstep the prescribed boundaries of feminine modesty." Dealing as she would with the world of children, not the world of men, retaining all her natural graces and virtues, the female teacher would be neither a threat to the position of women in general nor to society at large.

From other perspectives, however, Beecher's proposal was radical. She urged women to capture the profession and, once ensconced in the schoolroom, to reach out to shape their frontier communities. Teachers would, in fact, be crucial to the process of community building. "Soon, in all parts of our country," prophesized Beecher, "in each neglected village, or new settlement, the Christian female teacher will quietly take her station, collecting the ignorant children around her, teaching them the habits of neatness, order and thrift; opening the book of knowledge, inspiring the principles of morality . . . soon her influence in the village will create a demand for new laborers, and then she will summon from among her friends at home, the nurse . . . the seamstress, and the mantuamaker; and these will prove her auxiliaries in good moral influence, and in sabbath school training. And often as a result of these labors, the Church will arise, and the minister of Christ be summoned to fill up the complement of domestic, moral and religious blessing." Other women were even more explicit about the central cultural role women could play in their fledgling communities. "No clergyman, however well qualified, could have wrought such favorable changes in so short a time," one writer maintained, as a "young lady from New England" who taught school and who had an "unbounded, and almost transforming" influence in her community. Female voluntary associations, if carried to the frontier, had similar radical possibilities of capturing cultural and moral leadership. Emigration thus signified cultural and social opportunities for women.

Beecher's was not the only voice suggesting frontier life might modify woman's sphere. By the 1820's and '30's an abundant and readily available literature about the West joined a rich oral tradition. Though much of this material focused on the northwestern frontier of Ohio, Indiana, and Michigan, still in the process of settlement, rather than the unoccupied trans-Mississippi West, its message was less about place than about the significance of the frontier for American culture and society. During the first decades of the nineteenth century, many Americans wondered about the impact of the westward movement on American life and expressed their concerns by writing about the West. To the optimists, the West symbolized American growth and progress; the pessimists feared it represented the collapse of social stability and civilized values. Implicitly the literature raised questions about woman's place and mission on the frontier. Some accounts suggested the pioneer experience destroyed woman's sphere, others that it posed no threat to it or even inflated it. How influential the literature was in shaping the expectations of those women who would actually go west is impossible to know. Doubtless many were selective in what they read and absorbed. If expectations are difficult to measure, however, the messages are not.

Emigrants' guidebooks constituted one source of information with which most prospective travelers to the Far West were familiar. Commonplace between 1845 and 1865, the years of heavy overland emigration, the guides instructed emigrants how to take the long trip safely and efficiently. Prosaic in nature and form, they gave detailed information about equipment and average costs, and evaluated the different trails. Often they also included recent information drawn from letters and private journals. Although it is impossible to know whether women read the guides as avidly as their husbands, the fact that magazines like *Godey's Lady's Book* brought attention to them suggests their interest to the female reading public. As the reviewer of one guide told her readers, "This is one of the most useful books we have seen for a long time. The amount of practical information it embodies is immense, and possess what we Americans call a *cash value* . . . this volume is really worth its weight in gold," while she specifically noted that another was of particular interest "to the ladies." Some pioneer women recorded reading the books, though perhaps Lodisa Frizzell's account of devouring several of "the various guides of the rout to California" indicated she was more interested than most. Those women who did not read the books, however, could glean some idea of the messages by talking to husbands and by watching and aiding preparations.

On the most obvious level, the guides all but ignored women as they conveyed a wealth of practical information to the men in charge of the undertaking. This neglect suggested that, during the trip at least, women were at best irrelevant and at worst in the way. Certainly the descriptions of the course of the journey indicated that women, who were so closely linked with civilization and its values, were out of place. For emigrants would enter "a state of nature, amid the confused, revolving fragments of elementary society," a society in which they would be "surrounded only by . . . herds of wild beasts of prey, and danger and death." In this primitive and hazardous world also roamed Indians characteristically portrayed as both crafty and vicious. "They use every conceivable artifice at times, to elude the vigilance of the sentinels," warned a popular guidebook. On the journey west, then, civilized restraints were unknown. Obviously an aggressive man with "a good gun; at least, five pounds of powder, and twenty pounds of lead . . . prepared for any warlike emergency . . . [and] with the requisite energy and courage" was the model emigrant. The guides' advice on traveling light ("Do not encumber yourself with anything not absolutely essential to your comfort") reinforced the notion that women and their world were encumbrances. Too many belongings threatened the success of the trip by slowing down the pace. The significance of "home" and things from home which nineteenth-century culture believed helped to shape and civilize the family was rejected under the pressure of "long and arduous expeditions."

Yet if guides generally saw women as burdens, there was an occasional hint that the "gentle" sex would take on a vital role. Although women were usually not overtly discussed in the guides, provisions, appetites, and health were. Each guidebook specified what food emigrants should buy for the four-month journey, analyzed the size of appetites, and discussed the planning and cooking of meals. As for health, the guides warned that many would come "down with sickness, mostly bilious complaints," during the trip. Recovery was essential, since "in many places the wagons will have to be forced up the ascent or ravines by manual force." Here were tasks for women, but hardly for those who were soft and genteel. The trip entailed strenuous work for women, cooking, caring for the sick, perhaps even carrying wagon baggage up and down mountains. Women had to be ingenious (a "good pickle" could be made of a "prairie pea"; the limited number of cooking utensils presented culinary challenges), healthy, and strong. They could expect to eat twice as much as they did at home and anticipate "being subjected to continued and regular exercise, in the open air, which gives additional vigor and strength." The trip west was no place for a fragile lady.

The wild world into which emigrant wagon trains ventured would physically transform women into robust, hardy creatures and give them tough, crucial duties. Yet in the course of the trip, several guides suggested, conventional female attributes might come in handy. As *The Prairie Traveler* pointed out, "On long and arduous expeditions *men* are apt to be *irritable* and *ill-natured,* and oftentimes fancy they have more labor imposed upon them than upon their comrades." Contentious and ill-natured behavior threatened the success of the entire venture and those possessing "the greatest forbearance under such circumstances" deserved "all praise." "Cultivate a spirit of civility and accommodation," *The Emigrants' Guide to California* proposed. "Let there be no contention or intrigues in your camp. If dissensions break out . . . separate peaceably." Although men could be peacemakers, thus winning "all praise," and contribute "largely to the success and comfort of an expedition," nineteenth-century society had judged it woman's task to restrain men, to "lead and guide" them. A perusal of guidebooks suggested to women readers that they must develop male characteristics of strength, resilience, and resourcefulness to survive the trip and also to rely on their female qualities to soothe and socialize men, and to ensure social stability on the way west.

Women were to understand that they were to be all things to all people. Though such a message might well be disconcerting, the guides always offered the promise that any adjustments women made would be short-lived. For the books all presented a rosy picture of a pioneer West fast civilized. It took only a little foresight and imagination to see the frontier to which the emigrants traveled transformed. Wilderness would soon exhibit "all the enjoyments and luxuries of civilized life . . . numerous churches, magnificent edifices, spacious colleges and stupendous monuments." The West would boast of all the East had, and more. "Ignorance, superstition and despotism" would inevitably disappear forever, "before the march of civilization."

Guidebooks were, of course, only one form of reading material to which women were exposed, and although they certainly must have created expectations about the pioneering experience, few women were like the California emigrant Lodisa Frizzell, who read more than one. There was much greater likelihood that women read more in the growing popular literature about the West which flourished after the 1820's.

Much of the popular literature focused on the figure of the hunter/fighter, often represented by the folk hero Daniel Boone. By 1830 several regional variations of the Boone story existed, with specific sectional concerns. Like the guidebooks, most of the stories treated women only in passing, for they were, at best, peripheral to the tale of adventure in the wilderness. Yet, once again, there was an implicit but obvious message about the significance of the Western experience for the female sphere and its values.

The Eastern interpretation of the Boone story suggested that section's misgivings about an emigration which both lured the young to leave home and seemingly threatened values considered fundamental to civilized society. C. Wilder's 1823 edition of the Boone tale, for example, conveyed the fear that Boone (and the move west which he symbolized) represented the negative force of the wilderness with the resulting breakdown of society. Boone, Wilder pointed out disapprovingly, was "greatly prejudiced . . . in favor of the tawny inhabitants of the Western wilderness, whose manners and habits he did not hesitate to declare to the day of his death were far more agreeable to him than those of a more civilized and refined race." But in other versions of the story, there was an attempt to link the reality of emigration with the belief in the power of the section's values. In essence, writers, using frontier tales, insisted that Eastern values would dominate the westward movement. Thus, Boone became a symbol of civilization and a protector of "peaceable habitation[s]." In John Peck's 1847 *Life of Daniel Boone*, Boone, the hunter, was transformed into a domesticated creature, the model of a husband for the paragon of a wife who fulfilled herself as a true woman should, modestly and quietly. "His affectionate wife . . . was an excellent household manager," wrote Peck. When faced by one of her husband's departures, she "kindly and quietly consented to this separation, and called into requisition her skill as a housewife in assisting to provide the necessary outfit." Viewed through Eastern eyes, emigration had two possible outcomes. The earlier interpretations of the Boone material suggested social degeneration and implicitly the destruction of female values, the later the possibility of realizing these very values in a new environment.

In the South, there was much less interest in exploring the meaning of the westward movement through the figure of Daniel Boone. Western tales became the backdrop for stilted romantic plots in the hands of Southern writers. Boone was the aristocrat, his wife the genteel Southern lady with little control over events. As William Gilmore Simms, a novelist of the eighteen thirties and forties, pointed out, Boone, "in an age of chivalry—during the Crusades . . . could have been a knight-errant, equally fearless and gentle. That he would have been a Squire of Dames is very uncertain—but he loved his wife, and risked his scalp more than once to rescue beauty from the clutches of the savage." From this perspective, the West would be merely an extension of the prevailing Southern system and its ornamental and restrictive ideas of woman's place.

From the West came versions of the hunter story both more realistic in nature and more reflective of the oral myths of the pioneers themselves. Neither a natural aristocrat nor a domesticated family man, Boone became the man of action, the wilderness hero. Judge James Hall of Illinois, whose popular *Letters from the West* was published in 1825, described Boone as "the very prince of hunters." Explaining that the hero left the East, driven not by antisocial feelings (as early Eastern writers would have it) but by his love of the wilderness, Hall made it clear, nonetheless, that Boone recognized society's value. It was his understanding of civilization which led him to bring his wife, Rebecca, and their family into the wilderness. Rebecca, another model of the pioneer woman, shared her husband's love of the wilderness, although she helped domesticate it. Self-sufficient and hardy, she exhibited characteristics not generally included in the catalogue of domestic virtues. Above all, she was tough, resourceful, and courageous. When her husband was held in captivity, she rose to the occasion and "returned with her family to her father's house in North Carolina, braving the toils and perils of a journey through a wilderness of immeasurable extent and gloom." Other Western portrayals of the female pioneer prototype agreed. In 1835 the *Western Literary Journal and Monthly Review* published an article entitled "The Pioneer Mothers." The women going forth "as volunteers to act as hand-maids in rearing a nation in the wilds of the West" were at once heroic and noble. It was obvious that "they were not so refined, so deeply schooled in that which is delicate and beautiful," but "they had those [qualities] which were the developments of their nature's purity, uninfluenced by the fashion and artifice of society. We admit they were masculine, if you term that masculine, which prompted them to defend, aye die, for their husbands, their children."

To be both masculine and feminine at the same time was an uncommon message for the nineteenth-century female reader, but it did suggest that sexual distinctions would be blurred on the frontier. If some women found this interpretation troubling, they found the implications of the tales of Boone's alter ego, Davy Crockett, more so. *A Narrative of the Life of Col. David Crockett*, appearing in 1834, claimed to give Crockett's own account of his rise from poor frontier farmer to successful politician, land speculator, and hunter of wild beasts. Avidly interested in proving his prowess to the world, Crockett viewed women as merely another prize in the race for reputation and notoriety. Not surprisingly, he had three wives, who, far from being shapers of values, were insignificant in the story of his life and certainly far less important than the other symbols of his vaunted achievements, pelts, votes, and fame. The vulgarity of the swaggerer annihilated woman's sphere, while his sexuality threatened woman's purity and innocence.

That the West represented the threat of sexual vitality and violence was evident in the captivity genre, which identified the frontier with these qualities. Unlike other literature about the West, captivity narratives, which originated at the time of the early settlements in the new world and continued to be popular into the nineteenth century, frequently focused directly on women. In these accounts, whether actually or purportedly true, female captives underwent cruel and violent torments from the fiendish Indians. Readers were given their fill of sensationalism, but much of the dramatic impact of the tales stemmed from the uncertain fate of the women captives. Would they survive their experiences by losing their femininity altogether? Would they lose their purity by either rape or rape disguised as marriage to an Indian? Evidence on the sexuality of Indian men was only thinly concealed. As Elizabeth Hanson, former captive, noted, "The Indians are seldom guilty of any indecent carriage towards their captive women, unless much in liquor"—but who could count on Indians' sobriety? Finally, captivity tales raised the possibility that women might abandon white culture altogether and fight to stay with the adoptive tribe and family, as some in fact did.

Popular literature gave women conflicting hints about what their own experiences might be. Some tales characterized the West as the place where women would capitalize on their moral authority and participate in the transformation of the wilderness. But as the Western version of the Boone story made clear, this cultural task suggested the acquisition of "masculine" qualities, a disturbing message for some nineteenth-century readers. Finally, there was another even less appealing interpretation of the frontier, suggesting that the atmosphere of violence, cruelty, and sexuality victimized women in some way, rendering their sphere meaningless or ridiculous.

With so many interpretations of the cultural significance of the frontier available to literate women and to those women hearing the tales in their original oral form, it is intriguing to speculate what they actually made of it all. Although the numerous women who read or listened to stories, broadsides, poems, pamphlets, and novels about the West left little record of their thoughts, one clue to female perceptions is available. Articles, stories, novels, and poems written specifically by and for women treated the Western experience and, unlike stories about Daniel Boone or Davy Crockett, devoted full attention to the subject of women on the frontier. The number of these accounts suggests that numerous readers found the theme important and relevant, while the contents show how an influential group of women wished to interpret the West.

Women's literature often acknowledged the emotional impact of emigration. On the frontier, women could expect to "struggle with that feeling of isolation and loneliness which presses heavily on those who have severed all the endearing ties of home, where cluster those fond attachments only formed in youth." Each woman faced "many a sad hour" without her fond circle of friends, though, at best, a husband might become a "sympathizing friend." But women were hardly passive victims of fate. A song published in *Godey's Lady's Book* whose title and refrain repeated, "To the Prairie I'll Fly Not," pointed out that single women, at least, had options. They could refuse to go. "What, fly to the prairie? I could not live there, / With the Indian and panther, and bison, and bear; / . . . I'll not give my hand, / To one, whose abode's in so savage a land," the second stanza proclaimed, while the third disposed of the emigrant suitor, with a curt farewell. "Then tarry no longer."

Women's literature, whether fictional or "true," had a careful focus, as writers suggested that the West gave women the opportunity for influence and power. A favorite character, the pioneer mother and wife, was shown to be heroic and domestic. Danger, privations, and trials, duly acknowledged, became a means of realizing the female sphere. Mrs. Harper, an Ohio pioneer, for example, "was never known to yield to despondency, but with untiring energy exerted herself to encourage all within the sphere of her influence, teaching them to bear up against misfortune, and make the best of their home where their lot was cast. Her own family knew not, until the hardships of pioneer life had been overcome, how much she had endured." Truly, she was a "benevolent heroine." Nor did hardships force women to abandon the female sphere, for they were shown to have "a delicate sense of propriety" in both deportment and conversation. Though untutored, pioneer women learned from the Bible, wild birds, and even Indian powwows delightful manners and gentle ways. With the necessary addition of courage and heroism, each pioneer woman could be a perfect lady, "never be looked upon as . . . ordinary country-woman."

These supposedly realistic characterizations described pioneer women of the generation just passing away. Accounts of contemporary pioneering acknowledged the challenges to domestic ideology. Caroline Kirkland's series of books on the West, which appeared in the eighteen thirties, forties, and fifties, featured vignettes of "common-place people," and described incidents "in which the fastidiousness, the taste, the pride, the self-esteem of the refined child of civilization" might be "wounded by a familiar intercourse with the persons among whom he will find himself thrown." Yet despite customs which might appear at worst offensive and at best picturesque, Mrs. Kirkland assured her readers that "familiar intercourse" with rough-mannered frontier men and women had its compensating features. Women could expect, in time, to shape the lives and habits of their new companions. The "silent influence of example," she wrote, "is daily effecting much towards reformation in many particulars." Moreover, those who missed the comforts and niceties of civilized life could be "the first to attempt the refining process, the introduction of those important nothings on which so much depends." Finally, there was merit in being free "from the restraints of pride and ceremony." Too often women ensnared in genteel conventions lost sight of their true sphere and obligations. The West was a challenge for which true women were well equipped.

Moreover, the freedom of Western life meant that men would help women with their tasks. This did not imply a permanent confusion between the spheres. Generous male assistance would help realize the ideal of a harmonious home. For "if he is too proud or indolent to submit to such infringements upon his dignity and ease," Kirkland warned, "most essential deductions from the daily comfort of his family will be the mortifying and vexatious result of his obstinate adherences to early habits." If the conventional division of labor might collapse in the first stages of pioneer life, women need not fear they would become masculine. For men and women had different natures and, thus, different obligations. "To bring them into the same field of employment would be as absurd as to make the value of porcelain consist in its power to do the work of iron." Were women, for example, to do outside work as they did in European countries, they would lose their value in the eyes of society and their looks. "Their skin becomes shriveled, their complexions like coal, their features coarse and homely, and they fall into a premature decrepitude, more hideous than that of old age." Even worse, men finding little comfort and no refinement became barbarous overlords. Only by holding to "appropriate tasks" could women retain their beauty and exercise "just influence and power."

Those women who crossed the boundaries of their sphere could expect disaster. And the West, female writers insisted, did not demand this of women. Stories in *Godey's Lady's Book,* like "Beauty Out West: or How Three Fashionable Ladies Spent a Year in the Wilderness," or "May: The Squatter's Daughter," pictured genteel life not only flourishing on the frontier but even improving far from "the city with its vanities and false glare." The frontier offered a healthy and useful domesticity purged of the threat of vacuity. It provided "the truest and noblest life," with well-bred and marriageable youths, snug homes, and happy children, and the likelihood of a prosperous future.

If the frontier offered women benefits, one of them was appreciation, especially from their husbands. Without wives and lovers, men suffered deep depression. The fair sex, as a poem in *Ladies' Repository* pointed out, dispelled "the cloud of sadness . . . from [men's] soul[s]." It was women, poetess Lydia Sigourney insisted in her 1854 volume, *The Western Home,* who "strove, with still advancing skill,/ To make her home secluded bound / An Eden refuge, sweet and blest, / When, weary, he return'd for rest."

Women's literature was definite about the order of priorities in the West. If men gathered gold, one editorial observed, who was "to diffuse the wisdom which is more valuable than fine gold," and to instill the principles "of moral rectitude and social refinement" which could make the metal a blessing rather than a curse? Who else but women in their roles as mothers and teachers? Viewed from the female perspective, the moral and cultural success or failure of the venture west lay with women.

Gone, therefore, are the suggestions of female irrelevance, the loss of femininity, the threat of male sexuality. Literature by and for women consciously attempted to fit the Western experience into a framework which promised them the opportunity of fulfilling their social role. It shows an acceptance of social norms of domesticity and an expectation, or hope, that the norms could function on the frontier. The material is far more consistent in its treatment of the West than more general work about the frontier.

To point to the consistency in the literary approach to the role of women does not mean that women believed this interpretation corresponded to reality. They were familiar with the Boone and Crockett accounts and others. Many knew or heard folk songs about emigration which contained conflicting messages about the West similar to those which appeared in published form. Where women's literature was reticent about sex, for example, songs portrayed a frontier brimming with sexual vitality, illicit as well as licit, and indicated some confusion of sex roles. Despite what some women chose to believe, then, there were many cultural indicators during the decades of emigration to the Far West which suggested that the cultural and social framework established for women during the early decades of the nineteenth century might need modification and adjustment on the frontier. But, as the literature by and for women made clear, many women expected to resist the disintegrating forces of frontier life and hoped to realize and even extend their own social role. The goal was to shape the frontier in an image to their liking. Thus, a conflict between culture and environment was established even before emigration began. The tension would not work itself out before they left home, but the process would begin as families bade friends and parents farewell and set out for the West.

2

"Ladies Have the Hardest Time, That Emigrate by Land"

Many years after her overland journey to California in 1860 Southern-born Lavinia Porter found the experience as vivid in her mind "as . . . yesterday's events." The trip, she observed, had been difficult, so difficult that it was still "a constant source of wonder to me how we [women] were able to endure it." That she and so many other women survived the months of hardship suggested to Porter that her sex shared some important characteristics. "An American woman well born and bred," she wrote, "is endowed with the courage of her brave pioneer ancestors, and no matter what the environment she can adapt herself to all situations, even to the perilous trip across the western half of this great continent, ever ready to wander over paths which women reared in other countries would fear to follow."

Porter's choice of courage and adaptability as the traits characterizing American pioneer women suggests that emigration forced women to modify normal behavioral patterns. As she realized, the frontier, which for most women began as soon as they left home and friends, challenged conventional sex roles and accepted modes of behavior. During the five- or six-month ordeal on the Overland Trail to California and Oregon, thousands of women challenged domestic stereotypes by assuming male responsibilities and undertaking men's work. In extreme cases, when husbands became ill or died, women took charge of the whole venture of moving west. Just as women performed men's work, so too, at least occasionally, did men find themselves doing tasks which society defined as women's. The lines of differentiation between the sexes, theoretically and often actually so clear in a culturally established setting, blurred. The months on the trail offered women a taste of a West which could disrupt cultural arrangements between the sexes and question sexual ideology. It was an opportunity for women to question, to modify, even to challenge established stereotypes. Yet few women did so; most did not find it easy to throw off accustomed ways of thinking even when forced into new ways of behaving. Possibly the polarization of sex roles which cast women into the role of the dependent, if superior, sex made it psychologically difficult to create sexual alternatives even when the environment seemed favorable. More likely, the trail experience suggests that women found comfort and personal reinforcement in their own sphere and were reluctant to abandon it altogether, no matter what stresses and tensions existed within it, no matter how far short of its standards women's conduct was.

It is, of course, difficult to generalize about women's responses to the trail experience since so few left any evidence of their passage at all. As one emigrant pointed out, "Pioneer women were quite too busy in making history to write it." The majority of women as well as men lacked the time and perhaps the skills to keep a diary or journal. Those who did keep accounts of their trip probably agreed with Elizabeth Geer, an Indiana woman, who observed, "I could have written a great deal more if I had had the opportunity. Sometimes I would not get the chance to write for two or three days, and then would have to rise in the night when my babe and all hands were asleep, light a candle and write." Reminiscences written years after the trip supplement travel journals, but these must be used cautiously, since time often cast a rosy glow over events on the trail. Still, we may know more about pioneer women taking the overland routes west than we know about them before or after. Since the long journey was a major event, quite different from the three or four shorter moves many had made to other frontiers, women kept diaries or reminisced about it.

Then, too, men kept diaries about this significant adventure which also reveal information about women during the months of enforced and intimate interaction. For many men and women the trail saga constituted their only contribution to the historical record of the westward movement and, in fact, the only record of their own lives.

Their journals, which focused on the five to six months of travel, first along the valley of the Platte River, then through the South Pass to destinations in California or Oregon, described the most popular but not the only means of reaching the Far West. It was possible, if costly, to sail from East Coast or Gulf ports to Central America, cross by land, and then continue by ship to final destinations in the West, or to go by sea around Cape Horn. During the first year of the gold rush, about 40,000 of the 100,000 fortune seekers chose ships. But the majority always went by land. Between 1841 and 1867, the years of heaviest traffic on the trails, 350,000 took the overland route to California and Oregon; others traveled part of the way by trail. So heavy was the traffic that parts of the trail resembled a highway several miles wide. With the completion of the transcontinental railroad in 1869, traffic gradually declined, although wagons crossing the South Pass were reported as late as 1895.

During the decades of the eighteen forties, fifties, and sixties, the basic pioneer pattern diverged from the familiar one of moving from one area to the adjoining frontier to emigration to the Far West. Those who could afford to do so crossed half a continent to a destination two thousand miles from starting points like Independence, Missouri. The relative neglect of frontier close at hand was due to a number of factors. The depression of the late thirties and early forties hit the recently settled Mississippi Valley hard. The financial calamity was accompanied by bad weather, floods, and disease. Influenza, plague, chills, malaria, and yellow fever helped make the area uninviting, while propaganda from the West Coast painted the frontier there in rosy colors. California was the land of eternal spring and endless fertility, while Oregon possessed rich soil and peaceful natives. In any case, land directly to the West was still Indian country, closed to settlement, and considered unsuitable for farming. It was not until the seventies that pioneers pushed eagerly out onto the prairies of Minnesota, the Dakotas, Nebraska, and Kansas, and in the eighties that they moved to the chancy, arid frontier sweeping from the Dakotas and Montana on the north to Texas to the south. Finally, the trek to the Far West was clearly possible as emigrants in the early forties, testing the overland route, proved. In 1843 the first mass migration, helped by the return of good times, set out for Oregon. Each year thereafter saw more emigrants selling out and starting on their way to the coast. In 1847 the Mormons opened their own trail across the prairies. Eventually Salt Lake City would become a resting point for many of the emigrants headed for California.

Most of those who passed over the trail were young and often traveled with their immediate families or relatives. With the exception of the emigration of 1841 and the years during the height of the gold rush (1849–51), families rather than single people dominated the trail. In the forties, for example, approximately 50 percent of the emigrants were adult men, the other half women and children. After the excitement about California gold died down, the family pattern reappeared. Geographically, emigrants tended to come from rural and small-town backgrounds in the Midwest and upper South, although some hailed from the urban East or the newer cities of the Midwest. Many had moved several times before, however, often as children. The 1850 census of the Oregon Territory, revealing a cross-section of those who had emigrated, showed that almost half the adult men came originally from the East Coast, with only 11 percent born west of the Mississippi; most of the "native" Missourians were children of parents born elsewhere. The general composition of emigration, then, suggested a movement of families, many of whom had roots in the East.

Economically, emigrants were neither very rich nor very poor. Though family situations differed, all emigrants had to be financially solid enough to raise the substantial amount of cash necessary for the trip. Guidebooks estimated that emigration for four would come to over $600, although the sale of wagons and cattle at the trip's end might reduce final costs to $220. (A trip around the Horn was estimated at $600 per person.) Even those pushing out onto adjacent frontier land in the seventies and eighties required capital. Thousands began farming on the plains with *less* than $500, but the risks of doing so were high. Obviously emigration was not an option for the poor.

Women diarists, few when compared to the total number of women going west, seem representative of the mainstream overland migration. Most had lived most recently on Midwestern farms or in small towns there, though a few came directly from the East. Despite earlier moves to frontier settings (from Vermont to Indiana to Iowa to Oregon, for example), they were middle class in attitude and well acquainted with ideas of woman's sphere. It is, of course, true that there were other kinds of women on the trail, less obviously acculturated. Lavinia Porter, a Southern emigrant, described the rough and uncouth pioneers from Texas, Arkansas, and southwestern Missouri, the men blasphemers, the women "fitting mates for the men." She was not the only one to be disgusted with these emigrants, who, leaving little in the way of written records, cannot defend themselves. The trail experience may have differed by class or regional background, though how significant these differences were is impossible to determine. What we do know is what literate women thought and felt on the weary road west.

Their thoughts and emotions in the months preceding departure are, however, usually hidden. Most often their diaries start with the journey's beginning. Yet most must have suspected the arduous nature of the trip from their reading of guides and newspaper accounts. Folk music reinforced the theme of hardship. "The ladies have the hardest time, that emigrate by land, / For when they cook with buffalo wood, they often burn a hand; / And then they jaw their husbands round, get mad and spill the tea, / And wish the Lord, they'd be taken down with a turn of the di-a-ree."

Since emigration meant months of hard living, one wonders what motivated women to go west at all. Were they just dragged unwillingly by their men or did they participate in the decision? If they contributed to the decision, what were their reasons for doing so? Though the sources are meager, they do suggest some answers to these questions.

The major impulse behind emigrating appears to have been economic. To one Ohio woman, "going to the far west seemed like the entrance to a new world, one of freedom, happiness and prosperity," while a Southern woman candidly admitted the "imprudent financial speculations" and embarrassments which led to her family's decision. The West was a land of promise, though whether the promise was one of land, gold, or professional opportunity partly depended on the destination. An important secondary factor involved health and climate. "We were bound to search for a healthier and milder clime than Illinois," one emigrant woman explained, "to spend the remainder of our days . . . I do not in the least regret leaving the sickness and cold, sand piles and lakes . . . behind and am looking forward for the time to arrive when we may all get settled safely at the place of our destination." Other women focused specifically on their own health and their hopes for its improvement.

Men were, of course, expected to "make decisions," especially about economic matters, and the evidence suggests a pattern in which men brought up the subject of emigrating. Some women were taken by surprise, for, as one said, "the thought of becoming a pioneer's wife had never entered my mind." But this did not mean that women were passive spectators. Their style was to respond, to influence, even to argue. Certainly, there were enough women participating effectively in the decision-making process to pass into Western folklore. A popular folk song, variously entitled the "Wisconsin Emigrant," the "Kentucky Song" or the "California Emigrant," suggests the extent of female influence. In it, a farmer suffering hard times at home decides to go west. His wife, reluctant to emigrate, unwilling to accept his initial decision, offers one reason after another to change his mind. All fails until she points out, "Remember, that land of delight / Is surrounded by Indians who murder by night. / Your house they will plunder and burn to the ground, / While your wife and your children lie murdered around." Her appeal succeeds, and her husband gives up his scheme, confessing, "I never had thought of your dying before . . . you, my dear wife, are more precious than all." Other evidence corroborates female power to affect decision-making. Since the trip's success usually hinged on the participation of all family members, a wife's stubbornness could block her husband's plans. "All my father could do," wrote one woman, "was to read every item of

California news he could get and talk . . . for my mother would not be persuaded to undertake such a journey." Interestingly enough, this reluctant pioneer changed her mind only when her daughters and their husbands decided to emigrate for reasons of health. Even so, she insisted that their home be kept "unencumbered to return to in case we should not like California." The frequency with which marriage and emigration coincided suggests another facet of power. Whatever ideology had to say about the necessity of female submission, women felt free to disrupt male emigration projects and, because of the cooperative nature of pioneering or their single state, had bargaining powers. Of course, opposition to male schemes did not necessarily constitute a departure from female norms. Women, blessed with superior insight, had been told to direct and to influence their less sensitive husbands. The line between obstinacy and duty might well become blurred.

Others who shuddered at the idea of undertaking a "long and perilous journey" did not openly oppose their husbands. Their timid behavior reflected the standard interpretations of woman's nature at the same time that it highlighted an attempt to live up to the expected norms. For many women apparently forced themselves to acquiesce to the "dictates of duty." "My dear mother" did not oppose my father, wrote one daughter. "She tried to put down her fears for the perilous undertaking." Striving to act as a good wife, Abbey Fulkerath began her journal with these telling words: "Agreeable to the wish of my husband I left all my relatives . . . although it proved a hard task to leave them but still harder to leave my children buried in Milton graveyard but such is our lot on earth we are divided." There is no hint of resistance to her husband's plans.

But not all women were reluctant emigrants. Those who thought emigration "a romantic wedding trip," or who thought like Lydia Rudd—who wrote in her journal one May day in 1852, "With good courage and not one sigh of regret I mounted my pony"—were positive about the move west. Their support for emigration reveals that, despite an ideology assigning men the responsibility for making economic decisions, women also participated in decision-making and shared men's opportunism. "We had nothing to lose, and we might gain a fortune," one woman wrote, hardly sounding the disinterested female. The dream of easy circumstances often attracted women as strongly as it did men, even leading one woman to conceal her pregnancy and to suppress her fears about her health so that she could go west that year.

Lying at the heart of women's interest in the economics of emigration were contradictions in the concept of domesticity. Women, unsullied by material interests, were supposed to find fulfillment at home. Yet, their ability to do so depended in some measure upon their husband's economic success. Though ideology might proclaim that home was home, no matter how humble, most women knew better. Women wanted to live in easy circumstances in their own homes. All this took money. "Disinterested" women, therefore, were necessarily interested in economic questions, and in emigration if it seemed to offer a way of acquiring the resources needed for comfortable domesticity.

The vision of family life so central to domestic ideals also encouraged a positive female response to emigration. Mary Jane Hayden's explanation of the family decision to emigrate is revealing. When she learned her husband was contemplating a journey to California alone, Mary Jane told him she had resolved to go, too. "We were married," she said, "to *live together* . . . and I am willing to go with you . . . and under these circumstances *you have no right* to go where I cannot, and if you do, you need never return for I shall look upon you as dead." By insisting upon accompanying their husbands, women like Hayden showed how firmly they believed in the family and how determined they were that their husbands accept familial responsibilities. Letting a man go west alone, unless it were only to prepare a homesite, was a risky venture at best, even if the rationale was that of improving family finances. Women's magazines condemned gold fever because it unhinged men, making them feel "free as a bird" as they flew from "many a cheerful fireside . . . many a happy home." This "fearful curse" destroyed families and, in the end, the gold seekers themselves. Abandoning wives, children, and home meant "no fond arms wherein to rest . . . [a] cold brow as life fled!" So it was hardly surprising women willingly accompanied their husbands. "Where he could go I could," remarked one Missouri woman, while another pointed out, "It is the females that can improve your condition and make a home, and them alone."

Since the family provided meaning for women's lives and the basis for self-esteem, women might well wish to cooperate with emigration plans. How many were enthusiastic, how many reluctant, is unclear, since sources so rarely discuss the pre-trip scene. But those that do show a range of responses and suggest the need to avoid characterizing all women as reluctant emigrants. Of course, other factors also led to positive attitudes. The adventure and romance of emigration was appealing for some; a few mentioned their affection for their husbands. "I was very fond of my husband," recalled one, "and was nearly brokenhearted at the thought of the separation."

Missionary wives were a decidedly eager group of pioneers. To them the West was the means of realizing a religious vocation. This pattern of female commitment to religious work in the West became evident in the 1830's, when the first women participated in the short-lived attempt to convert Oregon's Indians. Early conversion experiences persuaded numerous single women that they must devote their lives to Christ. Since missionary societies generally frowned upon sending single women out into the mission field, however, they were relegated to teaching and good works at home unless they could find husbands. More often than one might expect, men who needed wives as assistant missionaries turned up; hasty proposals and marriages resulted. Although women might view such a marriage as part of a divine plan, the appearance of potential husbands was not entirely due to chance or God. Women like Almira David did pray "earnestly for some person who it appeared I was dependent on for going," but a network of friends and acquaintances often helped prayers come true. An Ithaca minister's letter to the mission board reveals the process of matchmaking at work. "A word in reference to their engagement and marriage," the pastor wrote. " 'Tis true their acquaintance had been very short—of but two or three weeks . . . But Mr. Gray came well recommended to the Rev. Samuel Parker, thro' whom he became acquainted with Miss Dix." Nor were the women themselves unresourceful. One young woman, who at twenty-six was considered an old maid, albeit one with a missionary enthusiasm, attended the General Conference of Congregationalists in Bangor, Maine. There she met a young man sharing her devotion to missionary work who, in turn, wondered whether "possibly his prayers were being answered in the person of this lady." After corresponding, the two married and set out for Oregon in 1856. Since Eastern missionary societies sent over 2,600 men to the West by mid-century, the number of enthusiastic wives was substantial.

In an April entry of his 1853 trail journal, Henry Allyn observed, "Miss Martha Wood wishes to go with us and we conclude to take her." Allyn's entry noted an unusual event on the trail, the single woman moving west without the protection of family or friends. Their motives are usually hidden. There are tantalizing references such as the one in the Bradley diary to "four lewd females" on the trail and occasional comments about young women moving west to join bachelor brothers. But certainly, whether they hoped to support themselves, find husbands, or just have adventures in the West, these women decided for themselves.

The motives of one group of single women—teachers—for going west are clearer. Like female missionaries, these women saw themselves as part of a national effort to save the West for Protestantism and civilization. Catherine Beecher's educational campaign, initiated in 1845 with her book *The Duty of American Women to Their Country*, helped to organize hundreds of these women to go west to teach. A group, formed at the Mt. Vernon Congregational Church in Boston in 1846, defined its goal as sending "competent female teachers, of unquestioned piety, belonging to the Congregational Churches in New England," to the West. Although sectarian aims were apparent, the group also recognized that it could provide "a merciful provision for hundreds of well-educated Christian young women, whose sex forbids their adventuring as their brothers do, and yet who, if such a Society will encourage them, and send them forth, may go cheerfully and understandingly right to the best spot for them in all that wide region." Acting as an agency for single teachers, the group sent 109 women west before merging in 1854 with the Board of National Popular Education, founded by Beecher in 1847. The board not only acted as an agency but also gave prospective teachers some job training. Although the religious mission was strong, the organization was nonsectarian. By 1858 it had sent over a hundred women across the Mississippi who, in turn, often found jobs for friends. The organization's work was publicized through magazines like *Godey's Lady's Book* and served as an informal stimulus for other women to leave home for a Western schoolroom.

The records of the Board of National Popular Education contain revealing applications from prospective teachers. Of course, no application was entirely candid; applicants provided the kind of information the board wanted to read. Candidates had to describe conversion experiences, for example, and to place their goals within a religious framework. So Augusta Allan told the board, "I humbly trust that I have sought, and experienced this change [conversion], and that my motives in going West, are a desire to benefit others, and to be benefited myself." Like Allan, most women said they wanted to be useful in a region they described as religiously and culturally destitute. But the women gave a variety of other reasons for wishing to go west which reveal not only their own situation but their expectations. Many of them were already teaching, and thought the frontier might provide more opportunity and even more money. They frankly acknowledged their financial needs. "Being dependent upon my own exertions," wrote Betsey Brownell, "I feel it necessary also to look at the subject, in another light, which I think is not inconsistent with the spirit of doing good." These applications reveal how industrialization was affecting single women in the East. No longer economically essential within their families, unmarried women found themselves in a hazardous world offering them few means of support beyond factory work, domestic service, and teaching. Teaching was the most respectable and offered means for independence; teaching in the West might be an improvement.

Women also spoke of their desire for a better climate and hinted at health problems. Some told the board of a long-time interest in emigration, for the lure of adventure could play a part for women just as it did for men. As one candidate explained, she was interested in the welfare of others, but she was also driven by the "love of adventure and desire to be acquainted with the manners and customs of the inhabitants of more distant parts." Taken together, these applications indicate that these unmarried working women had a variety of positive reasons for undertaking the journey west, ranging from the need to support themselves to the desire to see the world.

What evidence there is on women's motivation and involvement in planning the trip west, then, suggests the danger of viewing women solely as reluctant pioneers. This did not mean that they would not experience a sense of loss at leaving family and friends behind. Both sexes did. But it warns against describing women as passive victims of men's choices rather than as active participants in the process of emigration.

No matter how the decision to go west was reached, no matter how great or small a part women played in it, leave-taking was a traumatic experience. Weeks of activity preceded the day of departure and for some concealed the reality of leaving itself. Women were busy sewing, making dresses, sunbonnets, tents, wagon covers, and seeing their friends. As women attended to these female chores, men disposed of the homestead, either selling or renting it, and acquired the stock, wagons, and supplies the guides said were necessary. Finally, the moment came for farewells. Leave-taking occurred at home, or friends and relatives accompanied the emigrants for a day's journey. The occasion was usually a solemn and sad one as both the emigrants and the stay-at-homes contemplated the implications of the departure. "On the evening before [starting], the whole family, including my mother, were gathered together in the parlor, looking as if we were all going to our graves the next morning," one woman wrote. "There we sat in such gloom, that I could not endure it any longer, and I arose and announced that we would retire for the night, and that we would not start tomorrow morning, not until everybody could feel more cheerful."

Some diaries poignantly describe the tears shed by men and women alike as they set out. Others have terse, yet equally revealing, entries, like the one written by Amelia Knight, "STARTED FROM HOME." The very brevity conveys the emotion of the scene. Men and women both experienced a sense of loss. For the women, however, though emigration symbolized a means of realizing the domestic sphere, it also ripped away some of its supporting framework. True, the immediate and sometimes not so immediate family might remain intact when groups of relations and friends traveled west together. And equally true was the fact that women were socialized to expect the experience of losing family and friends when they married and moved away from mother, sisters, and friends. But this did not make it any easier to leave the current home with its familiar objects and rituals, with its groups of female companions and relatives who had contributed so much to one another's emotional life. And this move, unlike earlier moves to nearby frontiers, would separate friends by vast distances. It represented what well might be a permanent break. No wonder a deep sense of loss pervades the records. In her journal, Lodisa Frizzell asked herself, "Who is there that does not recollect their first night when started on a long journey, the wellknown voices of our friends still ring in our ears, the parting kiss feels still warm upon our lips, and that last separating word *Farewell!* sinks deeply into the heart. It may be the last we ever hear from some or all of them, and to those who start . . . there can be no more solemn scene of parting only at death." That women so often compared leave-taking to death was at once a realistic assessment that it was "not at all probable that we ever will meet again on this side of the dark river," as well as a symbolic recognition that the emotional void was like death itself. As for what lay ahead, it was "so far away and vague, that it seemed very unreal" to many of the women at the outset of the journey. What was real was what was behind.

Women's diaries, more than men's, tended to focus on the friends at home. An early entry in Anne Booth's journal suggests many others. "Nothing can atone for the loss of society of friends." The trip was hard enough, women wrote, without having "our hearts torn by the loss of dear ones." Although their marriage might be an affectionate one, a husband did not usually compensate for the loss of female friends. Men, too, of course, missed old companions, but Asahel Munger's reaction to his wife's grief typifies the male point of view. "This day has been rather long and lonesome to E," he wrote. "She thought much of home—friends—prospects—& present condition.

I tried to have her get above these things." Men did not dwell on absent friends in their journals; women did. Perhaps the long hours women spent sitting in wagons while men herded cattle, forded rivers, and drove wagons encouraged them to reminisce about absent friends.

Most women, however, did try to "get above these things." As they catalogued each sign of the passing of civilization, women coped with their sense of desolation by reproducing aspects of the world they had left behind. Thus, women arranged their wagons, writing in their journals of the little conveniences they had fixed, the pockets in the wagon's green cloth lining which held "looking-glasses, combs, brushes, and so on," the rag carpet to keep the floor of the tent snug at night, the bedding, sleeping, and dressing arrangements. As one woman explained, she was busy making "our home" comfortable so that there would be little time "for that dreaded disease, 'home-sickness.' " Another hoped to maintain some continuity by dressing as neatly on the trip as she might at home, in a blue traveling dress with white collar and cuffs rather than homespun, linsey-woolsey or calico.

These attempts to reproduce the rudiments of a home setting and to perpetuate a sense of the familiar, though they might appear trivial, were not. Publicists of domesticity had encouraged women to believe that the physical arrangements of their homes exerted a powerful influence over their families. The makeshifts of the journey were an unconscious way of asserting female power and reassuring women of their sexual identity. And, of course, the objects symbolized an entire way of life temporarily in abeyance. When her husband grumbled about the quantity of her baggage, Lucy Cooke revealed how vital her knickknacks were. Fearing that she would have to discard some of her luggage, she confessed, "I had a cry about it . . . as I seemed to have parted with near everything I valued."

Although Cooke's husband promised to stop complaining about belongings which provided so much comfort for her, other women would find it difficult to maintain symbolic ties with home life and the female world. The woman who started out in a traveling dress with clean collar and cuffs soon found she had to abandon it for clothes she originally had refused to wear. Indeed, changes in clothing hinted at the social disruption the frontier could cause women. By

1852, some women on the trail were wearing the bloomer costume, finding the "short skirt and pantletts" a "very appropriate dress for a trip like this." Although bloomers were practical, the costume, espoused by feminists as dress for liberated women, carried a radical sexual and political message and was, in the words of one magazine, "ridiculous and indecent." So one woman who had brought bloomers with her found she lacked the "courage" to wear them and vowed, "I would never wear them as long as my other two dresses last." Women bickered over the pros and cons of the costume. Supporters accused women in dresses of being vain and preoccupied with appearance, while they, in turn, replied that bloomers led to male gossip. Said one opponent, "She had never found her dress to be the least inconvenient . . . she could walk as much in her long dress as she *wanted to, or was proper for a woman* among so many men."

At the beginning of the trip, however, there were only hints of a disruption of "propriety" as both sexes attempted to maintain the comforting division of labor based on the concept of distinct sexual spheres. Generally men drove the wagons, repaired them, hunted, ferried the cattle and wagons across rivers, and stood guard at night, while women were responsible for the children, meals, and family washing.

"Felt very tired indeed—went to bed early," wrote Ellen Tompkins Adams in a typical journal entry. The refrain of constant fatigue occurs over and over again in women's diaries. On the trail women's work was difficult and exhausting. Maternal duties were taxing. Some women were in the last stages of pregnancy on the trip, although few of them mentioned it in their journals. Apparently pregnancy was a subject discussed among friends but not on paper (even in letters to female relatives, women approached the subject indirectly by talking about making baby clothes) until the baby had been safely delivered. Once the baby was born there was little time to regain strength. A day or so of rest before the trip resumed was about the most any new mother could expect. Some recovered quickly and resumed their chores, but for others childbirth proved a nightmare. "Her sufferings were so great," wrote one woman of her sister, "that she does not remember anything for quite a space along there. It all seems like a jumble of jolting wagon, crying baby, dust, sagebrush and the never ceasing pain."

Child care was complicated by traveling. Although older children often walked and herded loose cattle, mothers had to supervise their small children in the wagon all day. It must have been almost impossible to keep children good-tempered in cramped quarters; accidents were an ever-present possibility. Diaries refer to children falling out of wagons, under wagons, miraculously escaping harm, breaking limbs or even being killed in accidents. Their more careful older brothers and sisters caused concern by wandering or riding off or lagging behind and disappearing. Children of all ages came down with fevers, diarrhea, even cholera, and became fretful in a lurching, hot, and uncomfortable wagon. It is not surprising that journals often mentioned children as frightened, weeping, or disagreeable, but that mothers characterized their children in this way did not mean that they were necessarily unfeeling or that they did not accept conventional sentimentalized views of children. Hovering behind many of their comments lay the very real fear of a loved child's death, of leaving a "little body in that strange country for the Indians to dig up or wild beasts to devour." Part of women's exhaustion was psychological.

Preparing meals was also a challenge. Morning and evening cooking took place over campfires or camp stoves in all weather. "Unpleasant as it is, I have been cooking beans and stewing fruit and baking bread," noted one woman on a blowy, rainy day. Clothes were reduced to tatters "from coming into frequent contact with the camp fire," and occasionally serious accidents occurred. "Her dress caught fire from the stove," Mary Fisher observed, "and before it could be extinguished it was nearly burned off her." This she considered *almost* a bad accident.

Despite these trying conditions, women were satisfied when they carried out their traditional tasks successfully. As one woman observed, she suspected the other women "engaged in helping to cook supper . . . all enjoyed it heartily, as I did." In some trains, men had been hired to do the cooking. But rather than enjoying their freedom, privileged women in those trains often reported that they wished to take over the cooking, either because "the boys keep every-thing so dirty" or "because we liked it." When women did the cook-ing, one explained, the meals were more regular, less wasteful, and tasty. She could also have added that when women cooked it was more like home.

In numerous other ways women sought to continue their familiar round of activities during the early and relatively easy months of travel through the Platte River Valley. The journals noted the times when they cared for the sick and the dying of their own company and when they visited other trains in their efforts to help out. As at home, they sustained one another in the familiar rituals of birth and death. "Late in the afternoon a group of women stood watching Mrs. Wil-son's little babe as it breathed its last," wrote one woman describing an important moment of emotional support. And women made efforts to maintain the remnants of their female network on a daily rather than just an emergency basis. They reached out to construct new sup-port groups for the journey. "During the day," Catherine Haun, an emigrant from Iowa, explained, "we womenfolk visited from wagon to wagon or congenial friends spent an hour walking, ever westward, and talking over our home life back in 'the states'; telling of the loved ones left behind; voicing our hopes for the future . . . and even whispering a little friendly gossip of emigrant life." As women exchanged recipes, as they knitted and crocheted, they were keeping themselves "in the practice of female occupations and diversions." The journals indicate the feelings of satisfaction women felt when they visited, cooked together, or went swimming, and their frustra-tion when "the plain fact of the matter is, *we have no time for so-ciability.*"

But as the trip wore on, and the rolling prairies receded and gave way to harsh deserts and mountains, it became clear that women would be unable to keep the world they valued intact. Knickknacks, treasured belongings were cast aside in an effort to lighten the wagons and quicken the pace so that provisions and animals would survive until the journey's end. Female friendships were broken off as com-panies separated. When friends parted, women wept. "We had be-come so attached to each other having travelled so far together, and being dependent on each other in times of danger and accidents," explained one woman, while another, facing separation from her sister because of their husbands' "first class row," confessed that her sister "did not feel that she would ever be happy again." Troubling, too, was the prospect of being without the comforting company of other women. Ellen Adams, who nursed a sick woman in her train, finally had to leave the invalid and her husband behind at an army barracks. "I felt very badly to come away as there are no women at the Fort," she reported, evidently thinking the presence of soldiers and husband hardly compensated for the loss of female companionship.

Ultimately, even standard chores became unfamiliar and unfeminine. Cooking not only reduced women's clothes to rags and tatters but also forced women to take on jobs at which a lady would blush. As cooks, women found meal preparation often included gathering fuel. Since firewood was scarce on the trail, buffalo dung, called "chips," served for cooking. Some women saw the dung as the practical solution to the fuel problem. Others found gathering the chips demeaning and indelicate. "This caused many ladies to act very cross and many were the rude phrases uttered, far more humiliating to refined ears than any mention of the material used for fuel could have been," observed one of the pragmatists from Missouri. Some of the women wore gloves to avoid touching the dung, although eventually "most of them . . . discarded their gloves," and accepted unpleasant reality. Using the chips to cook food was another problem. "Mother thought at first she could not do that," recalled one daughter, and though, as always, her mother compromised, "she was never reconciled to that kind of fire, and never liked to think of those experiences afterwards."

Familiar patterns disintegrated under the trip's strain, and even the comforting sense of the flow of time vanished. Most striking was the disappearance of the Sabbath, which had become by mid-century a symbol of women's religious and moral authority. Initially many women had hoped to use the day for worship and rest. Parties lucky enough to have both a preacher and leaders who considered layovers no threat to the train's pace observed the Sabbath. But often the need to find water and food for the cattle, the need to make mileage, made traveling on the Sabbath necessary, especially as the months passed. Women had to agree, but confided in their journals that they were unhappy with the situation. Traveling "does not seem pleasant," on the Sabbath, wrote one, while another felt that the waters of the river her company had forded "seemed to reproach us."

Even when the caravan broke the journey to observe a day of rest, women found they had few moments for meditation or relaxation. "I was obliged to do many things I was very loth to do on the Sabbath," Esther Hanna revealed in her diary. Pennsylvania had been different. Baking, washing, mending, sewing all continued, Sabbath or no, while men had a break from their activities. Men, one sympathetic woman explained, needed "physical rest, so they lolled around in the tents and on their blankets spread on the grass, or under the wagons out of the sunshine, seeming to realize that the 'Sabbath was made for men' . . . [Yet] women, who had only been anxious spectators of their arduous work [during the week], and not being weary in body, could not fully appreciate physical rest." Whether men deserved the rest or not, "Does not seem like Sunday at all today—have been obliged to work nearly all day" was a constant refrain tired women echoed. The truth was, one sadly reflected, it was just impossible to have a real Sabbath on the trail. "And today is Sunday again. O what Sundays. There is nothing that seems like the Sabbath."

As civilization receded, some of the ways in which women thought about themselves changed. Domesticity suggested true women were feminine and attractive. However unlikely the attainment of this ideal, it shaped women's views of themselves and served as a normative goal. But it was a losing battle to be concerned about appearances on the frontier, and most women stopped thinking in these terms altogether. "As the days lengthened into weeks, our self-respect suffered somewhat in the matter of clothes," wrote one, who described her skirt as "a piece of wide fringe hanging from belt to hem." Another explained, "We were so worn out that we were not particular how we were dressed but presented a mixture of fashions." Only after the trip was nearly over did Luzena Wilson suddenly realize how thoroughly she had forgotten the female norms she had observed in

Missouri. As her party drew near to its destination, a man dressed in a clean white shirt came out to meet the travelers. The sight of someone in respectable clothes jolted Wilson and, as she recalled, "revived in me the languishing spark of womanly vanity." Realizing how she looked in her ragged sunbonnet, tattered skirts, "worn off in rags above my ankles," her face sunburnt, her hands "brown and hard," and, of course, gloveless, she shrank modestly away from the man's observation. By the end of the journey, Lavinia Porter agreed, "I doubt whether any of us could have been recognized."

"Getting tough, I can tell you," Mary Warner noted in her diary, after describing driving one of the wagons. If some familiar norms were forgotten, new ones were useful. For it was just as well if women got tough. As the trip progressed, women continued to be responsible for washing, cooking, and caring for children. But under the strain of travel, of parties splitting and hired hands quitting, women also took on jobs once clearly defined as male. They pitched tents, loaded and unloaded wagons, drove them, yoked the cattle. Some even drove stray cattle on horseback, and one surprised man noted "a couple of ladies" galloping full speed ahead after the beasts. Another disapprovingly noted that ladies even rode astride, "the greatest curiosity I have seen yet." Women whose husbands became sick or died on the trail, of course, assumed all the responsibilities for the family's survival and welfare, unless they were lucky enough to fall under the protection of another man. For many travelers, the line dividing the actual activities of men and women blurred and, in some cases, disappeared.

As women did men's work, men did women's. Single men shifted for themselves, but even married men sometimes helped with the washing and, when their wives were sick or out of humor, did the cooking. Some women suggested that helpfulness was a regional characteristic. As one wrote in her journal, she was lucky to have a Yankee for a husband, "so am well waited on." But another pioneering wife, from the South, felt that male courtesy and sharing was rare. "Men on the plains . . . were not so accommodating nor so ready to serve or wait upon women as they were in more civilized communities." If men helped with female work from time to time, this did not mean they did it regularly. Most of the disintegration of work roles affected women. A man assuming female responsibilities was doing a favor. A woman doing a male job was doing what was necessary.

Because of the many unavoidable difficulties of the journey and the exhausting grind of steady work, most women automatically cooperated with shifting requirements. There seemed to be no alternative. But some women welcomed the expansion of the female sphere. Rebecca Ketcham, a single woman from New York traveling west with friends, reported her riding adventures with glee. Others wrote that they enjoyed driving wagons and were proud of their ability to handle animals. They noted incidents which they felt revealed courage and skill. Some went so far as to adopt the symbol of masculinity, the gun. "I keep close to my gun and dog," commented one woman from Illinois.

But even when women seemed to enjoy their new responsibilities, few speculated on the significance of their actions or capitalized on their increased importance within the family. For most women found the trip neither exhilarating nor liberating. Far from welcoming the expansion of the female sphere, a few specifically found fault with it. "There were occasional angry debates while various burdens were being adjusted," noted one diarist. "Warner says I am cross for the first time," wrote a young wife. "Well none of the women think it their duty to help the cook, and he is cross if he doesn't get help, and of course he gets tired also." Women complained to their journals and to each other more about their fatigue, the monotony of the daily routine, the dirt and dust, than they did about their unaccustomed duties, but the point was the same. "This gy[p]sy life is anything but agreeable." "It is impossible to keep anything clean, and it is with difficulty that you do what . . . you have to do." The meaning of this catalogue of grievances is captured in a typical passage in the journal of a woman who had already moved once from Ohio to Iowa. "Oh dear," she confessed, "I do so want to get there it is now almost four months since we have slept in a house. If I could only be set down at home with all the folks I think there would be some talking as well as resting." Women hoped not to expand their domestic sphere but to recapture it.

Women's cultural values were also revealed when they came into contact with Mormons and Indians during the trip. Unable to see Mormons as the persecuted defenders of religious freedom or Indians as either noble savages or the victims of white civilization, women perceived both as threats to domestic culture. Only when the Indian or Mormon seemed to conform to their own standards did the women have anything positive to say. Thus, they admired Salt Lake City, a stopping-off point for California emigrants, for its beautiful plan, its cozy, snug homes, its prosperous and bustling air. Observant women approved of Indian mothers who made children's bonnets, or who dressed neatly and presented a "clean and wholesome . . . appearance," and even Indian men who seemed to be noble warriors and "well behaved."

But more often than not, women saw the similarities between their own culture and Mormon or Indian culture as superficial. Underneath it all, Margaret Hecox reflected, Indians were "just Indians." "I doubt if the savage instinct can ever be eradicated from the wild man's breast." Disgustedly, women recorded that Indians were thieves and beggars, little recognizing how their own civilization had contributed to the disintegration of Indian society. Indians were habitually described as filthy, lazy, dishonest, and harsh to women. As for the Mormons, the female writers found the men "very hard looking" and the women ugly. In the eyes of the overland emigrant woman, the two groups represented the collapse of civilized life and a negation of familial values.

Underlying the observations ran a fear of sex uncontrolled by all the conventions of nineteenth-century society. Women constantly commented on and obviously closely observed the nakedness of Indian men, who were "guiltless of clothing . . . very many . . . in the state of our first parents before they committed their first sin." Indians' sexuality was clearly suggested by many popular captivity accounts with their female victims who recollected savages whipping their "almost naked" bodies. Readers could easily imagine what other foul acts Indians perpetrated upon the "almost naked" female form. The actions of men seemed to reinforce the idea that they lusted after white women's bodies. A number of women recounted episodes in which Indian men tried to trade ponies for white women. The women's response was one of stark fear. Some described hiding in wagons to avoid the savage's flattery. Others became the butt of their husband's sense of humor. One revealed that her husband pretended to strike a bargain with an Indian, his wife for two ponies. The Indian, little realizing the joke, generously offered three, "then he took hold of my shawl to make me understand to get out. About this time I got frightened and really was so hysterical, began to cry."

If the intentions of Indians seemed clear to these diarists, so too were the polygamous practices of the Mormons. Women writers assumed polygamy exploited women sexually without giving them anything in return. "These demons marry some girls at ten years of age," wrote one horrified observer who emphasized that the demons often took on "a mother and her daughters and marry them all." To get "only one third or perhaps one twentieth share of a man" was hardly worth the hard work Mormon men expected of their wives. Indeed, Mormon wives were "all . . . a poor heart broken and deluded lot and are made slaves to the will of these hellish beings who call themselves men . . . They have not so much liberty as common slaves in the south." The fear of sexual license and the conviction that women in the other culture were men's slaves suggests the confidence these women had in their own values and social place as well as their fear of change.

These confrontations with an alien world and the hardships of travel which increased so dramatically during the second part of the trip caused women, at times, to feel fearful and bitter. Under stress, some women turned against their husbands and blamed them for the whole unhappy undertaking. "I felt as though myself and little ones were at the mercy of a madman," Mary Powers reflected, while Margaret Hecox, who had retreated into the family's wagon with her children as the rest of the party watched an Indian war dance, agreed. "I wondered what had possessed my husband, anyway, that he should have thought of bringing us away out through this God-forsaken country. I feared that we all were to be scalped or taken prisoners before morning." After a moving description of her younger brother's sickness and death, Ada Millington tersely observed, "Ma thinks if we had been 'at home he needn't have died.' "

Despite her bitter thoughts, it apparently did not occur to Margaret Hecox to confront her husband. Nor did Mary Powers, who noted in her reminiscences, "I said nothing." The ways in which women handled their frustrations most often testifies to their attempts to live up to norms of female behavior, at least in front of their men. Lavinia Porter confessed she often cried, wished herself at home, and then returned to chores with an air of assumed cheerfulness. For others, keeping journals must have served as a legitimate release of tension and as a place for cataloguing grievances. "This journey is tiresome . . . it is perilous, the deaths of many testify, and the heart has a thousand misgivings, and the mind is tortured with anxiety," explained one weary woman in her journal. Women also expressed their grievances to one another. "Husband is scolding and hurrying all hands (and the cook), and Almira says she wished she was at home, and I say ditto." And occasionally all the women gathered together to share their feelings. "The female portion of our little train are almost discouraged," observed one writer. "We sat by moonlight and discussed matters till near 11 o'clock."

On August 3, 1854, Mary Burrell wrote, "Worse than all, stuck my nose in where I had no business." Though she did not reveal what she had done, the entry suggests that though women most often seem to have tried to keep their place, they did not always succeed. Nor were men more successful. Both sexes indulged in disagreeable and petty behavior. "All out of humor" noted one woman, while another revealed she had hardly expected "to see so much selfishness and bad temper." "Being jolly when you are so tired yourself is no picknick," observed one woman still well enough socialized to feel it was her duty to cheer the "tired and cross" men. Men admitted in their journals to "heavy hearts," quarrels, complaints, and described shockingly inappropriate masculine behavior. John Minto told of coming across a father of four, "lying on his back upon a rock, taking the rain in his face, seemingly given up all thought of manly struggle." The cry of Indians sent some of the men of another train scurrying to hide in the wagons, courage fast forgotten. Vignettes of inept husbands unable to control their wives' behavior suggested how hollow were the claims of some to male authority.

It is not surprising that given the difficulties of the journey social restraints occasionally broke down and frustrations, usually controlled, exploded. As tension built up in one party, the observant Rebecca Ketcham noted how the behavior of all her fellow travelers changed. "It does seem as though we might have everything pleasant, but is all the other way. Mr. Gray [the captain] scolds when he is around, and when he is away the rest scold and find fault with him." As time passed, Rebecca detailed how the women finally stopped complaining to each other, abandoned all sense of woman's place, and "talked pretty plain [to Mr. Gray] me more so than ever. I don't know how he liked it, but I cannot help it." Other examples of what could be called female insubordination crop up in the diaries: women refusing to cook, women refusing to camp at the assigned spot, a few trying to bring the trip to an end altogether. One set flames to the family wagon; another beat her husband with a horsewhip. These were the extreme, but subtle resistance was, no doubt, more common and also less likely to be recorded. Lavinia Porter, who disapproved of her husband's barrel of whiskey, described what she did. Sure that complaints or reasoning would fall on deaf ears, she resorted to indirection, certainly a part of the female style. "I patiently bided my time, and one day when no one was around," she proudly recounted later, "I quietly loosened . . . the barrel . . . and by nightfall there was nothing left."

A 250-pound woman berated and abused her husband, "charging him with bringing his wife and children out into the God-forsaken country to starve and die"; she was, however, the exception and Lavinia Porter probably more typical. But neither open insubordination nor indirect resistance apparently resulted in any clear rethinking of the female role or of the relations between the sexes. Rather, women struck out blindly, angry at the tedium of the trip and the prolonged disruption of their female world. They were, perhaps, too tired to do otherwise. And as the journey neared its end, there seemed less and less need to rethink as women's thoughts turned more and more to the future and the reestablishment of their world, now so sharply contrasted with life on the trail. What had initially been vague now loomed close. "I am very weary of this journey, weary of myself and all around me," wrote one woman in late August. "I long for the quiet of home where I can be at peace once more."

The journals and reminiscences show the rich variety of responses women pioneers had to the overland experience. They noted the cheerful and lively moments as well as those of suffering and death. Many testified to the new and strong ties they had formed with one another, a good beginning for a new life. "I feel that the good friends we have made on the journey more than make up for the hardship," noted one woman. The trip had been a mixed experience. But now it was time to start anew. At the end of her journey, one woman wrote this artless poem which captures so much of the response of women to emigration.

> Day after day
> We wend our way; Through sage and sand,
> In hope to find,
> To please our mind,
> A home in a happy land.

3

"A Maid of
All Traids"

"My heart arose in gratitude to God that we were spared to reach this land," Esther Hanna wrote in her journal a few days before ending it in September 1852. "I can scarcely realize that we are so near our contemplated home." For women like Esther Hanna, the journey's conclusion was a joyous event. Misgivings about the frontier evaporated as families began their new lives. For others, however, the period of adjustment to new surroundings was trying. Physical exhaustion from the trip's rigors, a reduced emotional resilience, and meager family resources contributed to a sense of desolation in the days after arrival. Clothes were tattered. The trail was littered with treasured possessions, discarded as animals had weakened, then died. No matter how carefully the trip had been planned, few arrived with much cash, and even the lucky ones found their reserves could not replace what they had thrown away in desperation. "There were no luxuaries to be had even if we had ever so much money," one early pioneer recalled. But just as important as the physical and financial condition in which so many emigrants found themselves at the trip's end was the shock of confronting the reality of the frontier. Many women had survived the trip by fantasizing about their future "happy home in a happy land." When they reached their destination, they saw not a home but wilderness. "After the way we had suffered and struggled to get here," a Missouri woman wrote to her mother, "I had all I could do to keep from asking George to turn around and bring me back home." As dreams collapsed, some gave in to feelings. One band of women arriving in Puget Sound in November 1851 spent a long dreary afternoon helping their husbands carry possessions up the beach beyond the reach of the tide. Then, overwhelmed by their situation, one of the husbands later recalled, "the women sat down and cried." It was not long, of course, before some sort of shelter, however rudimentary, was constructed. But a permanent "home" often proved elusive. Journals, letters, and census data suggest several moves during the early years of settlement, as families sought the right claim or the right job.

Women settling the farming frontier, far from the Pacific coast, also found adjustment difficult in the early months and years after their trip. Although they were not so fatigued after a journey ending in Nebraska or western Iowa, their situation initially seemed bleak. Prairies and plains struck many women as depressing. "As long as I live I'll never see such a lonely country," was how one woman described her reaction to the Texas plains, while a Nebraska pioneer reflected, "These unbounded prairies have such an air of desolation —and the stillness is very oppressive." Like settlers of Oregon and Washington, emigrants pushing the frontier west from the Mississippi arrived at their destination with little capital to soften the burdens of homesteading. Like their counterparts in the Far West, emigrants found their dreams of a permanent home illusory.

The early years of settlement on the farming frontier, of course, differed according to time, location, and settlers' backgrounds. The mid-century plains and prairie frontier offered emigrants coming from Europe and the Mississippi Valley not only fertile soil and sufficient rainfall, for example (unlike the arid plains, sweeping from the Dakotas south to Texas, settled later in the century, where the rainfall could not support traditional farming), but also special problems stemming from the region's geography and climate. Although emigrants could use familiar agricultural methods, the weather, with its extremes of temperature and its high winds, could mean low yields, crop failure, and the destruction of valuable livestock. Timber for building and fuel, so abundant in the Far West, was rare on the prairies and plains, and its scarcity compounded problems of settlement. Hunger, poverty, and ruin hovered closer to the pioneers of this frontier than those of the Far West. There, however, though subsistence was assured, poor transportation and inadequate markets meant a continuing shortage of capital, which affected the quality of life.

Although different parts of the frontier challenged settlers in different ways, there were enough common threads to the pioneering experience to make it possible to generalize about pioneer life and women's response to it. During the initial period of settlement, women on all frontiers shared crude living conditions and similar domestic situations. Because of the shortage of capital and labor, early farming efforts were on a small diversified scale and demanded the participation of the entire family, especially women. The first years of settlement, therefore, continued the trail experience by demanding that women depart from cultural and social behavioral norms for the sake of their family's survival. The sense of dislocation some felt initially stemmed from this enforced departure from familiar behavior. The early years of settlement, in fact, would test many facets of the cultural framework which women had brought west with them. The test suggested how firmly women clung to the framework and the meaning which it could provide for their lives even on the frontier.

As one Oregon woman noted, the frontier was "a hard country for woman." It was hard, she knew, because "things . . . are rather in a primitive state." Crude housing was part of this "primitive state," which all women shared no matter where they settled on the farming frontier. A dugout or sod house on the plains, a small shack, cabin, or hole in the Far West served for shelter. Other more exotic alternatives appeared. "During father's trip he had seen two stumps standing a few feet apart," recollected one pioneer later, "and he laughingly told mother she might live in them . . . She insisted that father clean them out, put on a roof, and we moved in, a family of eight persons." Whatever the arrangements, home was often open to the weather, uncomfortable, crowded, with little privacy. Families lived for months in these dwellings, sometimes for years, as money and time went into other improvements. Early homes challenged domestic ideals and the concept of gentility, and women were sometimes discouraged. "What a contrast to the wheels of time unrolle to our view, compared with our home in Ill. one year since," sighed one.

The preparation of food, an important domestic duty, was arduous without the familiar ingredients and utensils. An Oregon pioneer of the 1840's described setting up housekeeping with her new husband with only one stew kettle (for making coffee, bread, and cooking meat) and three knives. Since the stoves with which many pioneer families had set out over the Oregon Trail had been too heavy to survive the trip, this woman, like so many others, did all her cooking over an open fire. No wonder some pioneers looked back to this initial period with distaste. "I assure you," Maria Cutting wrote, "we had many privations and Hardships to endure and O such makeouts sometimes having to use shorts instead of flour, sometimes sugar sometimes none."

Yet others took great pride in preparing tasty food despite all the obstacles; women's response to difficult living conditions often seemed related to their early attitude to emigration. As one Iowa pioneer explained, "I came here willingly believing it to be for the best and am determined to try with the assistance of Providence to make the best out of it." In any case, they knew they had no options beyond making "the best out of it." There was no returning home. As Margaret Wilson told her mother in a letter written in 1850, "You will wonder how I can bear it, but it is unavoidable, and I have to submit without complaining."

No matter how women reacted to primitive living conditions, few cared for their primitive neighbors. Oregon Trail diaries revealed that many women feared Indians, especially males. On the trail, however, the wagon train offered fainthearted women the protection of numbers; in any case, offensive natives were always left behind as the company moved on. Now settled, however temporarily, women on many parts of the frontier found themselves living in the midst of Indians.

They didn't like it. "I suppose Mother had more trouble there [in Oregon], really, than she had on the road; because we were surrounded by Indians," one daughter explained. Even friendly Indians made women anxious by their way of silently appearing, wanting food or just a look at the white woman and her children. Even though their accounts show them dealing directly and even courageously with Indian visits, women felt vulnerable in these meetings. Many were persuaded that the Indian men were particularly aggressive when their husbands were away. Whether this was true or merely reflected the women's view of themselves as the weaker sex is unclear. Certainly, their actions showed few signs of weakness. Sarah Sutton was typical. When Indians came for food when her men were absent, she dealt with them by jerking "a tent pole and laying it about her with such good effect that she had her squat of Indians going on a double quick in a very short time." At other times, she wielded a pistol rather than the tent pole. Still, the incidents were unpleasant, and unnerving.

Although women sometimes trained Indians as servants, they described them at best as shiftless and curious, at worst as treacherous, savage, and cruel. Only rarely could white women reach across the barriers of race and culture to establish sympathetic contact with Indian women. Most accepted cultural generalizations and were convinced that "the native inhabitants must soon submit to 'manifest destiny.'" Pioneer women were unsympathetic to the clash between cultures and unaware that white behavior often provoked the Indian behavior they disliked so much. In one sense they were right to be suspicious and fearful, since the settlement period was punctuated by Indian violence and hostility. The Indian Wars in Oregon from 1855 to 1858 were only one example that the so-called inferior race could strike out in a deadly fashion against white settlers and their families. But women's negative attitudes increased their sense of vulnerability and isolation. "We had no neighbors nor company save a straggling land hunter, or the native Indians," recalled Susannah Willeford, an Iowa pioneer. "The latter were seldom if ever welcome visitors as far as I was concerned."

Isolation from white women also shaped most women's responses to the earliest period of settlement. Although women had their own domestic circles, they missed female friends. A husband might be no substitute for a close friend or relative of their own sex, as Nellie Wetherbee discovered. "I have been very blue," she wrote in her journal, "for I cannot make a friend like mother out of Henry . . . It's a bore—and Mother is so different and home is so different . . . Oh dear dear." The difficulty of finding female friends stemmed, of course, from the scattered pattern of settlement (the Oregon Dona-tion Law, for example, provided each family with 640 acres, thus ensuring isolation) and also from the fact that there were fewer women than men on the frontier in the first years. As Mollie Sanford noted in her diary, "I do try to feel that it is all for the best to be away off here [Nebraska]. I can see and feel that it chafes mother's spirit. . . . If the country would only fill up . . . We do not see a woman at all. All men, single or bachelors, and one gets tired of them."

But the sexual imbalance was not so great as many popular ac-counts have suggested. The 1850 male-female ratio for the country as a whole was 106 men to every 100 women, while in rural Oregon that same year, there were approximately 137 men to every 100 women. By 1860, however, the sex ratio in frontier counties approxi-mated that in the East. Various studies of frontier settlements show, then, that the frontier was not overwhelmingly masculine. But given the role female friendship played in women's lives and the difficulties which made it hard for women to meet, the loneliness they felt was understandable.

Real isolation was, however, a short-lived phenomenon, usually lasting only two or three years on most parts of the frontier. Some of the men turning up in the census or in Mollie Sanford's diary were preparing homesteads for their families. The immigration pattern of Whidbey Island, near the coast of Washington, suggests the rapidity of the settlement process. Attracted by its fertile prairie land and pleasant climate, Isaac Ebey, an 1848 pioneer from Missouri, selected the island for his future home. By the time his wife, Rebecca, and their two sons joined him three years later, there were several other families on Whidbey and more coming. In June 1852 Rebecca was writing, "We have plenty of company four families of us here 12 children." Although her guests eventually moved to their own claims on the island, Rebecca's diary catalogues numerous visitors, both new emigrants and old. After Rebecca died in 1853, emigrants to Whidbey included the Ebey cousins, her husband's father, mother, brother, his two sisters, some children, and a single man who eventually married her daughter the next year. Nor was the Ebey clan the only one on the island, for other families as well as some unmarried settlers also migrated to Whidbey during these few years. Loneliness may have been a very real part of the frontier experience for women, but total isolation for an extended length of time usually was not.

If women shared common physical and social conditions on the farming frontier, they also shared a similar family environment. The stereotypical view of the frontier family suggests a familial experience which modern women would find oppressive and burdensome. Most historians have casually asserted that women on the frontier routinely married at fourteen or fifteen and that they then proceeded to bear children with monotonous regularity. Families with ten or twelve children are pictured as the norm. With such heavy maternal responsibilities, to say nothing of the arduous nature of pioneer life itself, pioneer women not only worked harder than women in the East, this interpretation implies, but differed from them culturally. Census data shows that throughout the nineteenth century the size of American families was shrinking, not because of reduced mortality rates, but because women bore fewer and fewer children. In 1800 white women who reached menopause bore on the average 7.04 children. Forty years later the figure had fallen to 6.14, reaching 4.24 in 1880. A dramatic difference in family size on the frontier would imply a "frontier" set of values.

Unfortunately, there are not enough studies of the frontier family in the trans-Mississippi West to allow a definitive description of frontier family structure, but the stereotype appears to be misleading. Western women's fertility patterns were not very different from those of other women in the country. One study based on the 1860 census returns ranging from New Hampshire to Kansas, for example, revealed lower fertility rates in frontier townships than those in the more populated areas directly to the east. Young children who were unable to contribute to the frontier family's welfare in those crucial early years were not an asset but a burden.

"Will I be a happy beloved wife, with a good husband, happy

home, and small family," Mollie Sanford, a Nebraska pioneer, had mused, "or an abused, deserted one, with eight or nine small children crying for their daily bread?" Scattered studies of different parts of the trans-Mississippi frontier suggest that Mollie Sanford's chances for marital satisfaction in the terms in which she posed them were good. The typical frontier household, though somewhat larger than those in the East, was made up of parents and a few children living together. An analysis of Iowa frontier families showed families with one to four children living at home, while a detailed study of a Texas pioneer area with 896 families turned up only twelve families with ten or more children. The "average" family household in this part of Texas contained four children, but fully *half* of the families had three children or fewer living at home. The 1850 manuscript for Oregon yielded similar results. Since none of these figures take into account children who were grown and on their own or include infant mortality figures, they do not disclose how many children women actually conceived and bore, but the figures suggest that pioneer households in the West were comparable in size with the American experience elsewhere.

Women on the frontier were, then, most often wives and mothers. Their small households suggest they believed in limiting the size of their families. Certainly contraceptive information was available. Newspapers between 1820 and 1873 advertised both contraceptives and abortifacients, while pamphlets, birth-control circulars, popular health books, and books also told women how to control conception. Contraceptive practices were long described in folklore. Although personal testimony concerning the use of birth control on the frontier is rare, a few references show that frontier women knew of and practiced birth control. An Oregon midwife, for example, described an abortion, a method of family limitation which increased during the nineteenth century. "I went to the woman's place several times," she recollected. "She had staged several sham battles. You see, they didn't do what was right, and had tried, too soon, to have the baby and get rid of it. When it was far along, it was a killing job. Hot salt water was what they used, and it sometimes passed. After the woman herself would be about to die as well as the baby, they'd call for help."

If pioneer women were not the fecund breeders of popular history, neither they nor their husbands were the excessively youthful group so often described. Most studies of pioneer families show husbands typically in their thirties or forties, with wives several years younger. Nor did women marry routinely in their early teens. One pioneer woman recalled a proposal when she was thirteen. "I said, *no!* Why I'm only a *child.* I have never given marriage a thought yet." Studies of age of marriage in Oregon and Texas turn up little evidence of early unions. Information which exists on the frontier family seems to suggest that married women on the farming frontier did not have the burdens of youthful inexperience or swarms of young children added to the difficulties of creating a new life in the wilderness.

These relatively small families, of course, provided the context for women's emotional and work lives during the initial years of settlement, when the interaction with outsiders was limited. Many pioneer women resolved consciously, as did Susannah Willeford, "to devote my time, life and energies to the welfare and interest of my family." This was no small resolve; women's work for and with their families was extraordinary. Since few pioneers arrived with substantial financial or material resources, and since hired help was unavailable, every family was thrown back on itself in the struggle to get started. All cooperated in the work of establishing the farm, but because women often were the only adults besides their husbands, they had to contribute more than a woman's share.

"I am maid of all traids," one woman remarked in her diary in 1853. As had proved true on the trail, necessity blurred the relationship between men's and women's work. The tasks seemed endless. Women did heavy outside "male" chores, helping to dig cellars, to build cabins, "as there was no other man . . . [Father] could get to help him," helped with the plowing and planting, again since "there were neither man nor boy that we could hire in the county." Then there were the conventional female jobs, sewing, "sweeping dusting churning ironing baking bread and pies dishwashing &c." And always there was laundry, an arduous undertaking which many women seem to have particularly disliked. "Dreaded washing day," wrote one, and added, "And as Mr. Taylor is not well he brings me water   I finish by noon then scrub in the after noon feeling quite tired." Women cared for vegetable gardens, cows, chickens. As farmers, cooks, seamstresses, and laundresses, their labor contributed to the family's well-being and survival in almost every way.

But women did more than these tasks, since they shared "a strong desire to provide the necessary comforts for our family." In many cases they seem to have become small-scale economic entrepreneurs. One resourceful but not unusual woman, for example, started out by cutting up wagon covers to make shirts to sell to the Indians. Then she moved on to making gloves for soldiers stationed nearby, a task with which her husband helped. "So, before spring, they were turning out very handsome gloves, also buckskin money belts." Later, as emigrants began to come into Oregon, she baked bread, pies, and cookies to sell. Female enterprises changed as opportunities changed, though the sale of butter and eggs seems to have provided a fairly steady source of income for women. These funds were especially important because of the chronic shortage of capital on the frontier. And as one observer pointed out, women often supported their families while their husbands learned how to farm. Occasionally women viewed their earnings as their own, but most often they were not a source of economic independence but rather a means of supplementing the family's income.

"Female hired help was not to be obtained," one man pointed out when reflecting on his pioneer years. "I assisted my wife all I could —probably did as much housework as she did." Continuing the pattern emerging on the journey west, men performed some female chores. Letters and journals show them helping with the washing, the cooking, and caring for children. But as on the trip west, men usually assumed these responsibilities only occasionally, when their wives were tired, ill, or in childbirth.

Much of the heavy labor women did initially could also be categorized as helping husbands out in the absence of male assistance. But wives more routinely assumed male responsibilities than their husbands took on female responsibilities. When men left their homesteads, as they did when gold was discovered, or when they went off to fight Indians, do political business, or herd cattle, they were often gone for months at a time. The women who stayed behind were left in charge. "As we live on a farm," wrote one, "whatever is done I have got to attend to and so I have a great deal of out doors work." As she listed her chores, they included caring for hogs, hens, milking the cows, and running the dairy. A hired man worked on the grain. On the plains, men often hired themselves out for cash, leaving their wives to oversee the crops and animals for weeks.

As their economic enterprises, their letters, and journals indicate, women were both practically and emotionally involved in economic matters as they sought to improve the family economic status. Even Kate Blaine, a Methodist minister's wife from the Northeast, wished she could be making some money. "If I were not the preacher's wife I should take in [washing] . . . It is very profitable," she confessed. Despite the claim of nineteenth-century culture that there was a gap between woman's world, the home, and man's world, the workplace, the two coincided on the frontier. Nor were women "disinterested" in economic matters. As women shared men's work, they adopted men's perspectives.

Home was not the quiet and cozy retreat that nineteenth-century culture envisioned, but a busy center of endless chores and economic ventures. Moreover, women were determined to defend it. One who recounted how a flood destroyed her family's investment added, "It did seem almost hopeless to start practically from the beginning again, but I was willing to do it." Destitution on the plains in the 1870's produced the same kind of female resolution when women refused to admit economic defeat. A spectacular case of courage and devotion to property was provided by the illiterate widow of a California squatter. When the rightful claimant to the land (who had killed her squatter husband) tried to drive her off the property, gun in hand, the widow seized her own pistols, approached her opponent, and dared him shoot her dead. Her defiance proved too much for him, and the woman retained the land to which she was so devoted.

If the frontier blurred sexual distinctions in the world of work, it also tolerated other departures from the female sphere. Women were occasionally involved in politics. Widow Sims of Arkansas noted, "The papers are full of Politics as this is the year for the Presidental election . . . of course I take sides as every one does so I espouse the cause of Filmore." At least one woman did more than talk. "During these years," David Staples, an early pioneer on the West Coast recalled, "Mrs. Staples cast as many votes as any man. Voters from Arkansas and Missouri, who could not read would walk around . . . and ask her for whom they should vote. She would take the ballot, and running her pencil across certain names, would say I would not vote for that man. By this means, she very materially altered the complexion of results." Women occasionally conducted religious services in the absence of preachers. They filed claims, took care of business, and, as one wrote, "I had a gun and could shoot with any of them."

The activities of these self-reliant pioneer women defied a number of nineteenth-century stereotypes about women. But this did not necessarily mean that pioneer women abandoned the larger conception of women's nature or that they ceased to value female culture. Nor did it mean that they attempted to work out a new definition of woman's sphere. Their behavior and their attitude toward their family, their attempts to replicate female culture suggest that their new environment, although it changed what they did, had only a limited impact on their views.

One might expect, for example, that women's economic importance to the family enterprise might result in a reordering of family relations and the reallocation of power within the family. Ideology, of course, characterized the nineteenth-century family as a patriarchy, with men making decisions and women obediently accepting them. Actually, all American women probably had considerably more power than this model implied. As foreign visitors to the United States noted, "Woman is the centre and lawgiver in the home of the New World." Ideology never tells all.

If ideology does not describe reality, the nature of power relations in families of the past is elusive. Power is difficult to measure at any time. Who wins or loses family confrontations obviously reveals something about the allocation of power and can more easily be observed than the ways in which family members may influence or modify decisions. Yet any judgment about who wields power and how much depends on the latter process as well as the former. In dealing with the nineteenth-century frontier family, the normal problems of analysis are compounded by the lack of direct information about the day-to-day decision process. The privacy of family life, symbolized by the notion of home as retreat, worked against recording situations which might reveal power dynamics. As Elizabeth Lord, reminiscing about her pioneer life in Oregon, pointed out, "Of many things connected with our family I do not care to speak in these pages, such as my marriage, the loss of my first child and the birth of my second, which meant much to all of us and was a great event in our lives, and is something that especially belongs to ourselves."

Conclusions about the power structure of frontier families are, thus, drawn from hints rather than from direct evidence. Census data provide a few uncertain clues. They show, for example, that there was no great disparity of age between frontier husbands and wives, which may suggest some limitations of male authority. The small surplus of males on the frontier gave single women some freedom to pick and choose before marriage, which could have affected the nature of the marriage relation. And the falling birth rate may signify female power or a process of mutual decision-making. Certainly we know that when husbands were away in the mines, at the legislature, or on the range, women had real authority in their families.

But what evidence there is suggests that though women were co-partners in the frontier adventure, husbands still made major decisions. Men seem to have determined whether the family would move on to a better piece of land or pursue a business opportunity just as they had decided to bring their family west. Yet, in both cases, men initiated discussions but did not dictate. They consulted their wives, and it may be that female power was really the right of consultation. Both men and women testify to the interaction. Milo Smith, a Colorado pioneer, pointed out, "There is not an enterprise that I have ever gone into that I have not talked the details over with my wife before hand," while another pioneer described a lengthy period of negotiation between herself and her husband, who wanted to take up a new claim. "Finally, after much deliberation on my part, and persuasion on the part of my husband, I consented to taking up a . . . claim," she reported, but only after learning that there would be a colony of thirty settlers from Baltimore nearby.

Women on the frontier did make many minor decisions, although they still deferred to men, negotiated with them, and often worked for their goals indirectly. A revealing account of an Iowa pioneer family shows how many women operated. Although the husband planned to support the family by doing carpenter work, "Mother had different ideas. During his absence she had accumulated nine cows. . . . She was able to support the family nicely . . . But milking cows did not appeal to father; one week from the time he returned there was only one left." Yet this was not the end of dairying after all, even though a definitive male decision appeared to have been made. The woman did not block her husband, but with an inheritance she again invested in cows. With the proceeds from dairying she bought winter clothing and supplies. The message was clear. Eventually the family acquired hogs to help consume the milk; stock raising ended as the family's main economic activity. Female deference and patience succeeded.

Throughout, women were careful to maintain the idea of male superiority. As Kate Robins explained to her mother in New England, "Abner would not like it if he knew I sent for you to send me things." The implication was that women would work behind men's backs and avoid direct confrontations with male authority. Frontier women were not attempting to upset the traditional male-female relationship; they did not consciously covet male power. Women's letters and journals describing the ways in which they managed when their husbands were away make this point explicitly. "My husband was absent so much of the time," wrote one woman, "engrossed in mining or in politics, that the care of the family and the farm was left entirely to me, and I was physically unequal to this double burden." Since her reminiscences show her to be a woman with great physical energy, one suspects that it was the constant responsibility which she disliked. Women were reluctant to take on the burden of decision-making alone, and when they did, it was with the expectation that they would do so only temporarily.

Mary Ann Sims, a widow at twenty-five, expressed her anguish at having to play a man's role on a more permanent basis. "I have been busy all day casting up accounts and attending to business," she wrote in January 1856. "I had no idie that it was as much trouble to superentend and take care of a family as it is   I feel tired sometimes." A few weeks later she added, "Allway beeing accostum to have some-one to depende on it is quite new to attend to business transactions and it pesters me no little." Two years later she observed, "I see a woman cannot fill the sphere of a woman and man too." By 1859 her thinking had crystallized. "It has often been a source of regret to me that my daughters were not sons a man can change his station in life but a woman scarsely ever arrives at more exalted station than the one which she is born in if we ecept those whose minds are mascaline enough to cope with men. a woman whose mind is supirior and whose feelings has been cast in a more exquisit mould to be compell to associate with *courser* minds who cannot understand is compill to feel loanly." Cultural prescriptions were so strong that the widow found herself physically and emotionally exhausted by male responsibilities. On the other hand, despite many offers of marriage, she remained single for several years. A study of frontier Texas illustrates a similar reluctance on the part of propertied widows to remarry. Perhaps the burden of decision-making lessened as women learned "to live alone and act for [themselves]."

Possibly women's fundamental importance in the early years of settlement set definite limits to female deference. "The women were not unaware" of their role in helping to support the family, one reminiscence noted, "and were quite capable of scoring a point on occasion when masculine attitudes became too bumptious." Though there may have been limits to deference and though women may have felt an underlying tension because of the contrast between the passive female stereotype and their own lives, most tried to observe cultural prescriptions concerning familial behavior. Direct confrontations occurred but appear to have been unusual. The evidence is, of course, weighted toward literate women, the very ones exposed to cultural role definitions. But studies of peasant women who prove to be less in-dependent than educated women suggest that a dramatic reallocation of power within humble pioneer families was unlikely.

An examination of letters, journals, and memoirs which touch upon marriage and courtship also indicate how many women carried conventional ideals west with them. Although it has been suggested that frontier women were drab work partners with few sentimental illusions, many of them held to romantic views appropriate for any true woman. Nineteenth-century society had glorified romantic love as a necessary precondition for marriage. Advice books, novels, and schooling described the rapture which a potential husband could be expected to inspire. The rigors of frontier life modified but did not undercut the value of romance.

In fact, the situation of single women on the frontier encouraged romantic fancy. Scattered studies of pioneer families indicate that single women married not in their early teens but in their late teens and early twenties. The sex ratio on the frontier meant that young women did not have to accept the first available suitor who presented himself but could bide their time and choose among several. Frontier demography made romantic ideas and love and courtship meaningful for a woman could wait for "one of those purely spiritual and intelectual creatures" to appear rather than accepting a humdrum and unworthy admirer.

The selection of a mate was not without a functional aspect, however, which it may have lacked in settled urban areas (but probably not in farm communities). "Young women were really sincere when they sought to excel in the preparation of household articles," one pioneer woman commented. "Their teaching was such that such excellence brought its reward in desirable matrimonial favor and the final fulfillment of woman's mission in life." Both sexes agreed that industriousness and competence were desirable for a marriage. A series of letters from a young Nebraska pioneer to his mother reveals this perspective. "You wanted to know," he wrote, "when I was going to get married. Just as quick as I can get money ahead to get a cow and to get married. I want to before I commence shucking corn if I can to Aunt Jennie's oldest girl. She is a good girl and knows how to work . . . A fellow cant do much good on a place when he has everything to do both indoors and out both. She says if we marry right away, she is going to do the work in the house and shuck down the row when I am gathering corn, but I will be glad enough to get rid of the housework." After his marriage, he reported with satisfaction, "She makes everything look neat and tidy and is willing to help me all she can."

The realization that marriage represented a working partnership hardly precluded romantic ecstasy, at least on the part of women. Capable as she was of seeing through some of romantic ideology ("How pleasant it would be to have a comfortable little home with one I *love*. I am afraid the anticipation is more pleasant than the participation would be"), Elizabeth Wardall faithfully recorded her raptures in a courtship lasting several years. "O: what a blessed thing is *love*," she wrote, while Harriet Strong told her future husband, "How glad I am *love* is indiscribable. I would dislike to think anything that *could be fathomed* could effect you and me as it does."

Nor did marriage necessarily dull tender feelings. Women did not see their husbands merely as work partners, although this aspect of the relationship may well have provided a strong basis for their affection. Susannah Willeford described her husband as "my first and only choice. The man to whom I had first given my heart and confidence. The man with whom I had sacrificed my home and friends, the man with whom I had shed tears and shared his gladness and with whom I had shared many difficulties and by whom I had borne eight children." Her words convey their warm relationship, as do the testimonials of many others about their marriage. Pioneer wives both expected and experienced the feelings which nineteenth-century literature suggested were part of married life. Separation often led women to express these emotions in romantic terms. Roselle Putnam called her husband "the idol of my heart" and remarked, "Never did I know what it was to sufer anciety untill I knew what it was to be seperated from [him]," while the long-married Mrs. Stearns spoke of her husband's "dear face." When husbands finally returned, women like Rebecca Ebey captured the emotional tone of their marriages: "And one thing which made [the day] . . . seem more exceedingly delightful, My dear husband arrived safe at home."

Nor was love without a sexual component. Although an argument has been made that nineteenth-century women neither wanted nor enjoyed physical affection, scattered evidence from married and single women on the frontier shows that passion had a place. Since nineteenth-century women were reticent about sex, these references are all the more remarkable. Wrote one woman to her husband in 1867, "Dear Husband you say you think that I could get plenty to hug me well I don't know whether I could or not I don't think I look very hugable now at least to any but your self as there is no-one knows how well I can hug but you." That a chaste hug was perhaps not what she meant is suggested by a letter written a few weeks later when she revealed, "I dreamed of seeing you last night and I thought I had a pair of twins." In a similarly suggestive manner, Kate Blaine told her mother she missed her absent husband as a bedfellow. "Now when I sleep alone the bed is so cold and my feet will not keep warm." A few women were less ambiguous than Kate. Mary Ann Sims lamented she had not met a suitable marriage partner and acknowledged the sexual satisfactions she missed. "I know that there is not a woman . . . that is capable of feeling a more devoted affection than [I] I am naturely impolsive and affectionate and I loved my husban[d] with all the intencity that my nature was capable of feeling but I must confess it was more the passionate ideial love of youth," she wrote. Though she implied that passion should disappear with maturity, it was not so for her. Her final diary entries show her struggling to overcome her feelings for a man she described as wild and dissipated.

It is certainly true, as Phoebe Judson pointed out, that "the inconveniences of our environment and the constant drudgery eventually took all the romance and poetry out of our farm life." Phoebe was, of course, talking not of marriage but of her idealized vision of farming life, but her comment raises a valid point. Pioneer women worked hard most of the time, and their difficult life certainly put limits on flights of romantic fancy. But they were more than work drudges and their occasional references to love suggest that the romantic revolution had affected their attitudes and expectations.

The majority of frontier women were wives and mothers during the early years of settlement; primitive conditions and women's workloads complicated motherhood. But the idea that frontier women had no time for the luxury of maternal feelings, considered so central to the conception of motherhood, and even less time to lavish attention on their children, needs some modification. Frontier women obviously worked hard, but this did not mean that they did not take their role of mother seriously or that they were unconscious of a nineteenth-century mother's duty. "How forsably I feel the responsability of a Mother," sighed one.

Only rarely did frontier women reveal how they felt about pregnancy and birth (which they called a time of sickness). Giving birth was, however, part of a "female ritual" which called for the involvement and support of other women on the frontier as it did in the East. To be alone at such a moment was a dreadful fate to be avoided. "I do not know what they will do when she is *confined* not having any Neighbours," wrote one woman, expressing the common fear of being without female support at such a moment. When it was at all possible, frontier women gathered round during childbirth, with little thought of monetary reward. The ritual had rules. "A woman that was expecting had to take good care that she had plenty fixed for her neighbors when they got there," explained one frontier woman. "There was no telling how long they was in for. There wasn't no paying these friends so you had to treat them good."

If women were reticent before birth, and gave few indications of what their views of motherhood were, not so afterward: "Well, old journal," Almira Beam exclaimed in 1861. "You have been rather silent these few months past: but it could not be helped. You have great cause to be thankful that we ever met. Arthur is asleep in his cradle below, and mother is getting dinner." In their letters east, women indicated their deep emotional concern for their children, recording the smallest details about their babies—their clothes, habits, small achievements. "I would tell you that he is the prettiest baby in the world," wrote Sarah Everett from Kansas, "if I was not intending to send his likeness." Occasionally mothers expressed ambivalent feelings about their female children. Two years earlier Sarah had described another baby as "the newcomer who seems to cause more rejoicing among her distant relatives than those at home—we think of calling Clara Elizabeth . . . It isn't of much consequence however seeing it's nothing but a girl anyway."

Yet four months later Sarah reported the death of *"sweet little Clara*—She brought a great deal of sunshine into our homely cabin this summer, and when she was carried out of it, it certainly seemed very dark to me." Whatever Sarah's earlier comment meant, Clara's death revealed the way in which her mother saw the maternal relationship as central and emotionally absorbing. A child's death robbed the mother of one "more dear to me than any thing ever had been." The sentimentalism of such testimonials strikes the twentieth century as maudlin, but it was typical in the nineteenth century. Though children's death on the frontier was a fact (twenty of the thirty-five reported deaths in Cass County on the Nebraska frontier in 1860 were children six or younger), the attitude was anything but pragmatic.

The nineteenth century defined the regulation of children and the formation of their characters as a mother's central tasks. Life on the frontier complicated them, as Mollie Sanford suggested. "Mother . . . fears I am losing all the dignity I ever possessed." "I know I am getting demoralized, but I should be more so, to mope around and have no fun." The pressure of other duties and the lure of the wilderness made regulating children difficult. Children remembered running "wild in the woods without any restraints," "carefree all through the woods and . . . hills." Mother, noted Wilda Belknap in her autobiography, seemed to have little time to devote to the children after infancy. But this hardly signified an abnegation of maternal responsibility. Children also remembered punishments and disciplinary measures. In later years pioneer women often pointed to their children as symbols of their lifework, testifying to the importance they attributed to their work as mothers.

When they could, then, pioneer mothers molded and educated their children. Rebecca Ebey, a pioneer from Virginia, taught her children lessons, but not just in reading and writing. "We . . . spend our time in training the young minds of our children in the principles of Christ and creating within them a thirst for moral knowledge," she explained. If knowledge of Christian principles was one goal, the inculcation of the habits of steady industry was another. Women expressed disapproval of idleness and indolence in children and sought to encourage them to be useful. On the frontier mothers expected their children to work, so much so that one recollection of a pioneer childhood stated the obvious, "You will gather from what I have related that work and plenty of it was the lot of pioneer children."

Tasks were not assigned solely on the basis of sex. Girls recalled plowing, herding cows, carrying wood and water, while boys helped mothers wash clothes and dishes. "I think the boys ought to do something," explained one mother. Just as responsibilities of the sexes overlapped in the adult world, so, too, did they in the children's world. But as time passed and children grew, sex distinctions were stressed. Daughters recalled mothers clarifying appropriate female behavior. Both sexes acquired knowledge of sexual boundaries, as records show. One reminiscence tells of "Margaret Isabell's sons, . . . teenagers . . . [who] had held their mother up so she could milk the cow. She was still weak from the birth of the baby, but milking a cow was 'woman's work' so they would not do it." Girls recalled their introduction to domesticity as they acted as a "mother's right hand." This was an apprenticeship for marriage, as Amanda Gaines explained. "I assist Mother in house-hold duties which are various. She is preparing me for a Farmer's wife." Another daughter wondered whether she had any existence aside from the domestic routine, for her life was "so prescribed for me by my family environment that I do not know who I am." She did know what she did, however: washing, cooking, and assisting "dear old mother." Even recreation could be sex-bound, with girls riding, visiting, and picking wildflowers, while the "boys swam with Father . . . and trapped animals."

Since the frontier family worked together, it was natural that women shared child care with their husbands, a departure from nineteenth-century theory, which assigned child care exclusively to women. Women expected and wanted assistance, not only because of the work involved, but because of the need to clarify standards. Women assumed that their husbands would introduce sons to the male world and take responsibility for their development at the appropriate time. This might occur relatively early in the child's development. As one woman explained, one of her boys was a problem. "His pa is gone so much that he is becoming a great deal of trouble to me I have often heard it said that little boys would not be industrious about everything under their mother's controll . . . I find it so, They become so accustomed to their mother's commands . . . that they get so they do not mind it." Her conclusion was predictably, "When little boys become old enough to do some work they need a father to show them and to push them forward to make them industrious."

In the first few years following emigration to the West, frontier women helped create a new life for their families. The ways in which they went about their duties and the ways in which they related to other members of their families were influenced by their culture just as much as by the new environment. Tired and overworked as they were, many of them still seem to have had the energy to worry about standards and norms. Necessary modifications were, of course, made. The concept of gentility was clearly inappropriate on the frontier, as was the notion of woman as ornamental (an extension of the concept of domesticity much criticized by its advocates, like Sarah Hale). Child rearing demanded encouraging traits not usually stressed in safer environments. "Children here have to learn self reliance and independence as well as their parents," explained one parent.

But the truth was that female culture shaped the ways in which women perceived the frontier experience and provided a means of orientation to it. Even though frontier conditions forced them into manly pursuits and led them to modify some of their standards, they hardly pressed for a liberation from female norms and culture. For much of the "freedom" which women experienced was the freedom to work even harder than they had before, with dramatic results. "I am a very old woman," wrote twenty-nine-year-old Sarah Everett. "My face is thin sunken and wrinkled, my hands bony withered and hard." Why should women lay claim to male tasks in addition to their own? The domestic ideal was a goal toward which women could direct their efforts, the promise of a day when their lives would not be so hard, their tasks so numerous. Domesticity, with its neat definition of woman's place, helped women bear what they hoped were temporary burdens and reestablished their sense of identity and self-respect. It served as a link with the past.

Frontier women gave many indications of their desire to hold on to the conventions of female culture no matter how unfavorable the circumstances seemed. "Home," crude and impermanent though it might be, received the kind of attention which would have pleased the proponents of domesticity. Though the cabin or sod house might not be the cozy nook pictured in stories of Western life, women hoped to make it one as they papered their walls with old newspapers or tacked up cloth to make the house snug and cheery. Old rags became rugs, old dresses curtains. A keg might become a footstool, upholstered with an old pair of pants. Thread turned into lace doilies. Outside, women planted flowers and trees from seeds they had brought with them and generally tried to maintain the standards of domesticity and hospitality with which they had been familiar before emigration. Although they often wore rough and rugged clothing, even buckskin trousers, pioneer women found "all these things . . . dreadfully annoying." As one pointed out, "We were always wishing for enough money to buy better clothes." The interest in fashion and the attempts to dress in style were symbolic of the intention to remain feminine. The "career" of a mid-century Oregon pioneer is typical. "Although I had now been absent from civilization—otherwise Ohio—for more than a year," she wrote, "I was still considered an authority on the matter of dress and fashion. I was consulted and acted as adviser whenever a new cloak or gown was made . . . I trimmed hats, literally, for the entire neighborhood, and I knew less than nothing about millinery."

The determination to maintain ties to the traditional female world and to create a female community where, in fact, there was none, was apparent in the energy with which frontier women sustained old friendships and associations. Mrs. Coe remarked in a letter to a friend in 1863 that she had written hundreds of letters, so many "that my Diary has dwindled away to almost nothing— All my romance has become reality—and as for poetry—it has vanish'd, resolved itself into and, mingled with the landscape around me." Pioneer women wrote letters to female relatives and friends in the East, detailing their lives, providing all the vital information which was the basis for an intimate female dialogue. They enclosed material of their dresses, described dress patterns, sent pictures of their children; they asked scores of minute questions about the health of family and friends, marriages and deaths, fashion, religion. "The most trivial things that you can mention about each other have a great interest to us way out here," Mary Ann Adair explained to her mother and sister.

Bonds of affection sustained the dialogue between pioneer women and their Eastern friends and relatives, but that dialogue had emotional costs. Slow and irregular mails which could take up to a year contributed to the natural anxiety women felt for the health and well-being of those far away. "My dear mother," wrote one woman, "you do not know how miserable I feel about you, for I have not received a line from any of my family." And as years passed, a new fear appeared. "Everything has changed so much at home since I left, that I expect I should feel like a stranger now." And with time, it was also possible that those at home would cease to care. "I have waited almost a year and a half hoping to receive a letter from you," Elisabeth Adams wrote from Iowa to her sister. "Why do you do so? Do you not wish to have intercourse with me? Do you not *love me?* I am sure I love you, and the longer I live the more I feel the want of affection from others, the more my heart yearns for kindness and love from my own family, I mean my *father's family.*"

A common theme runs through the correspondence. "I want you to come if you can and as soon as you can for no doubt I shal feel my self very lonesome." Women's letters are filled with urgent invitations to friends and relatives to emigrate. Often over a period of years, encouragement and advice about the trip poured out of the West in hopes that friends from the old life could become part of the new. "I want you all here, then I would be perfectly contented," explained Louise Swift, while another woman told her sister, "When we get together again we will not be parted so easy."

If relatives and friends did not come West, women sustained ties with them by nourishing hopes of an Eastern visit. Eventually this hope was realized for a lucky few; other women remembered that, in the end, all would meet in heaven. Although some of their discussions about a heavenly meeting sound strange to modern ears, the emotional well-being of many pioneer women was sustained by their faith that the network of friends and relatives could be eternal. There is, perhaps, no greater testimony to the importance women far in the wilderness placed on female culture than the conviction that parts of it would be replicated in heaven.

While many women on the frontier devoted considerable energy to keeping alive the home network, feeling, as one young woman put it, "Tis true we may have friends among strangers; but, ah, they are not parents, brothers nor sisters," most naturally attempted to establish new ties with other women as soon as possible. The trip overland had provided one opportunity for a new beginning. "Ever since I saw you in camp at Iowa (in '54)," Anna Goodell told Mary Bozarth, "you have looked and acted like my good Auth Sarah." Proximity (which was a relative term) also determined friendships. Although the nearest neighbor might be miles away, women made a special point of visiting one another. Reciprocity was understood. "Mrs. Terry came this morning," wrote Almira Beam in her diary. "She says she will not come again until I come to see her." Soon Mrs. Terry had become "the best neighbor I ever saw, or heard of." Although women might go for days or even weeks without visitors, when they came, they stayed. The visits provided a relief from work and the opportunity for mutual support and sharing experiences. Rebecca Ebey's diary revealed the many rewards of female friendship. "I have been busy all day ironing cleaning up and mend the children's clothes Mrs. Alexander came over this evening to spend the night I was very much pleased to see her and had been look[ing] for her for a long time . . . Mrs. Alexander is very cheerful and makes me feel much better than I have done to be awhile in her company."

Yet creating the new web of friendships on the frontier was difficult. Distance was an obstacle, at least at first. And cultural or social differences, usually overlooked, could stand in the way of intimacy. "Oh how I pine for association [of] some kindred mind," a young widow in Arkansas reflected. "All of my neighbours are good honest kind people but they seem to have no idie beyond their little s[p]here of action   they do not appear to have a feeling nor aspiration higher than the things of life satisfying their physical wants." Aware of such distinctions on the frontier, she decided, "I had rather be aloan for I feel aloan." Loneliness for another woman made "my mind meditate upon former scenes in my life when I had doting loving relatives all around me."

With time, however, the new network took shape. Ties became warm as marriage bound families together and family, relatives, and old friends emigrated to swell the circle of love. A recent study of kinship in Oregon suggests that this process could be relatively rapid. At least 40 percent of the households listed in the 1850 census had kinship ties with one other household and perhaps more. Census figures can only suggest the emotional significance of these relationships.

Despite the trials the frontier posed for them, many frontier women continued to see themselves as women within the mainstream of nineteenth-century culture. Although their courage, persistence, and physical endurance seem extraordinary to a later time, none of these women viewed themselves as extraordinary. Their diaries and letters show they expected to labor hard and long to achieve their goals. Though notes of weariness often creep into their accounts, they appear to have grumbled very little, at least on paper. Some complained of the monotony of farming life, though others seemed to enjoy the fact that there was "no bustleling crowd as in City or town to marr our peaceful happiness." They expressed discontent if family fortunes wavered. But they did not see themselves as drudges. Comments about Indian women invariably contrasted their own lot with that of the long-suffering Indian woman, who toiled like a slave for her husband.

The attitude of women during the early period of settlement was conditioned not only by their belief in hard work but also by limited expectations for personal happiness. Writing to her mother about a young niece's birthday, one woman advised telling the girl to remain a child "as long as she can, for the troubles of a woman, will come upon her soon enough!" The phrase "troubles of a woman" suggests something of the female frame of reference. Nineteenth-century ideology promised women fulfillment through marriage and motherhood, yet most knew the physical pains and dangers associated with bearing children and the disruption of female culture which marriage so often signified. In a highly mobile society, they witnessed the anguished separations which so frequently parted family and friends for life. The disparity between ideology and reality made it risky to assume happiness in any setting. The religious knew, of course, that God assigned both blessings and trials in life; Christians had to expect both. With such a frame of reference, nineteenth-century women were equipped to deal with the realities of their lives on the frontier far more easily than women of the present era could.

Their letters to friends and families in the East are good evidence of their plucky attitude to pioneer life. "Tell father I am not discourage and am not sorry I came," wrote Kate Robins to her brother, while Kate Blaine told her mother, "I could not have believed that I should have been as well contented as I am situated and must needs be here. We are deprived of all the conveniences I had considered indispensable before we came." Although most women were candid about the work required (Kate said, "A woman that can not endure almost as much as a horse has no business here, as there is no such thing as getting help") and frankly acknowledged their homesickness, they often were satisfied with their situation. "If our friends were here, we should be very contented, notwithstanding as we are deprived of many conveniences and comforts we might have enjoyed at home," Kate explained. Domestic triumphs, home improvements, new clothes, preaching in the vicinity were duly described and appreciated in the context of creating culture in the wilderness. The ultimate objective of many of the letter writers was, of course, persuasion. Still, the satisfactions cannot be discounted, nor can the women's underlying assumption of steady progress on the frontier. The future was promising in the West. So Phoebe Judson recalled, "The letters written back to our eastern friends gave such glowing descriptions of our fair dwelling place that some of them were encouraged to make arrangements to cross the plains the following year."

Women also told friends of the beauty of the West, of its good climate and healthy way of life. They noted the disappearance of old ailments and the feeling of bodily well-being they derived from the activities of outdoor life. And to their single relatives they described the "western gallant" perhaps not "dressed up gentlemen" but perhaps "better than anything you ever saw or heard of before."

Of course, it was in the interest of these women to attract friends and family to the West to aid in the task of building society anew. "I promise you a hearty welcome to my house" was a refrain of female letter writers. Yet the lures were real. As Pop from Arkansas pointed out, "If she was back and new as much as she dos she would endure as much more as she has to get back to Oregon."

4

"Am Beginning
to Feel Quite
Civilized"

In the early years on the frontier, women made their major contributions to and through their families. As the period of isolation came to an end, women's social contacts multiplied. The organization of churches, schools, and voluntary associations, the development of rural towns and cities, gave women a new and more public forum for their activities and opened another phase of female experience on the frontier. With growth came the opportunity to carry out the civilizing mission implicit in the concept of domesticity. This mission, heralded and inflated by publicists like Catherine Beecher, was one which proved to be at once satisfying and frustrating for women. For it was in their role as mothers of civilization that frontier women most clearly faced the conflict between culture and environment and experienced the complexities of their mission.

The growth of the rural community, which provided one basis for women's expanded role, proceeded in several stages. At first settlers had lived far from one another and regarded those living at some distance as neighbors. "We were . . . 'all told,'" Phoebe Judson remembered, "eleven families within a radius of six or eight miles, widely separated by our holdings of 300 and 20 acres to each family. In those days anyone residing within 20 miles was considered a neighbor." Lacking one central meeting place, group activities like preaching took place at a number of different locations. As more emigrants arrived, the initial spatial fluidity of the community gave way to established centers of activity. The local trading site, the schoolhouse, became foci of social, commercial, and religious activities. With time, differentiation increased. Congregations built their own houses of worship, and eventually school districts, with district schoolhouses, were established. Rural villages and towns developed. As the process of growth continued, the spatial and social simplicity of an earlier time disappeared. Families naturally created ties with the people they found most compatible and supported activities which corresponded to their vision of community life. Class distinctions and social divisions, which most settlers thought were absent in the early stages of pioneering, emerged. The very act of selecting churches and school sites created social divisions and alliances. "Each is afraid that the other will have some preference shown him or will derive more than his share of the benefit from the locality of the church," one woman explained. The evolution of the pioneer community might take place with some rapidity or be drawn out over five or ten years.

The rural community provided one basis for women's civilizing mission in the West, the urban frontier another. Many emigrants moved directly to the urban frontier rather than to the farming frontier. The trans-Mississippi West was, in fact, more of an urban place than popular views of the westward movement suggest. Most Western emigrants from outside the cotton belt did not settle on farms, for example; the percentage of the population living in cities nearly corresponded to the average of the nation as a whole.

Some of the cities settlers chose were advance bases of settlement. Rather than emerging as a response to the farming frontier, cities like San Francisco and Denver sprang up in advance of it. Their pattern of development surpassed their speculators' wildest dreams. Other sites became cities because they supplied the emigrant trade. St. Joseph and Kansas City fitted emigrants for the trek across the plains, Salt Lake City functioned as a rest stop for travelers, Portland as a destination. Writing from Portland in 1865, Harriet Williams vividly characterized the pace of urban growth on the frontier. One thousand people had arrived one Saturday, she reported, with not a house to be had for rent.

Whatever the basis for the development of any one city, commentators noted the general explanation. American frontiersmen were not only farmers but also enthusiastic town builders, planners, and speculators. Foreigners marveled at the rapidity of urban development in the West. "Nothing earns our admiration as much as the rapid rise of towns in those parts of the American Union . . . twenty-five years ago . . . still inhabited by Indians," wrote one in an 1854 Missouri immigrant guide. Urban growth was like "a stroke of magic." Phoebe Judson conveyed the drama of the urban frontier, starting with the "nightly spectacle" of "glowing fires" which cleared the land. "New buildings," she wrote, "spring up in all directions, and everything wore that indescribable air of excitement and thrill that accompanies the carving out of a town in the wilderness."

The Western frontier as it passed beyond the first stages of development, then, provided urban and rural settings for women's cultural activities. Some of the characteristics of these communities should be highlighted so that female contributions to community growth can be placed in their proper context and so that the nature of women's experience during this stage of frontier development can be appreciated.

One of the most striking features of growing rural communities on the farming frontier which was to affect both individual women's lives and their attempts to create culture was the transiency of the population. Wapello County, Iowa, offers characteristic evidence. Less than one-third of the pioneers listed on the 1850 census were there ten years later. Mobility may have been more a pattern of single pioneers than of married, for an investigation of another Iowa county during the same ten-year period revealed that 91 percent of the single men but only 73 percent of those with families picked up stakes. Only 27 percent of the pioneer families there stayed put over the ten-year period.

Census data give no information about why settlers on the rural frontier moved so quickly. The Wapello County data show that those who stayed until 1860 had been more successful than those who left. Moving in itself, however, was not necessarily a mark of failure. Of those emigrating into the county in 1850, for example, those who had moved several times owned more valuable property than did first-time emigrants. Still, it was apparently the more successful who stayed in Wapello County while the less successful left. This picture of a geographically mobile lower class on the frontier resembles but is more extreme than the pattern of urban lower-class transiency which urban historians have established for Eastern cities in the nineteenth century. Other studies of frontier farm laborers, tenants, and land consolidation also indicate that the frontier community rapidly departed from the egalitarian, homogeneous model so often described.

Transiency, social and economic inequality, community conflict were the characteristics of the growing rural community. On the one hand, they suggest the ways in which the pioneer experience may have differed according to class (although the written records which reflect the experience of the more successful and prosperous settlers yield little evidence). On the other hand, they also suggest some of the barriers faced by those who wished to establish stable institutions and moral habits on the frontier.

The urban frontier differed from the rural frontier in a number of ways. Demographically, Western cities were distinctive, with youthful populations and fewer and smaller families than rural areas. During Portland's twenty-year pioneer period, for example, 41–50 percent of the women were childless, while 20–30 percent had only one or two children. At least half the women were under thirty during this period and most were married. And they were surrounded by young men. The actual ratio between the sexes depended on the nature of the town or city. In 1850, Portland, a center of trade, had more than three men for every woman; mining and cattle communities had proportionately more men than Portland, rural villages fewer. Although the ratio evened out with time, the implications for urban female life and activities were manifold. One woman commented, "There is plenty of men here. They cast sheeps eyes at Lib and Lucy's girl but they have not popt the question yet." Courting was only one leisure activity for a predominantly male society which also drank, gambled, and supported prostitution. Female concerns might not fare so well, as the editor of the Houston *Morning Sun* pointed out: "It is a source of much astonishment, and of considerable severe comment . . . that while we have a theatre, a court house, and a jail, and even a capitol in Houston, we have not a single church."

With few families and numerous single young men, the urban frontier had a character of its own which was a far cry from the ideal community of families. Many of the men lived in boardinghouses or hotels which were, in essence, male dormitories. Though most married women did not work, they often chose to live in hotels and boardinghouses rather than set up their own household. Hired help was in short supply, while "city" dwellings could be just as rough, crowded, and hard to maintain as the rural cabin. Housekeeping, all too often, signified drudgery, and many young women wanted none of it in the early days of urban living.

Like rural communities, towns and cities also had unstable populations. Roseburg, Oregon, a county seat and center of trade in the Umpqua Valley, was described by an 1862 visitor as "a gem of a village." He remarked upon its well-laid-out streets, its "neat, white, frame cottages." On the surface, Roseburg was a stable frontier town of some charm. Yet census data suggest that beneath the surface, the picture was one of instability. The 1860 census revealed that over half the youthful adult work force was composed of restless single men. Few of them stayed long in the charming town. Eighty-five percent of those appearing in the 1860 census were gone within five years. Some wives shared male mobility, but marriage was a factor which seemed to diminish men's urge to move on. While only a third of the single men stayed for more than five years, 68 percent of the married men did. Still, the majority of the town's men settled in Roseburg only temporarily, and economic information suggests their stay was not a very successful one. Those with little or no personal property were the least stable.

Economic data point to the existence of social and class distinctions on the urban frontier. Although the early days of Roseburg's growth saw little in the way of economic specialization, there was an emerging sense of social differentiation. The newspaper's designation of some inhabitants as "respectable" or "leading" local figures was echoed in private correspondence. By 1876 the *Plaindealer* was referring to an *"elite,"* mainly composed of merchants and professional men. These successful residents were politically and culturally active in town affairs; they were men of prestige. Their wives shared in their social position. Long-time residents like artisans and laborers were also considered respectable, solid members of the community. Paupers and minorities were at the bottom of the social scale.

On the urban frontier, which Roseburg exemplifies, marriage seemed to retard transiency, while length of residence was associated with wealth. These correlations suggest that some married women were in a favorable position to participate in community growth, for as wives of respected men they had power and prestige. They also stayed long enough in the community to contribute to its culture. And these were the women most likely to be familiar with cultural imperatives because of their social status and, in Roseburg's case, because of settlers' New England ties. But a New England background was hardly necessary. The rapid appearance of Eastern papers, magazines, and novels on the frontier ensured that literate women would be reminded of their mission as mothers of civilization.

Yet the civilizing task was far from easy. Women residing for a lengthy period on the urban frontier, like their counterparts on the agricultural frontier, were only a minority of the population as a whole and also a minority of their own sex. Urban and rural areas were often divided by community differences. The large floating population of young men in a Western city or town had little stake in that place's future, while families on the agricultural frontier also were often only temporary residents. Attempts to establish standards of behavior and to shape culture would run up against these conditions time and time again. Mrs. Stearns, a prominent Roseburg resident, gave a graphic picture of the atmosphere which made her task difficult in a series of letters to her husband. Their sons were "running in the streets," and she trembled for their safety because of "this drink and gambaling . . . the chief Amusements night and day." The teacher played billiards, the town was agog at the latest scandal. Mrs. Kearney's baby was born and announced full term by the doctor, early by the mother, illegitimate by the husband, who talked of divorce.

Still, Mrs. Stearns reported that the town had taken the first steps toward establishing a free school. Residents did not abandon the vision of a good society just because conditions seemed unpromising at times. But her reference to the school meeting indicates that, as a woman, she was not directly involved in the formal efforts to organize the school. In Roseburg, as elsewhere, it was the men who usually established the political, social, and economic institutions which would help to integrate the community and who founded its official cultural groups like lyceums and debating societies. At least they took credit for these activities. Newspaper accounts, recording the process of community growth, focus on male achievements but provide little information on women. Occasionally, however, there is a glimpse of married women who helped to organize and staff formal social institutions. Mary Staples, for example, recalled, "Through the efforts of the ladies in 1860, a purchase of 150 volumes was made as the beginning of a Free Library," while Esther Pillsbury recorded her election as vice president of the Okoboji Literary Society and her activities in the club. But most frequently frontier women lent support to formal institutions rather than founded them.

The social ties which women made with each other, however, constituted an informal kind of institution which was instrumental in establishing culture on the frontier, though few newspapers commented on its activities. Letters and reminiscences, however, attest to the early and spirited efforts of pioneer women to create their social world. Lois Holman told her mother that no sooner had she arrived in Sergeant Bluff, Iowa, than "the lades have all called on me that live here in the City whitch concists the whole of six." She went on, "I have not retirned them yet but I must begin soon or I shant get round this summer." Although visiting might be regarded by the male world as frivolous, it created a female support system and assisted women in their attempts to regulate society. As the previous chapter suggests, early female networks probably included women from different backgrounds, but with time, women probably became more selective in their choice of companions. The comments which women made referring to women of whom they had heard but with whom they did not associate suggests this was the case as communities grew.

The informal network existed as a means of sharing information about fashion and styles. Although it might seem puzzling as well as superficial for women in frontier communities to talk of fashion, these discussions reinforced their sense of identity and increased their feeling of control over their environment. Appropriate clothes, the end product of discussion, helped to encourage and reinforce correct behavior and establish a proper society.

Informal social exchange also consoled women and clarified group norms. Louisiana Strentzel reported spending part of a day listening to Mrs. Chase, who was "in great trouble" because of her husband's drinking. Kate Blaine listened to a homesick woman pour out her unhappiness. The "little frail creature" loved her husband, Kate explained, but "will smother her homesickness and other trials, rather than permit him to know she is not happy. It really seemed a relief to her to be able to tell me how she felt." Female confidences helped women who were discouraged and frustrated in their roles as frontier wives by allowing them to share their feelings. As they did so, they could reaffirm the correctness of their world view, whether it involved the necessity of female submission or the necessity of temperance.

Female companionship also helped relieve the tedium and burden of female work on the frontier. Women helped one another cook festive meals in preparation for community social occasions. Sewing and quilting were often done among a circle of friends. "I went to Mrs. Low's quilting   There was 15 to quilt   had 2 quilts and there was indeed meery faces about them," reported one young Iowa pioneer. While they worked together, women also "gossiped." "This afternoon," wrote Elisabeth Adams, "I go to Sewing Society at Mr. Pierces. I suppose the affairs of the town will be discussed over the quilt." Gossip made work go fast but, like individual exchanges, probably served as a means of expressing anxieties, reasserting standards, exchanging important information, and even covertly or overtly attacking male society. Unfortunately, gossip rarely gets recorded, but the few references to it suggest these were its functions. Gossip, then as now, may also have had a folkloric aspect and been one means of artistic verbal expression.

The group setting made necessary work more enjoyable and also provided an occasion for sharing the creative skills fostered by female culture. There was "commendable reciprocity in the exhibition and distribution of new patchwork quilt designs. The display was made with quite as much pride as is the showing of artistic fancy-work today," one woman reported. "All plans, patterns, ideas or innovations were pleasantly passed along . . . This was true, likewise, of clothing cutting. Exclusiveness in the cut or trim of apparel was unthought of."

As a community developed, the informal pattern of female interaction could take on a wider social purpose. Voluntary female associations, staffed by women who had decided along with Mary Jane Hayden that "the time had come when I must do my part socially," provided a variety of services for the community at large. Even quilting became a means of social assistance, as Ellen Strang noted when she described a surprise quilting at the Lewises': "They being in great want of a [quilt]," with the guests providing the materials.

Women's cultural contributions were not limited to these informal group settings with other women. Although women were not listed on school boards in the West, or on the boards of trustees which founded early schools, they played a significant part both in establishing and servicing educational institutions. Private educational efforts were important on the frontier, since many Western communities were laggardly in establishing common schools. Even bustling frontier Kansas City, for example, had only one public school in the late 1850's, which most city children could not attend. A school census indicated that 90 percent of school-aged children were not in school, though other estimates had less gloomy figures. Although a writer for the *Journal* pointed to what seemed an obvious truth, "If our city would employ the most effectual means for a steady growth . . . let her do for education what other cities have done," it was not until 1867 that the city's children had classes, and then in rented quarters.

The failure of Western communities to provide early public education for their children reveals much about the state of Western society and the staged process of community building. A majority of men and women failed to see free public education as an important enough social goal to press for it or to pay for it in early years of community development. Only a minority of the pioneers (often of New England backgrounds) worked to set up public, quasi-public, or private schools, thus ensuring that some children at least would be exposed to the moral, religious, and educational values normally part of a nineteenth-century curriculum. Their efforts, while important, were often marked by financial crises and temporary failures. Their influence was limited, all too often, to those children whose parents would pay. (Even as late as the 1870's and '80's, only about 40 percent of those eligible to attend school in Jackson County, Oregon, went to school. The $5 charge helped to deter the others.) In the long run, of course, their efforts succeeded, and free public schooling became the norm in the West as in the East.

Although men served on the boards of early community educational institutions and played a crucial part in raising money, women helped to staff them. If the frontier was anything like the East, as many as one-fifth to one-quarter of the women taught at some time in their lives. In many cases, women started the educational process. Reminiscences and letters almost always point to a mother or female neighbor as the first teacher. In the earliest stages of community growth, married women often set up simple schools in their own homes, realizing, as did Mollie Sanford's mother, "that the children ought to be in school." These impromptu schools had little permanence, serving neighbors and family for a few months a year when nothing else was available. Later, as communities built schoolhouses, women were drafted to teach. "Next arose the question of teacher," one woman wrote, describing the informal process of selection which existed in her frontier community. "Somebody suggested that Mrs. Lewis, the wife of our community doctor, would be a good teacher. I do not know how it was determined that she was qualified, but she was chosen by a show of hands, and accepted the post." As the process of selection became more sophisticated and as public education finally became a reality on the frontier, women continued to staff city and country schools; most often they were confined to the primary department either as teachers or directors.

Although women's ability to provide financial support for education was limited, they did provide some monetary assistance for hard-pressed schools. Tabitha Brown, a widow and grandmother, showed generosity which was exceptional, not only for the size of her gifts, but also because her benevolence was recorded. Instrumental in establishing an early private school in Oregon, Tabitha Brown donated land, a house, $550 of her earnings, and a bell before her death in 1857. Perhaps just as important as these contributions were women's attempts to bolster and support boards and trustees in their difficult education ventures. Tabitha Brown's contributions are again instructive. "On one occasion it was actually resolved [by the male trustees] to discontinue the school, but the resolution had been heard through the cracks in the ceiling of the cabin by Mrs. Clark, Mrs. Smith, and Mrs. Brown, and they plead with the men to reverse it, with the result that the school continued."

For married women, teaching could be viewed as a natural extension of motherhood and, thus, an eminently respectable occupation for them. Some saw teaching also as a means of capitalizing on women's moral and religious influence, as Catherine Beecher had suggested, while others stressed the importance of maintaining social and cultural standards on the frontier. In advertising for the second term of her early log-cabin school in Oregon City, Mrs. Thornton assured prospective students and their families that "strict attention will be given not only to the intellectual improvement of the pupils, but also to their morals and manners." Even on the frontier female teachers offered instruction in "all the branches usually comprised in a thorough English education, together with plain and fancy needle-work, drawing, and painting in mezzotints and water-colors." The early appearance of female academies run by women and teaching the "female arts" in rough towns like Houston suggest their determination to pass on female culture.

Of course, moral and cultural goals did not preclude pragmatic concerns. Agnes Sengstacken found "my school teaching quite a relaxation" from "my family and my housework," while Sarah Everett hoped to make money for her dairying by teaching. Sarah even considered leaving her baby with a neighbor and taking her five-year-old "boarding around" with her so that she could take a teaching job. Whatever the motives which led them to teach, married women helped both to establish and to support educational institutions in their communities in the years in which support was most needed.

Single women, though always a minority of adult women on the frontier, made up the majority of female teachers, and it was as teachers that single women helped shape their society most directly. Teaching was for a woman, as Catherine Beecher had pointed out, "the road to honourable independence and extensive usefulness where she need not outstep the prescribed boundaries of feminine modesty." Women in the West, as they had in the East, gradually came to dominate the teaching field. In the early days, even though women set up schools at home and taught spring schools, men usually taught winter schools, which the teenage boys attended. In Iowa Territory, for example, only 23 of the 124 teachers were women in 1848; by 1862, however, women had taken over the profession. An 1854 report suggested the reason for the change. Women would work for half what men demanded. Teaching, then, became women's work as the community matured and men found better-paying opportunities.

At least two sorts of single women decided to teach in the West. Women like Mollie Sanford wanted a job to earn money and pass a few years until they married. Teaching was their most attractive alternative, but it was viewed as temporary employment. As Fannie Case confided to a friend, "I cannot say that teaching is perfectly congeniel to my taste—but—well, I might as well say it, but it is very confidential, you know, I think there is nothing so nice as housekeeping, in a little home of one's own, and I have no hopes that there is such bliss in store for me, think teaching second best." Others, however, came from the East as part of the crusade to save the West or shared the crusading viewpoint that education was the key to civilization on the frontier. Teaching was their vocation. The Board of National Popular Education sent over a quarter of its teachers to the trans-Mississippi West. Most of them stayed in the West; some married, an event "incidental to the main purpose of sending teachers . . . West," but one allowing them to "form connexions which will increase their power of doing good."

No matter why women chose to teach, the job itself had little security. When schools failed to materialize or collapsed through lack of support, would-be teachers found themselves unemployed. When they worked, many discovered, often to their dismay, that they were the focus of community interest. Some of this was to be expected. Settlers had raised the schoolhouse and saw it as both an educational and a community center. Their proprietary sense was evident in the process of teacher selection, in their attendance at periodic school exhibitions, and in the practice of having teachers board with members of the community. But the constant surveillance in and out of school, the need to prove competence and character, the bad food, poor quarters, and even the household chores sometimes involved in boarding around, led some to bemoan their situation. "I find among strangers we are judged by outward appearances," one Iowa teacher sadly observed, "and that we cannot be to careful in giving the world's people occasion for slander."

Teaching itself was hindered by classroom conditions. Short terms of three months were educationally limiting. The wide range of students' age forced a teacher to do a little of everything. One Ashland, Oregon, schoolhouse, for example, had twenty-eight pupils, all in one room, during the 1859–60 term. Seven were between five and nine; thirteen ranged in age between ten and fourteen, four from fifteen to twenty, and another four between twenty and twenty-nine. Not only were students of different ages, they were differently equipped. Each student brought books from home, thus complicating instruction even more. Finally, a casual attitude toward school kept attendance irregular and unpredictable.

Teachers' letters and journals stress the effort and the unpleasantness of the authoritarian task which conditions and pedagogical theory suggested. "I have only 11 scholars," wrote one woman to her aunt, "but I am glad I have no more for it is all I can do to manage them. I have to use my ruler pretty often." Mollie Sanford's response to the requirements of the classroom was similar, and she appeared torn between an image of woman as nurturer and the reality of teacher as disciplinarian. "I was thinking the other day how nicely and smoothly I was getting along," she wrote in her journal. "Not an unpleasant event had occurred at school . . . But a day or two ago I had to inflict my first corporal punishment. After exhausting my powers of moral suasion with little Johnnie Morton, to establish my authority and make an example, I chastised him very mildly."

When Johnnie didn't come to school for a few days, Mollie, conscious of possible criticism, paid the troublesome Johnnie a visit. Discipline, necessary as it was, might provoke community disapproval. An irate father suggested limits to the teacher's authority. "I am very sorry to informe that in my opinion you have Shoed to me that you are unfit to keep a School," he wrote, "if you hit my boy in the face accidently that will be different but if on purpos . . . you are unfit . . . I shall in forme the Superintendant in which this Scool has been commeced and how it Seames to go on." An Iowa schoolteacher fared even worse and was brought to court, charged with "assault and battery by punishing in an immoderate and cruel manner one Peter John Matthew," and found guilty. No wonder some of the teachers confessed, "I wish this term was through. I am becoming tired of teaching." Few probably stuck with teaching for more than two years.

Teachers whose goals included attention to their pupils' "precious undying souls," and the advancement "of culture and refinement among the female of the regions," faced similar problems. Moreover, their high sense of purpose and their single status often made them feel lonely in their new communities. Perry, Arkansas, was a "benighted portion of the west," Maria Atwater commented to the Board of National Popular Education.

Hope of providing an education which would "soften the asperities of tempers, check the waywardness of . . . appetite and train . . . [the] habits of industry" was checked by what was perceived as the "stupor" of pupils and parents. Ambitious goals may well have made students appear even more backward than they were and progress slower. Efforts to establish Sunday schools to complement the common schools were sometimes hampered by parental indifference, although as one Missouri teacher reported, "They have plenty of time to buy and sell, and many of them desecreate the Sabbath by drinking, horse racing and gambling." Another described her successful Sunday school, which attracted mothers and children. Even so, she found herself not altogether pleased. It was hard, she admitted, to adjust to mothers' nursing their babies during her instruction.

Sensitive to their Christian responsibilities, these teachers confronted their own inadequacies. "I do feel very incapable," of doing good, wrote one teacher from Missouri in 1853. "I have had so little religious experience myself. Pray for me that I may be taught of God how to teach and that my feeble efforts to serve Christ, may be blessed." For all the difficulties they encountered, however, most of them were aware of a great opportunity to extend culture. And their communities responded with occasional raises and even appreciation for their good "influence in the community."

Somewhat unexpectedly, these missionary teachers found themselves departing from the very norms they expected to maintain. In the absence of permanent churches, they took on religious responsibilities themselves. "It seems rather hard that neither of these men are willing to open the [Sabbath] School by prayers," one teacher reported, "but since they are not, I feel it my duty to do so." Another teacher, similarly situated, indicated how fast she forgot proprieties when duty called. "The question whether a woman should pray in such a public place was . . . easily answered in my mind," she wrote.

Their comments highlight a paradoxical side to women's civilizing activities. Devotion to "duty" and efforts to build community could result in unconventional behavior in the same way that early burdens of pioneer farming had done. Yet few of the women went beyond the rationalization of duty to claim that their new activities were appropriate for all women. As a group, they were very conscious of conventional female norms, eager to observe and spread them.

Although the highest hopes of these teachers may have been dashed as they embarked on their ambitious program of molding minds and souls and of spreading civilized values, although they were often depressed, many eventually saw signs of progress on the frontier. Perhaps the culture they were able to communicate was diluted, but as the prejudice of the communities disappeared, as teachers succeeded in imparting even simple standards to children, they felt they had achieved something worthwhile. The test was that so many sent out by the Board of National Popular Education stayed. "I like the West so much, and see so much need of teaching here, that I have no intention of ever going home to stay," wrote one, while another confessed, "I do *not* feel like a stranger in a strange land." For all its frustrations, teaching seemed to offer proof to some women that their civilizing mission was succeeding.

Certainly teaching offered the most satisfying career for single women. Although most adult women on the frontier were married or would marry, there were increasingly numbers of single women who might need or want to work. In Portland, for example, single women constituted 22 percent of the adult female population in 1860, but by 1880 the percentage had risen to over 29 percent. Women who worked often expressed the desire to be useful and to avoid being an economic drain on their families. "Next winter *I must* be where I can make some money for myself," Irene Calbraith wrote to her father, "instead of being a dead expense on you. I *must* and I *will.*"

Rural communities offered few opportunities for paid employment aside from teaching, and so enterprising young women, like Mollie Sanford, went to urban areas to "look about for something to do to help myself . . . duty and necessity call me." They found jobs as domestics, nurses, teachers, seamstresses, clerks, even as prostitutes. None paid much, nor were they particularly rewarding from other perspectives. Mollie found herself a dressmaker and seamstress and reflected, "I do often wish that I might be something more than a mere machine. There is something dull in sitting here day by day, planning this garment and making that." Despite her pluck and initiative, she considered the unappealing job "my destiny just now. There does not seem to be much that a girl *can* do here." Census data support her complaint. The 1870 census showed 45 percent of the single women in Portland working, for example, mostly as domestics. These jobs were temporary and considered so by those who held them. Only marriage offered relief from the monotony, and most women eagerly accepted it as such. With the coming of industrialization to the West within a generation, the number of job opportunities multiplied, but women's position did not improve much. Working women in Kansas in the late eighties did not make enough to break even. Working women in the West were undervalued and underpaid.

It was as married women, then, that most women on the frontier made their most significant contributions to their communities. Maintaining Protestantism on the frontier represented one of their greatest challenges. From the beginning of the vast migration west, many had feared that the frontier would become a center of religious indifference. By 1850, Eastern missionary societies were spending $500,000 a year on Western missionary work and had sent out and helped support over 2,600 ministers for "destitute" frontier communities. By giving significant aid to missionaries and by preparing the way for them, women helped to establish religious institutions on a firm basis. As they did so, they, too, discovered unexpected opportunities for autonomy, although, like the teachers, these women rarely capitalized on the unexpected.

Westward migration posed many difficult problems for Protestant denominations. Creating and sustaining new congregations when members of the community were scattered, with different denominational loyalties, when they were out of the habit of regular churchgoing and giving, was difficult. Buildings had to be constructed, maintained, and then used. Yet as the Reverend Milton Starr lamented, "Even the New England element among us seem in some measure to have forgotten their early training," while the Reverend Oswold in Kansas agreed, saying, "It has become entirely easy and natural, to remain at home all day Sunday."

Apparently, however, women in the West, like their Eastern counterparts, remembered their religious duty better than men, so much so that the frontier "congregation is mostly (*femenine*)." These steadfast women were particularly important at the beginning of missionary work, when ministers were trying to establish the habit of regular worship. Perhaps just as crucial as their attendance was the encouragement women gave to missionaries, who were often deeply depressed by their apparent failure. So Mrs. Thornton lifted the spirits of the Reverend Gray, who recounted how she "assured that the *result* was greater than I was able to perceive. She said she had observed a marked increase in the piety of some of our church members since I came here; that the young people were more interested—that I was well fitted for this place &c." It was this kind of support which comforted missionaries as they sought to Christianize the West.

By mid-century ministers judged success by conversions and membership figures. Women not only swelled membership rolls but were quickly recognized as recruiters and forcibly reminded of their responsibilities. The Reverend Reuben Gaylord, an Iowa missionary of the forties, "took occasion before the meeting closed to make some remarks upon the duty of mothers and the power which God had given them over their children. Several wept freely." Circuit rider John Dyer pointed out that maternal recruiting must even be done at life's last moments, for a mother's parting religious advice "often brings the children to Christ." Women were also encouraged to exercise their influence on their husbands and gain them and incidentally their assets for Christ. "Some of the female members have husbands," wrote one candid Oregon missionary, "who are not professors—who might give much more than they do—that is allow their wives to. which they would willingly do—but they feel a restraint in that particular—of course the wife must always exercise prudence in such a case."

Many women found that church membership and activities satisfied deep spiritual needs. But their support for religion was also related to their role as community builders. During the long trip over the Oregon Trail, numerous women had noted how they missed observing the Sabbath. The reestablishment of services was a link with the world they had left and symbolized the determination to make the West like the East. Christian fellowship reinforced and publicized social and moral standards and clarified values. Skimpy church records show how congregations tried to foster certain behavior by disciplining errant members and rejecting them if they refused to mend their ways. Such incidents must have provided the substance for many lively community discussions. The Pleasant Grove Presbyterian Church, for example, recorded the case of Mrs. Pira Rudolph, who "having absented herself from the stated ministration of the word for the past year or more and various reports derogatory to her character as a christian coming to the ears of the Session she was visited by them, and she expressed a desire to have her name striken from the roll." The West Union Baptist Church records described an unseemly altercation between Sister Zachary and Sister Constable. Sister Zachary, the minutes noted, "having circulated Slanderous reports against the character of Sister C and having failed to prove them and haveing refused the call of the church when cited to attend and wilfully so, is considered disorderly, and unworthy [of] the fellowship of the church." Mrs. Constable was later in trouble for a party given at her house. While these policing activities may seem unattractive to the modern observer, they did define for the community what the highest standards of conduct ought to be. They gave believers the courage to struggle on. Jane Walrud's diary shows the impact religious fellowship could have as she reported how she had been able to resist "the tempter [who] came and gave a hard try."

Religion also offered some women the opportunity for leadership. In the days before formal churches were organized, women could become key figures in providing religious exercises for their communities. In Kansas, Lois Murray became church school superintendent and began to read sermons in the community Sabbath school. Although she was careful to seek her husband's approval, the "mission" God had given her led her to speak at numerous meetings and even to officiate at funerals. It was "from a sense of duty I complied; and felt I had merely filled a servant's place," she explained. Though few women probably interpreted their religious duty so expansively, others did work in Sunday schools, often the only continuing religious activity in a community served by itinerant preachers. Women instituted Sunday schools, recruited students, taught them, and even attended regional conferences to report on their progress.

Participation in camp meetings, revivals, and prayer meetings also gave leadership possibilities to women. Prayer meetings, for example, provided opportunities for women to become charismatic figures. Prayer meetings ideally were held at least once a week. Some were open to both sexes, others were segregated. The format was generally fluid, and women took advantage of this looseness. "Everybody who wished to do so could take part by offering a prayer, making a talk, or singing a song as the spirit moved." The Reverend Atkinson's 1848 prayer meeting was typical. "I preached, after which a prayer meeting was held. The impenitent were invited to the anxious seat. Some women spoke. Two screamed very loud and grasped hands, uttering many things incoherently." Although Atkinson's Congregational background made him downplay the women's behavior, it was clearly the focus of the meeting both for him and for the group. And though he might disapprove of moaning women, Atkinson was shrewd enough to realize how instrumental they were in bringing about conversions and membership. They could hardly be discouraged.

Women's church groups also thrust them into a position of potential power. The Reverend Knight attested, "As is always the case in the infancy of Christian efforts, we have been greatly indebted to the ladies of our congregation for material aid. By their sewing society &c. they have furnished fuel and lights and kept up repairs." The financial aid women provided from their group activities was often substantial; it was desperately needed on the frontier, where Eastern support for missionary work was inadequate and where religious expenses were so high. Women's fund-raising abilities thus gave them a real, if limited, power. Although the minister might point out specific needs, the women made the money and the decisions. Records of the Ladies Guild of St. Paul's Episcopal Church in Oregon City, for example, reported that the rector requested aid to build a rectory porch. "After some talk on the subject," the minutes revealed, "it was concluded to lay it on the table until the next regular meeting." Not until the following year did the rector get his porch. And that same year saw the vestry begging the women for $150 to meet year-end expenses.

As Ephraim Adams evaluated the contributions of women to frontier religion, he commented, "What wonder if there were some praying and talking then, and voting too, other than that done by the brethren?" His comments suggested the freedoms and implied the boundaries of the church world for women. Although religion on the frontier offered women scope and influence, in the end it also confined them to their socially established role. Instrumental as Lois

Murray had been in supporting the religious life of her early community in Kansas, she wrote the letter "requesting that ministers might visit us, when God might direct." Women were excluded from formal church organization. Despite her position as assistant superintendent of the Sabbath school, and her appearance at the quarterly conference to report on it, Ketturah Belknap found herself not on the church board but driving "home with perhaps two or thre Lady visitors for we al ways expected friends from distant parts of the curcuit to be entertained." And when in Keokuk, Iowa, a few Episcopalian women gathered into a society in 1850 and determined to form a church, the vestry was composed entirely of men who were not even Episcopalians.

Even on the frontier, church women as well as church men continued to operate according to the social definitions of woman's sphere. Most women viewed the minister as "sent of God" and expected men to regulate the larger affairs of the church. It was hardly surprising that men expected to do so. Ministers, for all their dependence on women, shared the prevailing ideas of society. And, financially pressed, they still anticipated that the bulk of their monetary support would have to come from men. The Reverend Chamberlain was only expressing a typical attitude when he wrote, "We greatly need a few *faithful laboring* male members. I sometimes feel I stand almost alone in the great work."

It may be that the religious activities of women in their frontier communities eventually contributed to a broadening understanding of women's roles in their churches. But women's records show little evidence that they overtly resented their displacement or their secondary position. Subconsciously some of them may have harbored rebellious feelings. Certainly the fact that Lois Murray continued some of her informal services even after the circuit rider served her Kansas community is suggestive. Her justification indicated she was unwilling to accept the common definition of women's role in the church. "From a sense of duty, I complied [and attended to religious services] and felt I had merely filled a servant's place," she explained. And the decision of St. Paul's Ladies Guild to keep the rector dangling in the matter of his rectory porch may imply a similar resentment of their lack of power within the church. But the signs of discontent are few.

Of all the women involved in establishing Christ's kingdom in the West, the missionary wife was doubtless the one with the highest religious and cultural purposes and the highest standards. An examination of their work suggests both the problems and successes involved in building frontier communities. The women constituted a small but influential group. Most of the 2,679 missionaries sent from the East to spread the gospel on the frontier probably were married, for they were counseled and counseled others to bring wives with them. An Iowa band received typical advice when they brought up the marriage question. "Wives are the cheapest things in all Iowa. Bring wives! Bring Yankee wives, that are not afraid of a checked apron, and who can pail the cow, and churn the butter."

Women who went west as missionary wives viewed themselves, however, as missionaries first and as wives second. If young Cushing Eells's proposal lacked some of the standard romantic trappings, it was certainly appropriate for a woman who had written in her school copybook, "I go, my friend, where heathen dwell; / Then if on earth we meet no more, / Accept this cordial, short farewell, / Till we meet on Canaan's shore." Asked if she were willing to be a *missionary* (rather than a wife), she replied, "I doubt whether you could have asked any one who would have been more willing."

Few anticipated the potential conflict between the two roles. Nor did their religious enthusiasm and lofty idealism prepare them for the reality of missionary work.

Although often initially impressed by the frontier's potential for fruitful church work, couples soon discovered how hard it was to attract steadfast supporters. The realization that much of the support was female resulted in wives taking on heavy recruiting and social responsibilities, which had both emotional and physical costs.

As the Reverend Tenney testified, "The only reputable social circle rallied about the church as a center, though the town ladies did not enter the church organization. The pastor's wife became the center of female influence." The Reverend Atkinson described his wife's constant entertaining. "In a new country," he pointed out, "it is difficult to avoid company unless we become boorish and inhospitable and the minister cannot consistently be either. It is very important for me to have visitors."

As teachers in Sunday schools and regular schools, as organizers of prayer meetings and other church groups, the women also worked to create Christian society in the West. Saving souls turned out to be no easy matter, but at least the task was central to the religious mission. But few wives had realized that religious duties might take second place to their efforts as fund raisers. They were, of course, pulled into fund raising for the church, organizing and canvassing for church operating funds. But the women soon discovered they must also help support their own families. Missionary subsidies were woefully meager, no matter what the denomination. Men had the responsibilities of preaching, visiting, and traveling; women were left to earn money. So women taught not only because teaching offered a religious opening but because it paid. Milton Starr, reporting from Tacoma, wrote, "Our first effort here was to instruct a few of our neighbors children in our own house. My wife is now teaching . . . about 12 schollars on an average . . . . this helps a little by way of support." Missionary wives also took in boarders for cash, even sold butter, and almost always did their housework without hired help, all the while practicing rigid economy. Their husbands' letters are full of descriptions of the workloads of their wives and breakdowns caused by fatigue.

The trials of missionary life were increased as women discovered the necessity of playing several roles simultaneously. At the beginning of missionary work, most of the women were young and childless. But with the coming of children, domestic demands clashed with religious vocations and with a wife's duties as helpmate. The life of the Walkers in the 1850's was punctuated with strife as he sought to persuade her that her first obligation was to him. As an itinerant minister, he wrote, living "without you is the greatest earthly sacrifice I have to make and if I could have you with me, I should regard it as the greatest earthly comfort. You have no idea how strong is my feeling on this point. You gave yourself to be a minister's wife before you became a wife & mother." Mary Walker was not to be persuaded, but other women sadly set aside their original hopes for domesticity. "How forcibly do I realize that my husband has got to be the laborer for the church . . . for the Lord," wrote one wife in the early 1850's, "whilst my duty is to take care of him and make *home* my paramount field of action. I fear I am not reconciled to this my views being so different from the duties of a minister's wife especially a missionary's wife I have literally as much as I can do to take care of myself, my husband, my dear babes, whereas I thought my duties would be almost wholly spiritual I have felt unhappy because I have not been able to teach. I came here for that purpose. I love to teach but if domestic toiles are to be my care I will yield obediently." Though the appeal to duty may have helped, submission was difficult and at times tinged with resentment. Mrs. Eells, who "yielded with regret" to her husband's dutiful decision to move to the rough frontier of Walla Walla, announced flatly when their house burned after ten years, "We can leave now; we have nothing to leave." Her son's comments that those years "were ever uncongenial to her" suggest her embittered feelings.

Mrs. Eells disliked Walla Walla because of "the life, the lonely farm work, and the want of society." Perhaps she disliked it, too, because, in that remote place, it was difficult to realize the many goals of missionary life which sought a West populated by industrious, faithful people living moral, pious, and temperate lives. Such a social vision for the West was noble and corresponded to the nineteenth century's understanding of woman's civilizing mission. But this was not the West which emerged. Although Western society did not lapse into barbarism, drinking and other social vices flourished. Many stubbornly refused to attend church. Secular amusements continued to attract a spirited following despite denunciation by the godly. One young woman captured the flavor of the confrontation between the secular and the religious. "The Church members did not like [dancing]," she wrote, "and some of them got a little 'huffy' about it, but we did not care a fig for them. One of the young ladies told the minister that if he would preach a sermon, we would not dance, but we must either have a sermon or dance. The minister took his hat in hand and left."

By so narrowly defining the nature of the good society, missionary women felt defeated at times, even though they actually played a significant part in the development of the West. As ministers' wives and as teachers they occupied positions of visibility and respect in their communities. They used their positions to make others aware of the highest standards of nineteenth-century culture and provided a clear frame of reference for evaluating the frontier life. Their work made it impossible for new communities to forget their links with American society as a whole.

Yet, for years, the women could see only failure. This was not altogether surprising. Religious commitment appeared to be weak in the West, and missionaries and their wives seemed unable to do much about it. Denominational rivalry tempted the "faithful" to transfer allegiances, but no denomination had impressive growth statistics. One study of church membership suggests that only one out of every three or four persons was a formal member of any church in the West as a whole.

No wonder missionaries and their wives were often deeply discouraged. Yet the frontier was not so irreligious as they thought. Formal church membership nationwide included no more than 23 percent of the population in 1866. But missionaries judged their achievements by their ambitious hopes and contrasted their gains with an idealized picture of religion in the East. And they correctly noted the different atmosphere of Western society. Many of the props which maintained the semblance of religion in the East, churches, bells, the quiet Sabbath, were absent in the West, while the competition of visiting, horseracing, and relaxing was all too visible. The West was a godless place for the godly, although a modern observer might say it was only less hypocritical.

The depression that missionary couples seem routinely to have experienced was sometimes lifted by consolation from the home missionary board. But low spirits soon returned. Because they were certain their objectives were righteous, they came to question the vitality of their faith. Finally, some shifted to more promising fields of endeavor. "The question I asked my self," the Reverend Kellogg wrote, "was this: in which sphere can I do the most good?" For Kellogg it was college teaching, for Atkinson a major church in Portland, bringing affluence and a Chinese houseboy by 1870. For others the answer was to return to the East. Although men ostensibly made these decisions, the evidence suggests that exhausted and frustrated wives played a part in motivating career changes.

"It is not wise to overdo and thus sacrifice the future to the present," Atkinson noted. "Many do this and die before their time." Eventually, many who, like Atkinson, stayed with their religious vocation reinterpreted their mission. Rather than using conversion and membership figures to assess their effectiveness, they turned to counting the number of church buildings and clergy, adding up financial assets, and finally counting members. Institutional growth assuaged consciences. What part women played in redefining the religious mission is not clear. Yet women as early fund raisers and church builders may well have been involved in the increasing emphasis on institutional expansion. Certainly, their recollections of their husbands' careers tell not a story of defeat but one of gradual success.

Of course, most women did not define success as narrowly as missionary wives once had. Those who flocked to church and joined sewing circles but never became church members sympathized with some but not all the goals missionary women espoused. Yet even less ambitious attempts to establish social institutions on the frontier ran into obstacles. Activities which women supported were only partially successful at first. Most institutions had an unsteady existence as a shifting population undercut attempts to create stability; schools were not maintained every year, literary societies and sometimes newspapers disappeared within months; even churches disappeared. Habits like drinking and gambling persisted.

Yet, by and large, there is an accumulation of evidence that women fulfilled important aspects of their Western mission. First of all, family life survived. Reminiscences of pioneer women were often cast in dramatic terms, picturing their families triumphing over wilderness. Domestic ideology and the hard work of women deserve much of the credit. Communities were established and grew, with goodly if not godly institutions offering opportunities for social interaction.

The mere existence of Sabbath services, whether they produced conversions or not, symbolized community progress and provided the
congregation with the opportunity for friendly intercourse. Rachel
Applegate's enjoyment of the Sabbath was social not spiritual. "To
day is sunday," she wrote, "and I have just got back from Church
—seen every body." Likewise, dances, frowned upon by the clergy,
and parties indicated a goodly society which was "very enjoyable
compared to our earlier pioneer life," as one woman pointed out.

As such comments suggest, women, in time, used a new frame of
reference to judge the progress of their pioneer communities. Instead
of comparing the new life to the old in the East, settlers compared
the present to the past on the frontier. From this perspective, the
advance of society was clear. Isolation had disappeared and institutions had emerged. Women could see the part they had played in
initiating, supporting, and maintaining community growth, and found
a sense of satisfaction in their contributions. As material conveniences
became more readily available and better communications with the
East were established, women began to "feel quite civilized," and even
told themselves that their pioneer experiences and the pioneer stage
of society had ended.

As census data suggest, only a minority of women actually lived
in one community over an extended period. At first, their efforts to
establish and sustain social institutions and civilized habits may have
seemed inadequate and unsuccessful. They may well not have imposed
their views on temporary residents, although the institutions they
supported must have influenced them. But they too could see progress
when they contrasted their present situation to their earliest days on
the frontier. Moreover, the few who remained within one community
eventually had the satisfaction of seeing their standards established
as the community's, just because they stayed and because they belonged to the most prominent and prestigious social groups, with
visibility and the means of expressing their point of view. And, as
one study of frontier culture indicates, later emigrants, attracted by
a community's character, tended to reinforce early cultural patterns
and strengthen dominant values. The transients became less impor-

tant as the number of like-minded settlers grew. Local histories of pioneer communities which describe growth from the perspective of the stable minority tell a story of success.

That the frontier experience served to reinforce many conventional familial and cultural ideals is apparent in an examination of domestic ideology in the West. Frontier images of women were closely tied to images of women current in the East. The concept of woman as lady, the heart of domestic ideology, survived; it was vivid in songs and poems. However hard it was to live the genteel life, the image's persistence indicates the continuing desirability of the ideal and the efforts made to attain it. More common was the characterization of woman as wife and helpmate. This view deemphasized gentility and stressed the desirability of initiative, resourcefulness, and energy in women. The image reflected the qualities needed on the frontier, but essentially the image was still a domestic one, and, in keeping with conventional nineteenth-century ideas, women were perceived as selfless creatures living to serve others rather than themselves.

Although the frontier experience resulted in the emphasis on certain "masculine" qualities as desirable for Western women, the necessary domestic framework remained intact and was, in fact, strengthened by frontier life. Women were extolled as mothers, wives, and civilizers. Their confrontation with the wilderness reaffirmed their image as molders of civilization, through church, school, and social activities. The reality of the frontier, far from rejecting the civilizing mission, reaffirmed it.

5

"The Rarest Commodity . . .
Are Women"

In 1849, a disease which had swiftly assumed the proportions of a
national epidemic struck the pioneer inhabitants of a simple log
cabin on the Missouri plains. Mr. Wilson, a farmer in his early
forties, exhibited all the telltale symptoms of a sickness which affected
males most virulently: an unquenchable thirst for fortune, a firm
conviction that he had nothing to lose by abandoning his home, and
a compelling desire to be off to California at once. What was unusual
about the course of gold fever in the Wilson household, however, was
the fact that his young wife was equally infected and was determined
to accompany her husband west. "I would not be left behind," she
recalled over thirty years later. "I thought where he could go I could,
and where I went I could take my two little toddling babies." Un-
daunted by their relative ignorance of California and gold mining,
the Wilsons set off across the plains to make their fortune. Thousands of Americans and Europeans, including the Wilsons, flocked to
California by land and sea. For, as Luzena Wilson explained, "the
gold excitement spread like wildfire," not only sweeping through
Missouri, but through all the other states and Europe as well. California, with its promise of instant riches, attracted newcomers at a
rapid rate. On the eve of the gold rush, the territory had only about
14,000 inhabitants (excluding Indians), but a year later the population approached 100,000; by the end of 1852, it had more than

doubled. The Wilsons were thus part of a vast migration of fortune seekers, but they were unusual because they came as a family. Probably a mere 5 percent of early California gold rushers were women and children.

California was the first and the most spectacular of several mining frontiers in the trans-Mississippi West. Although flush times petered out there in the fifties and gold production declined, continuing dreams of striking it rich provided emigrants for subsequent rushes to other areas. In 1858, rumors of the discovery of gold in British Columbia sent 25,000–30,000 to Canada, many of them coming from California. In 1859, reports of gold in Colorado triggered what was to become the second largest mining rush in the West, attracting experienced forty-niners as well as "tenderfeet" from the Midwest and South. Within three or four seasons, the easily mined placer deposits were depleted and by the mid-sixties the central Rockies mining frontier had collapsed. But discoveries in the Pacific Northwest during the early sixties and in Montana and Idaho toward the end of the decade kept the dream of riches alive and the miners moving. In the mid-seventies, prospectors thronged to the Black Hills of South Dakota, lured by gold once more.

Over several decades, then, the mining frontier shifted its location as metal deposits were discovered, exploited, and exhausted. The earliest stages of a mining rush saw fortune seekers working alone or in small groups, hunting for loose "placer" gold (loose because it had eroded away from its original rock formation). As these deposits ran out, it became apparent that retrieving gold or silver embedded in solid rock or in deep gravel would demand a more sophisticated technological approach and more capital. In time the necessary expertise was developed. Later mining frontiers were exploited less by individuals operating independently or in small groups than by corporate and industrial concerns with miners working as wage earners. Even as early as 1852 in California, the financial demands of mining had transformed most of the miners into wage earners.

Dramatic stories of the gold rushes, the dazzling riches, the life of the mining camps caught the imagination of contemporaries, and the lore of the gold rush became a part of American popular culture. Except for the acknowledgment of the mining frontier prostitute, pictured either as the woman with a heart of gold or as the predatory female ("Hangtown Gals are plump and rosy, / Hair in ringlets mighty cosy, / Painted cheeks and gassy bonnets; / Touch them and they'll sting like hornets"), women were not remembered. In some ways, this was hardly surprising. In 1850, California's population was over 90 percent male; in the mining camps, the figures were probably higher. Yet if women's participation in the mining rushes did not catch the popular imagination except in the most marginal way because there were so few of them, women like Luzena Wilson were there. Although Eliza Farnham advised her readers in her 1856 book, *California, Indoors and Out,* that "none but the pure and stronghearted of my sex should come alone to this land," both strong and weakhearted, single and married women came to California first and to the other mining frontiers later.

Because there were so few women on the mining frontier, they were particularly visible and the focus of eager attention. The arrival of four women in Nevada City in 1853, for example, "caused a great sensation . . . there has never arrived more than one lady at a time before. The men stand and gaze at us with mouth and eyes wide open, every time we go out." The arrival of a woman on the mining frontier was, of course, more than a time for men to feast their eyes on the female form; it had a symbolic significance for the new and rough society. California and the later mining frontiers posed one of the nineteenth century's greatest challenges to the conventional wisdom that women were shapers and civilizers of society. Despite the sex ratio, and despite the belief that gold fever reduced rootless men to a condition far more debased than that of ordinary men, nineteenth-century society still expected women to tame and refine. As Farnham pointed out in her influential publication, "There is no inviolate fireside in California that is not an altar; no honorable woman but is a missionary of virtue, morality, happiness, and peace, to a circle of careworn, troubled, and often, alas, demoralized men." Farnham believed that it was only "in the presence of women" that there would be an "efficient remedy for these great evils" which California was experiencing. But she realized that the mining frontier was a test. "It is hard to natures, that have not more than common strength," she wrote, "to live uprightly and purely, when they feel that there is no sympathy with their life, in those who surround them —and, still worse, no faith." Would women shape the new society on the mining frontier as Farnham hoped or be shaped by it as she feared? This was just one of the questions California and the other mining frontiers raised for the women who came there and for the culture which accorded them such significant moral influence.

How women participated in the mining rushes and what the experiences meant to them and to American culture make a complex story. Its complexity is immediately apparent in women's varied responses to the mining frontier. Luzena Wilson arrived in Sacramento to find that a miner was willing to pay her ten dollars for a biscuit made by a woman. This triggered fantasies. "In my dreams that night," she confessed, "I saw crowds of bearded miners striking gold from the earth with every blow of the pick, each one seeming to leave a share for me." Yet Martha Hitchcock wrote to her sister-in-law in 1851 that she was disappointed with California: "The more I see of men, the more I am disgusted with them—they are rather worse too, in California, than anywhere else—this is the Paradise of men—I wonder if a Paradise for poor *Women*, will ever be discovered —I wish they would get up an exploring expedition, to seek for one." Paradise or purgatory? As a first step to placing such conflicting female responses in perspective, the nature of the mining frontier should be considered. Despite diversity, certain characteristics common to mining communities contributed to making them unique places for the women who went to them.

Perhaps their most striking feature was the rapidity with which mining communities developed after news of a strike spread. California's spectacular population increase demonstrated the pattern of instant growth which became typical of the mining frontier. While the agricultural and commercial promises of the farming or urban frontier might attract a thousand, the mining frontier would lure ten thousand. The White Pine silver mining district, in Nevada, illustrates the pattern on a small scale. News of discoveries in 1867 brought a handful of eager miners to the district by the summer of 1868. Despite bad weather, the town of Hamilton had grown from 30 to 600 by midwinter, while the district as a whole had drawn about 3,000 newcomers at the rate of about 50 a day. By the spring, 75 to 100 were arriving daily; the total population of the White Pine district reached 12,000.

Another significant characteristic of the mining frontier was also evident in the White Pine area. Most of the "residents" were young men, for few women or family groups came during the early boom times. The demographic profile of a typical mining camp, Walla Walla, shows that the sexual imbalance there was more severe than on the urban frontier. Fifty-nine percent of Portland's population was male in 1860, for example, as compared to 80 percent in Walla Walla. The age distribution also differed. In Walla Walla most of the men were between twenty and forty, while in Portland there were many men both younger and older. Many of the young men who thronged to mining centers obviously had had little or no worldly experience. Gold seeking represented one of their first ventures out of the school-room and away from the confines of home.

Most mining districts not only had a youthful male population but a heterogeneous one as well. Gold seekers came from every state and many foreign countries. About one-third of California's inhabitants in 1850 were foreign; ten years later the new boom area in Colorado's Comstock Lode region also had a high percentage of foreign miners. This heterogeneity set the mining frontier apart from the agricultural frontier, which was often settled by groups of Americans with similar regional backgrounds. Although mining society was, on the surface, cosmopolitan, it was not cohesive. Having varied backgrounds and few ties beyond the hope of striking it rich, miners were not members of a community but temporary residents, virtually transients.

The rapid influx of large numbers of fortune seekers resulted in ramshackle camps filled with fire and safety hazards. Little as these unsightly camps resembled Eastern cities and much as they were temporary stops for a disparate group of transients, the camps had a definite urban character. Miners needed and demanded a variety of supporting services, and although few found the riches they envisioned, they earned enough to support numerous urban occupations and activities. Merchants, saloonkeepers, cooks, druggists, gamblers, and prostitutes accompanied miners to provide for their needs and to share in their profits. Since farming usually followed discovery, freighters, bringing in both essential and luxury goods, joined this motley group. Even in the most feverish moments of the '49 gold rush, only about half of California's residents were involved in mining. The rest serviced the miners. The pattern was typical.

Within a relatively short time after the discovery of gold or silver, mining camps and towns boasted of a variety of urban amenities, not found in the same-sized community in the East or on the Western agricultural frontier. Newspapers, theaters, debates and lectures, sporting events, suppers of champagne and oysters broke the monotony of mining life and proved to the outside world that the strike had succeeded.

Because few communities established an adequate government, because drifters and ne'er-do-wells flocked to new mining centers and because of the boom-and-bust cycle, most mining centers experienced disorder, too. "In the short space of twenty-four days," wrote Dame Shirley to her sister, "we have had murders, fearful accidents, bloody deaths, a mob, whippings, a hanging, an attempt at suicide, and a fatal duel." Although most camps were not so lawless as Dame Shirley's letter suggested and as stories later insisted, social standards and conventions broke down. Without a legal mechanism for settling conflicts, in an environment full of young men, physical solutions to disagreements were common. Fist fights and murder occurred. Plentiful liquor spurred on the foolhardy and even the wise. Vigilante justice, glorified as a means of dealing with disorder, was itself often violent and brutal. Vigilante justice, in fact, symbolized how much turbulence had become a part of mining life and how standards of justice and order had become perverted.

Some men had set out for the land of gold with every intention of maintaining standards, but their resolve often collapsed under the realities of mining life. The story of one group from Boston epitomizes the breakdown. Bountifully supplied with Bibles and thoroughly instructed about the necessity of carrying New England culture west, the group's resolve evaporated almost immediately. After only two days in the placer mines, all the Bibles were gone, not given away in hopes of reclaiming sinners, but exchanged in a Benicia bar for whiskey.

Many miners felt that they were not accountable for their actions. They had no long-term stake in the camp and gave little thought to the consequences of their deeds. The *Denver Daily Tribune* printed a blistering article dealing with this irresponsible attitude and the behavior it encouraged. "Men of decent appearance seen elsewhere, as soon as they reached Leadville jibed, sang low songs, walked openly with the painted courtesans with whom the town teems, and generally gave themselves up to what they term 'a time' each one promising the other not to 'give him away,'" the article commented disgustedly. "Secure in the fact that their boon companions would not 'give them away,' that their women folks were safe and snug in their distant homes, that their children, prayers said, were tucked in their little beds, these whilom gentlemen announced that they were going 'the whole hog or none.'"

Joel Brown's letter to his wife, Ann, in 1852, sets the collapse of standards into perspective, however. "In fact when it is dig, dig, dig, work, work, work, there is not much time for immorality," he wrote. "Gambling and drinking is the worst crime I see here and this vice is carried on nights and Sundays." Miners had neither the time nor the energy to carouse or to brawl day and night. But there was usually nothing to stop them when they decided to have a spree or when they sought companionship in the saloon or gambled away their gold dust.

Much of what the nineteenth century saw as vice came from the monotony and difficulty of mining life, the availability of cash, and the belief that morality was a woman's concern. Without good women, many men simply did not feel it was up to them to do a woman's job. "I attribute so much gambling and drinking to the fact there is no women in the country," wrote Brown. William Perkins agreed. "The want of respectable female society, rational amusements, and books, has aided greatly to the demoralization of many whose natural character would have kept them aloof from temptation had there been other means but the gambling tables and drinking saloons, to have assisted them in whiling away the hours not devoted to labor," he wrote in his journal. "Notwithstanding the best efforts of a man," he continued, "it is impossible not to be more or less infected by breathing continually a tainted moral atmosphere." If proof were needed that ideology was realistic in its assessment of men, the openly male temper of mining towns with the frank acceptance of vice provided it.

The appearance of the miners suggested the peculiarities of mining life. Shaggy hair, untrimmed beards, faces coarsened by exposure, old shapeless hats, baggy pants, and flannel shirts, high boots became the marks of the miner and fused into an image which passed into popular culture. Just as women's interest in clothing and fashion on the agricultural frontier signified their determination to remain civilized, miners' sloppy clothing suggested that they had in fact left civilization behind. The mining frontier was a world of its own, a world marked by singular uncertainties.

Unlike frontier cities and towns which flourished either because of their strategic position or because of agricultural development nearby, mining camps, frequently in remote areas, mushroomed because of the promise of riches. Urban growth on the frontier usually suggested some stability and some future, but on the mining frontier it had no such meanings. Within three or four years the cycle of boom and bust had occurred, the hordes of people had come and gone. A few mining districts avoided disaster by developing different kinds of mining operations or by finding alternative sources of prosperity to replace the precious metal. Their social and economic patterns came to resemble those of other urban areas. California, for a variety of reasons, never experienced the slump that most mining frontiers did. But the death rate of mining communities was impressive.

The discovery of precious metals created two major cities, San Francisco and Denver, to supply the mining communities. Though they were instant cities (San Francisco had been a modest settlement in the forties, Denver a wilderness), they survived and grew. Still, like mining towns, their pattern of growth was erratic. Neither city, for example, had a stable population (even in nineteenth-century terms) but accommodated vast and fluctuating crowds of miners and suppliers. City residents themselves shared a mining-frontier mentality. They had little interest in building a city or creating a culture for its future but harbored dazzling visions of striking it rich by speculating in mining stocks or building sites, by providing supplies and services, or by doing anything else which might pay. They sought just enough order to protect their gains until they left.

In the early days, the appearance of the two cities was chaotic. San Francisco in 1849, for example, was a picture of confusion and disorder, with most of the temporary inhabitants camping in tents. Its two-story buildings were either gambling halls or hotels. Within a few years, however, the city had elegant buildings, churches, libraries, schools, and shops offering a profusion of goods. A new arrival even wrote home that San Francisco reminded her of Boston. But the transplanted New Englander was wrong. Buildings and urban amenities did not signify a civilized or stable community; in fact, many of the improvements were made only after devastating fires which so often swept through the carelessly built-up city. Little physical long-range planning had occurred because few expected to remain. The profusion of buildings was no more a sign of stability than the size of the population.

Further indications of the impermanent character of San Francisco were revealed by the kinds of buildings which were constructed. While offices, hotels, theaters, restaurants, opera houses, and saloons were erected with alacrity, the construction of family housing lagged. The number of people running boardinghouses or hotels to house transients far exceeded the national figure. In 1850, for every thousand Californians gainfully employed, over nine were in the hotel or boardinghouse trade, more than double the figure for the country as a whole.

The population explosion which created the two cities suggested unavoidable urban confusion and stress. In 1848, a mere thousand inhabitants lived in the Bay area. Within four years, 36,000 more had flocked to San Francisco. By 1860, city dwellers topped the 56,000 mark. Ten years later, one-third of the entire population of the state lived in or within a few miles of the city. While it had taken Boston 250 years to attract a population of one-third of a million, it had taken San Francisco only twenty-five years.

The pace of urbanization certainly magnified problems which had baffled city dwellers in more slowly growing areas, while the social composition of the cities contributed to a lack of interest in solving them. The social hierarchy, initially based on the whimsy of fortune, was inherently fragile and irresponsible. The heterogeneity of the population, as in the mining camps, was probably an additional factor contributing to social instability. Half of San Francisco's population in 1853 was foreign, and the vast majority of all inhabitants were unattached men. Out of the total population of 50,000, there were only 8,000 women and 3,000 children.

Yet city life in Denver and San Francisco was exciting, amusing, and novel. Early years were hard, but before long all the signs of culture appeared: theater, opera, restaurants, balls, churches. Visitors to the cities remarked upon the numerous diversions and the relaxed way of life which had emerged. As John McCrackan explained to his sister in a letter of the early fifties, San Francisco society was far less demanding than Eastern. "Here we are left to indulge our own peculiar views," he wrote, "dont attend church but half a day, believing that I can spend the ballance more profitably amid the beauties of nature." Drinking and gambling were two popular amusements which attracted more adherents, no doubt, than all the charms of nature. The number of drinking establishments far outnumbered hotels and restaurants, and skimpy Recorder's Court statistics show twice as many arrested for drunken and disorderly conduct than for any other offense. Another amusement brought more to the hospital with venereal disease than any other complaint in the early days of the gold rush.

A Denver woman recalled that her introduction to the city as a girl had been the witnessing of two murders: "These were terrible experiences to us, and we wondered what kind of a place we had come to." In fact, the nature of mining society raised the question whether women ought to participate in mining frontier life at all. The leading San Francisco newspaper, the *Alta*, thought the question not worth debating, since its policy was to attract women to California. "We are pleased to see that each succeeding steamer is bringing to California the wives and families of many of our merchants and mechanics who have preceded them and built for them a home among us . . . The happy influence of woman in a new country is a great one." In agreement that the presence of women was essential to the future of California, the 1849 political convention gave married women property rights, at a time when few other states had done so, hoping to lure them west. Yet even among boosters, there were mixed feelings about the presence of women. Nothing was done to establish a statewide system of public schools, and efforts to eliminate or to license gambling were defeated.

Whether in Denver, San Francisco, or a remote mining center, men were not easily persuaded either to bring their families west or to marry and settle down. They observed the characteristics of the mining frontier which seemed to make it inappropriate for family life. Robert Effinger, for example, claimed, "I would much prefer that a wife of mine should board in a respectable bawd house in the city of New York than live anywhere in the city of San Francisco." Charles Tuttle pointed to "the privations and fatigues which females undergo" in a country with few women and told his wife she would be "deprived of the society of those of your sex and exposed to all the severities of the weather" if she joined him. Other men never considered bringing families west because they had no idea of staying but planned to return east with a fortune. Most of them discovered that fortune was elusive. In the early fifties, the average California miner was making only about three dollars a day, two dollars more than an Eastern coal miner, but hardly striking it rich. The pattern was similar elsewhere. The high cost of living ate up most of those modest earnings, but dreams die hard. Some gave up and returned to their families, but others stayed on, still alone, still determined to make the whole venture worthwhile. As one miner explained to his sister, "Everybody in the States who has friends here is always writing for them to come home. Now, they all long to go home . . . [But] it is hard for a man to leave here, when there is so much money to be made, with nothing . . . I have no pile yet, but you can bet your life I will never come home until I have something more than when I started." The longer they stayed, the harder it was to return or to settle down in California or anywhere else. They had become dreamers and footloose adventurers for life. Finally, the cycle of boom and bust discouraged men from bringing their families to the frontier. No one could know how long a strike would last or how profitable it would prove to be. It often just did not seem worthwhile to bring a family on a long, tedious, and costly journey when there was no certainty there would be anything but a ghost town when they arrived. Even miners living in those remarkable communities which survived the rush were reluctant to marry. Twenty years after the initial gold rush only 25 percent of the men in one California mining town and 33 percent in another were married and living with their families.

Yet the youthful miners were lonesome for mothers, wives, and lovers. "I expect that you will think . . . that I am crying to see my wife," Joel Brown wrote home. "Well suppose I am and what then? I am not the only one that is crying to see the wife and baby." The lines of anxious men waiting for hours for letters on Steamer Day in San Francisco mutely testified to homesickness and loneliness. Yet there were other reasons why men yearned for women. On their own, for perhaps the first time, miners had the unforgettable and unpleasant experience of doing women's work and found it monotonous and dreary. Then, too, some miners were quick to realize that if mining was an uncertain way to get rich, providing services was not. Deciding in favor of settling and serving, a proportion of forty-niners returned home to get their families or brides and returned to begin a second and hopefully more lucrative career on the mining frontier.

Whatever the reason for bringing women west, most men believed that their arrival would also signal the advent of respectable society. Yet their very desire to have women on the mining frontier was ambivalent. As the legislators of California had given married women property rights but refused to curb gambling, so men on the mining frontier expected women to be agents of civilization, but they did not always want to give up the habits acquired in a time of relative freedom. Their ambivalence toward civilization was reflected in other aspects of mining life. As mining camps grew, for example, efforts were made to acquire the symbols of Eastern life: architecturally appropriate buildings, stable social institutions, civil government. At the same time, however, there was often a profound unwillingness to pay for them.

If men had a variety of motives for sending for wives and families, women had many reasons for coming. Initially, many women had bade a reluctant farewell to their husbands for what they thought would be a relatively short separation. But as months passed, some realized that they had either to join their husbands or to give them up altogether. As Augusta Knapp told her husband, "Do not imagine that I want to come, for I do not, and think that you will be a real goose to stay, for all the gold in the mines; but if you do stay, I am coming, or else I will get a divorce . . . And whatever you do, Gid, do not *imagine* even that you can live without me, for you cannot and shall not." Gid eventually came home, but other men did not, and their wives went west to maintain their marriages. Many seem to have shared the expectation, however, that the sojourn in the West would be temporary and left their children behind.

Whether single or married, virtuous or fallen, most women also responded to the lure of riches. Maria Tuttle, one of the wives left behind, soon discovered she could not tolerate staying at home. Her letter, written in early January 1851, revealed her anguished feelings of loneliness: "I have not heard from you since October and my mind is well nigh wrought up to a fit of desperation." But later in the month she was carefully contemplating the financial advantages to be gained by going west. "I used to think to meet you at my father's door would be my choice," she wrote, "but now I have no desire that you should return if you can do well there, it would be better that I should go to you." Other women realized their own opportunities for making money by servicing miners. Margaret Frink, who was as fired up by visions of gold as her husband, described hearing tales of women's earning power. "I began at once to figure up in my mind how many men I could cook for, if there should be no better way of making money," she confessed. Once on the plains, the sight of the other emigrants filled her with dismay. "I was half frantic over the idea that every blade of grass for miles on each side of the road would be eaten . . . And, worse than all, there would only be a few barrels of gold left for us when we got to California." A few like Sophia Eastman responded to the sheer adventure of it all. As a schoolgirl in Lowell, Massachusetts, she realized, "I shall be obliged to go into the mill unless I get a passage before or by fall . . . I cannot submit to it, and I am willing to go with a small fitting out, or none at all, in the capacity of a servant, or any way, rather than be disappointed." As her brother-in-law noted, Sophia had "devoured all the reading about California," and finally, after borrowing money to pay for her trip, she set off for the West.

Some women, as one might expect, went to the mining frontier with the explicit intention of battling the materialism and vice. Gold, wrote Sarah Gibbons, a missionary wife, was the god of adults in California, but she hoped to save the children. With similar idealism, Mrs. Harmon told her friend, "she thought it a pity for educated women to come to this country and spend their lives over a washtub and around a stove, and so she is going to teach." Even Mary Jane Megquier, a New Englander quite candid about her materialistic aspirations, still remembered a greater mission of being a "good influence upon society." Being a "good influence" in California was a heroic challenge.

Some of the first women to arrive on the mining frontier regarded female obligations very lightly, for, as prostitutes, they planned to profit from vice. "The hordes of shameless women, whose presence had," in the opinion of the Reverend Martin Kellogg, "done incalculable mischief" seem to have made rapid decisions to come west. They came alone, in pairs, or in small groups. They may have constituted 20 percent of the female population in California in 1850 and outnumbered respectable women in early mining camps by 25 to 1. Not all were American. Robert Effinger observed that "the cities of New York, Philadelphia, and New Orleans are pouring a portion of their prostituted population into our Market," but also noted the "pretty French dancing girls," and the Australian women who arrived to take advantage of the ready market of miners.

William Perkins noted an astonishing feature about prostitution in early mining society. A number of the "soiled doves" who paid "a nominal tribute to virtue," mainly by behaving decorously in public, were considered socially acceptable during early gold-rush years. San Francisco's first piano concert, in 1849, saw the front seats reserved for the "doves"; respectable men appeared openly in their company with little risk to their reputation, and the women were "treated with the greatest respect and gallantry the same as would be extended to the most respectable women by men in general." The mining frontier's sexual demography and the ability of some prostitutes to observe "all the exterior rules of respectability" explained this social phenomenon so shocking to conventional moralists.

Some of the prostitutes did well on the mining frontier, especially during the boom days, when competition was limited and prices were high. Edward Ely speculated that one madam, "although she has not been in the place one year . . . must be worth a hundred thousand dollars. It could scarcely be otherwise considering the high price of everything . . . and more especially where there is a monopoly. To speak plainly one night's enjoyment of the society of the charming mistress of the house, costs the man the moderate sum of one hundred dollars, and the same indulgence with the girls, fifty dollars." These women were high-class prostitutes, working in a good house, but there were many opportunities for the early comers. Some acquired substantial possessions, as Ely suspected. Probate court records on the estate of Mary Lee, who died in Sacramento in 1853, for example, catalogued her white window curtains, two leather trunks, jewelry, $1,520 in cash on deposit, and an opulent array of clothes, including twenty-one skirts, eleven chemises and thirty-one dresses of linen, muslin, brocade, satin, silk, gingham, merino, wool, along with a white silk cape and a red jacket. Successful prostitutes considered their occupation a business, and a prosperous one at that. A famous Denver madam, unusual because her views were recorded, insisted that this was the case. "She defended calmly but without emotion—the life she had led. And she said at the first, 'I went into the sporting life for business reasons and for no other. It was a way for a woman in those days to make money and I made it.' "

The madam's response highlights the point that other occupations for women in the early days and even later were strenuous and un-glamorous. Although prostitution as a career may have represented degradation in the eyes of the moralists, for the prostitute it prob-ably symbolized economic opportunity. Although little is known of mining-frontier prostitutes as a group, the majority of them prob-ably came from working-class families with few attractive economic alternatives. As the frontier symbolized a fortune to the miners, it no doubt suggested golden opportunities for women who may have already been in the business elsewhere. Court records show, for ex-ample, that Mary Lee, whose real name was Mary Butler and who was the daughter of Irish immigrants, had worked at Mistress Ann Wood's house in New Orleans. Certainly the prostitutes from France and South America were no novices. Some women may have drifted into prostitution after losing their virtue on the mining frontier. Moralists emphasized adultery's inevitable conclusion was the brothel, but others agreed that the loss of virtue meant the loss of self-respect. A Denver madam pointed out, "I never took a girl into my house . . . who had had no previous experience of life and men. That was a rule of mine. Most of the girls had been married and had left their husbands or else they had become involved with a man. No innocent young girl was ever hired by me."

Yet prostitution was not always gilt-edged on the mining frontiers. Within the group as a whole, social and economic gradations quickly emerged. At the top were madams and women who lived in good houses with elaborate furnishings (at least in comparison to the rest of the mining frontier) and had rich wardrobes. Just below them, and scorned by them, were the women who worked in dance halls and theaters, where the lines between a courtesan and actress were sometimes imperceptible. On the bottom of the economic scale and far more marginal were women working in dens or out of their own cribs, small dwellings with a front bedroom and a window on the street and a kitchen to the rear. These women's earnings must have often been minimal, especially when youth and good looks faded.

No matter what the prostitute's class, age, or race, her profession was hazardous. As mining communities matured and respectable women came west, prostitutes were often harassed. The tempo of the campaign against prostitution picked up as a community matured and the number of its families increased. By 1860, in Nevada City, for example, the respectable community's intention of cleaning up the town became evident when angry citizens raided the house of a prostitute. Not long after, other irate citizens were dragged into court, accused of wrecking the dwelling of a "notorious prostitute." In 1866, ninety people signed a petition requesting the government to ban all "bawdy houses." This hot issue landed in the city council, which passed it on to the police commissioner, who, typically enough, chose to do nothing beyond continuing an informal policy of occasional arrests. But the result of this agitation was the confinement of prostitution to one area of town just as if there had been some legislative action calling for it.

There were other hazards in addition to outraged virtue. Mary Lee, despite her material success, died at the hands of another prostitute, who felled her with a bowie knife. Brawls between prostitutes and between their customers were part of the sporting life. The Nevada *White Pine News* reported a typical event in 1869: "A man got on a spree Saturday night, went to a house of ill repute corner of Treasure and Dunn streets, and pitched into the nymphs after the most approved style of 'knock down and drag out.' He dragged two of the women into the street, knocked them down and trampled them in the mud. He was finally captured and locked up." And because the status of prostitutes in the law was so unclear, they were easy victims for crime. So Sarah Church, who worked at Mary Jane Carswell's house, made change for her client James Brown, explaining, "We had some business together that caused us to make use of some money." Then she claimed that he robbed her of over $5,000, "mostly in gold coin & some dust, also a lot of jewelry."

What happened to individual women over the course of years is unclear. Those who stayed with the trade followed the miners as they sought out new boom areas. Some of them, memoirs insist, escaped through marriage. "Sometimes a good citizen, wealthy and respectable," one women maintained, "marries his wife from some one of these corrupt houses, and he seldom ever regrets his choice. He builds her up to be respected and respectable. I have heard of several cases." Others made enough apparently to retire to respectability. "Red Stockings," who appeared in Colorado in 1860, was supposedly one of the lucky ones. Her background, whether real or fabricated, included a rich Boston family, seduction in Paris, and, of course, humiliation. A year after plying her trade in Colorado, however, she departed with thousands of dollars, supposedly reformed, and married respectably.

But the picture given of prostitutes in court records and newspapers is one with few happy endings. Violence, drink, drugs, and youth (some prostitutes apparently were in their early teens) were linked with prostitution along with growing social hostility. "Of all the human wrecks caused by the maelstroms of vice and dissipation," suggested the *White Pine News*, "there is none so sad to look upon as that of a young and beautiful woman. We saw such a one in Hamilton. She was young, perhaps not twenty, but intoxicated—beastly drunk. She had staggered in through the back door of a gambling den, and had been ejected from the room into the backyard . . . where she fell, amid the jeers and ribald jests of the rabble, the mass of whom were doubtless less refined and no more virtuous than even the degraded target of their vulgar wit. In this helpless, maudlin mood, she began singing, in sweet and plaintive tones, the very words above all others most suited to her case: 'Once I was happy, but now I'm forlorn.' "

Respectable single women arriving early on the mining frontier found less colorful and less dangerous jobs, though their early opportunities for making money also faded. Like women on the agricultural frontier, mining-frontier women performed "female" jobs. And despite the initial acceptance of unorthodox females, there was a clear line dividing reputable female work from disreputable. In Sonora, Perkins pointed out, women could either become prostitutes or "ostentate a decent profession, such as sewing, washing, pastry making and selling knick-knacks." The respectable occupations paid well at first in a male society hungry for services. As one young woman explained to an Eastern friend, "A smart woman can do very well in this country—true there are not many comforts and one must work all the time and work hard but is plenty to do and good pay

If I was in Boston now and know what I now know of California I would come out here If I had to hire the money to bring me out. It is the only country I ever was in where a woman received anything like a just compensation for work."

Married women, whose skills were far more in demand than their counterparts on the agricultural frontier, in the early years found themselves taking on the same kind of jobs as single women. They ran profitable boardinghouses, took in washing, hired out as nurses, sold pies and cakes, in addition to caring for their own families. They shrewdly recognized their assets and capitalized on them. For they not only tended to miners' physical well-being but also to their emotional well-being by creating the illusion of home. "A room in a private family was a treasure," one woman pointed out, and men were willing to pay for the comfort and the semblance of family life. By catering to men's needs and nostalgia, women often made more than their miner husbands and recouped family finances in times of misfortune.

In time, however, economic conditions changed for these women, as they did for their erring sisters. As the boom began to peter out, miners abandoned the mines and flooded the job market, as they did by the early eighteen fifties in California. Lower wages, unemployment, and poverty resulted, and women who had serviced mining society suffered. Some opportunities just disappeared, some just paid less. As Sophia Eastman told relatives, by the summer of 1854 in California, "Wages are becoming low, and it is quite difficult to obtain a place. As soon as I can get my pay, I think I shall leave for Sacramento, or some other place." Yet a month later she was still unemployed. "I find every day people are more and more unwilling to employ me." Although Sophia attributed her trouble in finding a job to her refinement, which she thought made people unwilling to hire her, the contraction of the economy and competition which occurred on every frontier were really the problems. Cheap Chinese laundries, for example, threatened women who made money by washing clothes. In Helena, Montana, the operation of Chinese laundries constituted such a serious threat that the town's laundresses warned the Chinese in a newspaper article to leave town or suffer the consequences. By the time the first phase passed in the mining West, few signs of women's early economic opportunities remained.

Even if the early years were financially rewarding, they were also hard on women and left them little time for relaxation or rest. Some claimed they hardly had time to leave their houses. It was not surprising that now and then they reflected that the monetary rewards were not worth the hard labor involved. After describing her primitive kitchen, the large meals she cooked three times a day, the washing, ironing, and odd jobs she performed, Mary Ballou concluded, "I would not advise any Lady to come out here and suffer the toil and fatigue that I have suffered for the sake of a little gold, neither do I advise any one to come. Clark Simmons wife says if she was safe in the States she would not care if she had not one cent."

But the early loneliness and fatigue which women experienced in the early years had some compensations. There was, of course, the satisfying ability to earn money, far more than women could earn in the East. But equally rewarding was the position working women occupied in early mining communities. They provided basic services which a predominantly male society desperately wanted. Their work as cooks, housekeepers, seamstresses both enhanced their standing in the community and led to unexpected responsibilities and privileges. Some women reported, for example, that they became bankers for miners, while others noted that their word went unquestioned. And, of course, the attention which men paid to the women after they left their work could not help but feed their vanity. When Elizabeth Gunn went to church with her husband and children, all the men sitting on Sonora's main street rose to salute her as she passed by. Every available woman was avidly sought out for social occasions and became a belle. The middle-aged Mary Jane Megquier, who ran a boardinghouse in San Francisco, reported to her daughter that she was a social triumph at dances. Eliza Wilson, younger than Megquier but no beauty, remembered, "Even I had men come forty miles over the mountains, just to look at me, and I never was called a handsome woman, in my best days, even by my most ardent admirers."

Women who secluded themselves at home eventually found that domesticity was no protection from masculine attentions. Elizabeth

Gunn in Sonora, Rachel Haskell in Aurora, and others initially tried to shut out the male world of the mining camp and to devote themselves entirely to caring for their families. The free-and-easy atmosphere of mining camps made their task difficult. As one mother explained, "Virginia City [Nevada] is a very hard city in which to bring up children, for all classes drink, high and low . . . Nearly all play and gamble. Two-thirds swear, and the other third uses by-words of every kind—some very laughable ones—while others use coarse and rough ones." In light of the threats to family life which the mining frontier posed, Rachel Haskell's feeling of achievement in a simple evening at home is understandable. "How comfortable and cozy the sitting room did look this evening by twilight," she wrote in her diary. "The shelves laden with books, specimens, minerals, shells. The Piano, the Sewing Machine, comfortable sofa and easy chair, with healthy, happy, prattling, chippy, little children."

But eventually even these retiring women could not avoid becoming centers of interest. On the streets, men stared. Women who rarely ventured outside their house were sought out. Rachel Haskell's music attracted numerous evening visitors, while the Alverson girls' piano playing drew a crowd in Stockton in 1852, "scores of men in the street as far as the eye could see, and some were sobbing." Women at home had male visitors, some of whom spent the entire day. Eventually the most domestic of women recognized their position in mining society carried social obligations. As Elizabeth Gunn remarked: "I have never attended concerts and lectures as I have done here! The folks are talking about a Lyceum and I hope it will be formed; it will be something to draw the young men from the gambling places and houses of ill fame which abound here. The reason we go to everything good is to set an example."

Since she was careful to fill her letters with " 'particulars' . . . for I am 'a woman and a sister,' and am writing to women and sisters," Elizabeth Gunn's correspondence gives a vivid picture of her early experiences on the gold-rush frontier. The nature of her life as a woman and her female perspective becomes particularly clear when her letters are compared with William Perkins's journal for the same years in the same town. Elizabeth described family, religious, and cultural news, while Perkins spoke of the teeming life of prostitutes, parties, and mining. Perkins, in fact, witnessed the family's arrival and captured Elizabeth and her perspective in a few vivid phrases. "What chance has virtue in the shape of tall, gawky, sallow, ill-dressed down-Easters," he wondered, "in rivalship with elegantly adorned, beautiful and graceful vice . . . It is too much to expect from weak male human nature in California, that a man ever so correctly inclined, should prefer the lean arm of a bonnetted, ugly, board-shaped specimen of a descendant of the puritans, to the rosy cheeked, full formed, sprightly and elegant spaniard or Frenchwoman."

Perkins's comments were clearly more than unsympathetic remarks about Elizabeth Gunn's appearance and unfashionable clothes. Rather, Perkins was uneasy about the social role he rightly perceived women like Elizabeth would eventually try to play on the frontier, especially when communities matured and respectable women found they were not alone. If Perkins, on the one hand, underestimated the power of these middle-class women to affect their communities, he perceptively suggested the limited nature of their victories on the other. The character of the mining frontier, its population, its life style, its illusions, its cycle of rapid growth and decay, combined to prevent women from realizing their cultural mission in the way Eliza Farnham had envisioned in her book *California, Indoors and Out.*

The editor of the *Montana Post* vividly sketched what respectable women, most probably the wives of the town's professional men, had confronted the year before on the mining frontier. "Public resorts there were none," he pointed out, "save for those where lawless men and shameless women made night hideous with their unlawful revels and midnight orgies." Unlike those who settled on the agricultural frontier, women in mining camps faced not an institutional vacuum but flourishing counterinstitutions. Gamblers, saloonkeepers, and prostitutes were always among the first in any new boom town. By the time ministers, teachers, and wives arrived, they had to deal with these counterinstitutions, which were providing very real services for the mining community. Although editors and merchants who realized the relationship between profit and permanence sympathized with efforts to establish a respectable society because it signified stability, this goal was clearly at odds with the values and tastes of much of the transient mining society. Their support would have limits.

How many women were actually involved in efforts to tame their mining communities is uncertain. Studies show links between marriage and class. The more affluent and successful tended to have wives with them. In one California mining town, for example, the families of professional men (6 percent of the total population) accounted for 24 percent of the families there. We may be able to assume that the wives of these professional men were the ones trying to establish respectable society, but we have no idea whether they received support from other women (whether married or single) less well placed than themselves. In any case, the uncertainty of mining life, the crowd of miners focused on getting rich and leaving hindered all efforts to establish familiar institutions on a firm foundation. Attempts to raise money for schools and churches faced general indifference, if not hostility. Church attendance was abysmal. The Reverend James Pierpoint reported a Sunday attendance of only 40 out of a total mining population of 3,000–4,000, and his report was not atypical.

Yet women had some advantages, the main one being their scarcity. Because there were so few women, there were always some men who would conform to female views in order to spend time with them. Whether they wished it or not, women's homes became the centers of a select social life as men lonely for female company dropped by to spend a few hours during the day or evening. Visiting was easy in a well-populated mining community where much of the work was seasonal. Once visitors arrived, women could insist upon proper behavior and maintain standards themselves in the meals they served, the music they played, and the conversations they encouraged. "Had a spirited evening," Rachel Haskell remarked in her diary, as she recounted yet another night spent entertaining men at home. "It was exciting to meet two new gentlemen both good looking and interesting . . . Talked of books." Men, apparently, were careful not to lose visiting privileges by inappropriate behavior or language. As Dame Shirley explained to her sister, profanity was a way of life in California, but "the most vulgar blackguard will abstain from swearing in the *presence* of a lady."

If home was one small center of traditional social life, church became another. Missionaries to California bemoaned the materialism and godlessness of gold-rush society. What they, in fact, witnessed was the fragility of ties to organized religion when there were few social pressures to encourage conformity and many distractions. "Multitudes of young men who bore with them from their Eastern homes the fairest reputation and the fondest hopes," wrote Baptist missionary Osgood Wheeler, "are here thrown into the whirlpool of confusion, this maelstrom of evil, to be heard from no more, unless by some fortuitous chance or Providential interference . . . they seem to wake up when I take them by the arm . . . But unaided by the restraints of an organized moral and religious community, they soon return to all their vice with renewed energy." The combination of breeding and religious indifference, even viciousness, shocked clergymen. The Reverend Tuttle, an Episcopal bishop, remarked how "men were kind personally, generous . . . respectful and courteous; but I was appalled to discover day by day how almost universally given up they were to vicious practices."

Many apparently poised on the brink of perdition occasionally came to Sabbath services. Although the arrival of respectable women did not have a great impact on the size of church membership, it did at least make attendance at church services and social functions more desirable. As one missionary candidly wrote to the American Home Missionary Society, "We must send no more unmarried men. California needs woman's influence . . . a devoted intelligent woman *can do more than two ministers.* A ship load of *female missionaries* would be the greatest blessing California ever had."

As women enlivened religion by their presence, they also took on their familiar but vital role of raising money to furnish and finish churches, to pay off debts on the buildings. The building program was seen as particularly crucial, since missionaries reasoned that a steeple or the sound of a bell would revive the memories of religious obligations. James Waren, a Nevada City missionary, reported, typically, the importance of women's fund raising. "We received very timely and efficient aid, by a *Fair* of the Ladies of this place," he wrote. Using $200 of borrowed money and putting in four or five weeks of work, the women netted $1,100 for the church. A miner, Charles Ferguson, also recalled some of these Nevada City church festivals. They had few bargains. The men paid for the smiles.

Social occasions like fairs and balls became vehicles for fund raising, entertainment, and the affirmation of proper behavior. It was again the scarcity of women that provided the opportunity to use social occasions for their own ends. And as respectable women began to use social occasions to insist upon polite behavior, they also began to demand proper clothing as well. William Perkins, along with many others, noted how, with time, "the epoch of flannel shirts . . . disappeared for townsfolk. We now dress like christians, and I smile to think of the change as I witness myself equipped in a silken lined cloth frock."

Because there were so few of them on the mining frontier, women may have moved beyond some of the social conventions of Eastern life to adopt a more inclusive approach to female friendship. Elizabeth Gunn, who longed for more "good people" in Sonora and lamented because bad weather prevented her from visiting a New England woman located five miles from town, made friends with Mrs. Yancey from New Orleans, who "seems to have little education" although "she does not make mistakes in talking, and dresses and acts as though she had moved in good society," then with the minister's wife, and finally with Mrs. Lane, "a catholic. I like her as well as anyone I know here." Even more surprising, she had positive things to say about the neighboring French woman living with her mother, younger sister, and brother who made "her money by going to the gambling houses and dealing out the cards to the players." Yet, as women's insistence on decorum and dress at fairs and parties suggested, culture and class were hardly forgotten. Ellen Fletcher proudly reported that, despite the lack of formality, "it is said that there is the most respectable society of ladies in Summit City of any Settlement in the Territory." One of Elizabeth Gunn's friends had, she reported, counted "sixty virtuous females" in Sonora. The list was an ominous sign.

Since one of the objectives of respectable women on the mining frontier was to change its social atmosphere and particularly the open acceptance of sexual immorality, women used social occasions to make their disapproval clear to erring women and their gallants. Sarah Royce recounted with evident satisfaction a typical episode. The setting was an entertainment sponsored by women of four churches. In attendance was a wealthy man who had brought "a splendidly dressed woman, well known . . . as the disreputable companion of her wealthy escort." The couple made themselves comfortable, and were probably more than willing to give generously to the churches. But the sponsoring ladies would have no tainted company or money, and contacted a group of men to ask the sinners to leave. Sarah Royce concluded, "The events of the evening proved to him, as well as to others, that while Christian women would forego ease and endure much labor, in order to benefit any who suffered, they would not welcome into friendly association any who trampled upon the institutions which lie at the foundation of morality and civilization." Other women made the same point by refusing invitations ("I understand some are invited that are not fit for decent people to associate with," wrote Clementine Brainard) or by refusing to call. The identification of woman's sphere with morality and the seriousness with which many women took their cultural mission clarified the boundaries of the world of female culture and friendship and set the would-be civilizers apart from other women.

As these moral women counterattacked and sought to eliminate wicked flourishing institutions and the habits and attitudes which supported them, they soon discovered how few men shared their perspective. Prostitutes were social and sexual companions, and some men, at least, realized that it was impossible to lump them into a category entitled "bad women." Some prostitutes were, indeed, disorderly and did little more than satisfy male sexual appetites. But, as many men noted, there were also "adventuresses of a better class, some of them educated; all of them accustomed to the forms of society; many with innate feelings of delicacy and womanly decorum, even after virtue has been discarded as an unnecessary appendage to California life." Conventional standards defining virtue and vice did not do justice to women who were, in fact, good companions and not vicious. Sexual transgressions did not result in an automatic collapse of character. Edward Ely's trip to the California mining frontier in 1851 led him to this conclusion. His initial view of prostitution was unfavorable, for it was, he wrote, "demoralizing to the community." But when Ely found himself on a coach with the madam responsible for the business he condemned, he found not only was "she . . . a really goodlooking girl . . . [but] had I not known her character would have thought her to be quite respectable. However we did not stand upon moralities in a California stagecoach and as she was witty and talkative the ride passed away very well."

Some men, of course, detested the prevailing acceptance of prostitution. The mere presence of prostitutes on the streets of a mining town "polluted" them, Charles Tuttle thought. Missionaries agreed and stood steadfast in their belief that prostitutes were "shameless [and] . . . hopelessly irreclaimable." The fall from virtue apparently cut prostitutes off, more or less permanently, from any hope of salvation. They were viewed as the devil's agents, corruptors of innocent, if weak, men. As William Taylor, a Methodist missionary in San Francisco, pointed out, if the devil "can lead men into bad company, familiarize them with debauchery, and fill them with rum, they fall an easy prey to his diabolical designs." Where else could this scenario take place as easily as in houses of ill fame, described by a missionary in Columbia, California, as "hatefully fixed up, with gilded signs and wide open doors." Such men called respectable women to the mining frontier and supported their efforts to safeguard values and institutions.

Clearly many, if not most, of the respectable women condemned prostitution, although its very openness suggested that the men who agreed with them were very much in the minority. Their condemnation did not stem only from outraged virtue, however. Respectable women's attitude had elements of envy and anger. High-class prostitutes in a city like San Francisco and even in boom towns enjoyed an opulent life and a freedom of behavior probably attractive to hard-worked virtuous women. In Sonora, Elizabeth Gunn wrote, "a judge . . . sold his house to some women who came here from San Francisco." The women had "a man servant to clean their house, and they eat in a restaurant." In contrast, Elizabeth's life was epitomized by her comment, "I am cleaning all the time." Generally, high-class prostitutes were among the first to be able to buy expensive goods like pianos or elegant clothes, while women like Elizabeth Gunn or Luzena Wilson had "for several years [as] my best dress . . . a clean calico."

Moreover, prostitutes were competitors. Instead of visiting moral women in their homes, one outraged woman wrote, "young men . . . nightly spend their evenings, like dogs, smelling out all these vile excrescences, peeking through the cracks of doors, windows, and blinds in our crowded thoroughfares, in the full face of ladies and gentlemen going and returning from church!" Even worse were young men who "pass the early part of the evening in the society of virtuous females, discoursing upon the charms of democratic life, and the solace of home, and virtuous associations! and directly upon leaving, *cross the street and enter a house of ill fame.*" The visibility of prostitution and the continuing support the male community gave to it not only established the limits of women's moral authority but also the limits of their charms. Women's pleased comments about the attention paid to them on the mining frontier suggested the anger and jealousy they felt when their charms were denied.

The saloon, often a gambling hall as well, was another target for female anger. Once again male and female perspectives diverged. To lonely men, especially in the early days of mining, the saloon was the place to find companionship and good cheer, a place to forget failure and hard monotonous work. There might be a good hot lunch there for free, and one might see "pretty, saucy looking, active girls behind the bar." It was obvious that saloons might foster disorderly conduct and excessive drinking, but these did not outweigh the real contributions saloons made to the men who frequented them.

Women, however, knew that gambling destroyed habits of industry and thrift, while drinking reduced men to the level of "their own animalized selves" and bred irresponsibility and violence. Furthermore, the saloon had a clear link with overt sexuality. Not only were questionable women employed there, but abandoned women visited them. The decoration of saloons explicitly coupled drinking and sex. "In the gambling saloons," noted a horrified Elizabeth Gunn, "are pictures of naked women, and women half dressed, dancing on the tables. I never saw a place where there was so much need of teaching and preaching and living as we ought to live." Finally, women saw their husbands spending time and money in saloons rather than at home. Rachel Haskell, a resident of Aurora, catalogued her husband's bouts with the saloon in her diary. "Felt very much concerned . . . worried in mind a good deal . . . rather a forlorn, angry feeling at heart" were phrases expressing her anxious response to "those growing peccadillos" which included all-night bouts. Saloons were a threat to the whole structure of domesticity which women like Rachel Haskell tried to create on the mining frontier and, at times, even a threat to their physical well-being.

Women's strategies for modifying life on the mining frontier included establishing desirable alternatives to vice and working on an individual basis to reform sinners. Rachel Haskell's diary shows how she dealt with the saloon problem at home. The problem was all too clear. "Papa came home very late with a dreadful headache. He laid on the sofa saying 'He never was so sick in his life.' Threw up. And I went to sleep with Ella." Her tactic of making her errant husband sleep alone, "in his cold bed for home penalty," seems to have been one of her favorites, though she also reported "sharp" talks with him. Her diary breaks off, so whether she reformed her husband or not is not known. She apparently did not, however, move beyond a very individual response to the problem. Because "Mr. H. refused" to sign a temperance pledge, for example, she did too. Other women, again most probably middle class, did organize around the liquor issue. In 1855, for example, San Francisco women lobbied for the prohibition of liquor. But women did not easily move into the public world in their attempt to reshape it.

The issue of Sunday closings was one which encouraged well-organized collective efforts, for individual grumbling was ineffective. Many middle-class women saw the elimination of business activity on Sunday as a vital part of the struggle to create order in mining communities. Few men agreed with the militant women. For hard-working miners without families, Sunday was a day for mending clothes, washing, and going to town for supplies and relaxation. It was the only day of the week during the mining season when they did not work. Merchants found Sunday one of their most profitable business days, as did saloonkeepers, restaurant owners, and prostitutes. Few of them could see much point in Sabbath closings.

So women in a few communities organized. The Reverend Hamilton, a missionary in Columbia, California, described one campaign for Sunday closings which women spearheaded there. Complaints from what he admitted was a "minority" about business operations on the Sabbath were commonplace, but no one did anything specific to pressure businessmen until the women decided to mount a petition drive. Collecting over 160 signatures on the petition requesting Sunday closings was but the first step; advertising a public meeting was the second. At the meeting, the women themselves read the petition "with a marked effect." Apparently the merchants were impressed by the "unanimity" on the issue and took "the matter into immediate consideration, and after strenuous efforts, on the part of those deeply interested in the object, secured concert of action and closed their stores." This victory was, Hamilton pointed out, entirely due to the ladies. Whether it would be temporary or not, he was not willing to say.

The growing courage of women to tackle vice in an open manner was evident in San Francisco's famous "Cora affair." By 1855 the city had a nucleus of married women and families. Because these virtuous few had to walk through the parts of the city favored by prostitutes in order to reach the shopping area, they could hardly overlook the "offenders" who, they noted, had "splendid houses" and who endeavored "to attract attention by sitting before their open windows and doors." The urban organization of San Francisco was typical in forcing this envious and outraged confrontation between virtue and vice, for lack of planning and rapid growth often brought the two together in mining communities.

Women met not only in the streets but in other public places as well. The Cora affair began with an encounter at the theater. Charles Cora, a well-known gambler, accompanied his mistress, Arabella

Ryan, or the Belle Cora, as she preferred, to the theater one evening. The Belle Cora's moral standing was not only clear in her status as Cora's acknowledged mistress but as a proprietress of a chain of houses. She was also notorious for the scornful glances she returned to virtuous women while walking the city streets. The same night U.S. Marshal William H. Richardson and his wife were also in the audience directly in front of the infamous couple. Mrs. Richardson was horrified and urged her husband to have the gambler and his mistress thrown out of the theater. Though her husband tried to follow his wife's instructions, the pair would not leave. In the end, the Richardsons retreated.

The next evening, no doubt fortified by his wife's inflammatory rhetoric and more whiskey than usual, Richardson sought Cora out, provoked a quarrel, and was shot and killed. While Cora pleaded self-defense, the papers whipped up sentiment against him and the town's general immorality. "Let something be done," proclaimed the *Fireman's Journal*, "so that a man may be able to walk through the streets with a virtuous woman." Much of the journalistic campaign was directed to women, who responded enthusiastically. Their part was to create the heightened emotional atmosphere necessary for a moral campaign. As one angry woman wrote, "The ladies of San Francisco hold the power in their own hands . . . to purify this city, to drive hence the gambler and the harlot, and restore the tone of moral health and purity, and make it a suitable residence for the virtuous and the good."

Meanwhile, the Belle Cora hired the best lawyers she could find for her man. During the trial, one of them described the lovers' relationship as "a tie which angels might not blush to approve." The response from the women of the city was violent. As one woman wrote, "Has the man who thus endorsed the sinful union between the gambler and prostitute, a mother living? Has he a wife or daughters, who can read his sentiments? Has he a son?" Tempers continued high; the jury reached no agreement on Cora, hardly surprising since Richardson had clearly been the aggressor. Cora returned to jail. James King, leader of the editorial campaign, continued to bait "moral offenders," and in May 1856, one of his targets shot him down for his efforts.

In all the excitement, the women had aired their views in letters to the paper and enjoyed an influential forum in King's publication particularly; yet they had not organized themselves to deal with the conditions they found so offensive. Nor did they organize after King's death. It was the men of the city who pressed forward and formed a vigilante justice committee to cleanse the city. Again, however, women lent vocal support. "What is to be done with that villain, Casey [King's murderer]?" one wrote. "If the men don't hang him the ladies will!" The ladies didn't need to worry that their bravado would be tested. The vigilante committee found King's murderer guilty along with Cora. The Belle Cora, who married Cora just before his execution, and others like her, had been given violent warning that virtue would not tolerate vice. As the reform movement continued, different schemes were brought forward to eliminate gambling and prostitution or, at the very least, to decrease its visibility by confining it to certain districts.

The San Francisco *Chronicle* had declared that it was "the duty of the lawmakers to drive all such practices into the dark recesses of night, where the young and unsuspecting will not find them, unless they seek them out." By 1857, vice was less visible to the innocent young and their virtuous elders. Although neither gambling nor prostitution had disappeared or had even moved off the main streets, the offenders were far more discreet than they had been in the past. On the surface, then, San Francisco seemed reformed, but underneath little had changed. The Belle Cora ran her house until she died in 1862.

The "resolution" of the Cora incident suggests that the efforts of those women committed to changing the mining frontier's atmosphere had, at best, mixed results. As flush times faded, some of the activities that depended upon easy money departed. High-class prostitutes and gamblers left a dying town to search out others, and many of the hardened miners followed. The moral improvement was the victory of decay. In those mining areas which found new sources of prosperity and in cities like San Francisco and Denver, the victories were more apparent than real. Sabbath closings worked for a few weeks but often not permanently. Serious institutions like churches never attracted the kind of support that committed believers thought necessary. As late as 1890 only 31 percent of San Francisco's residents were church communicants, while in Cincinnati, a city of similar size, 39 percent were.

Women were capable of agitating and publicizing their position, though they were less successful in organizing to deal with social problems. No matter what approach they took, they were not able to impose their views on a heterogeneous, transient male society in any but a superficial manner. Their allies lacked the influence or the will to push through the reforms. Protestant clergymen, of course, supported women's causes, but as Elizabeth Gunn pointed out, missionaries themselves had only limited prestige on the mining frontier. "The minister is not regarded with the reverence that was given him at home. They respect his learning as they would that of any educated citizen and think he is a good man, and that is all." Editors and merchants favored improving society, for they knew the illusion of permanence worked to their financial advantage. But for them the illusion of order might well be sufficient; moreover, they differed with women over issues like Sunday closings, which had financial repercussions and which were also opposed by the majority of the male population, many of whom were European and horrified by the vision of the Protestant Sabbath. City governments proved to be more interested in making money out of vice than in ending it.

Earnest women did succeed, however, in making many of their standards clear. The lines between acceptable and unacceptable institutions and behavior became more distinct with time, and certain conventions were observed in the presence of respectable women. Men left off their flannel shirts and wore topcoats; their support of vice (if they wished to be received) was discreetly concealed. Social distinctions were sharpened. Then, too, women established and supported institutions which competed with vice as centers of attraction, and here numbers again worked in their favor. Ice-cream parlors, for example, favored by women, flourished. In San Francisco they served up to three thousand customers a day, "lovers with their sweethearts, and husbands with their better-halves." "No one visits here who is not willing to see and be seen," the newspaper pointed out. Balls and pleasure excursions, reputable theaters patronized by respectable women, were other lures. Churches served as both social and religious centers.

Women emigrating to California, Eliza Farnham advised, ought to have "fortitude, indomitable resolution, dauntless courage, and a clear self-respect which will alike forbid her doing anything unworthy." Her list of virtues necessary for women on the mining frontier testified to her conviction that mining society had the capacity to shape women or to be shaped by them. How far her fears that women lost their female virtues on the mining frontier were justified is hard to say. Like the trans-Mississippi agricultural frontier, the mining frontier did not encourage women to move very far beyond conventional social roles. Although men were not always willing to change mining society, they were just as insistent about female nature as the most traditional woman. What California wants, one article in 1854 pointed out, is woman "in her highest and holiest nature . . . the companion, the friend, the co-worker with man in the great cause of humanity." Male conservatism in regard to woman's place was clear when men failed to give women the vote in early gold camps although miners in their mid-teens voted. Newspapers derided feminism and praised Western women who "never talk of 'women's rights'—never parade the streets in bloomers and high heeled boots—never mount the stump . . . telling of the tyranny of men. In this respect [they] are angels in contrast with their strong-minded sisters in the East."

But if there were no radical innovations in female behavior or in nineteenth-century norms, there were changes. Women, just as men, felt the effect of loose or nonexistent community standards. The same voices which exhorted women to come to save the mining West often noted the numbers of women already there who had failed that task. Certainly many women supported the familiar institutions which reappeared on the frontier, although the proportion of women doing so is unknown. But ministers pointed out that there were far fewer women in church than they had expected, and a variety of reasons lay behind this neglect. As Elizabeth Gunn explained, "We do not go to meeting now, as the preacher is a Southern man and favors slavery and there is no other meeting near." Certainly the presence of a cosmopolitan attitude toward Sunday as a day for relaxation and pleasure contributed to religious indifference. Another factor isolated by missionaries was secularism. There were fifty ladies in Crescent City, wrote one missionary in 1854, but only twelve church members. The influence of woman, he continued, "has not been *what is expected of her at home;* women of religious professions at home step into the deep stream of worldliness along with their husbands and instead of leading them out, *drag them down.*" Worldliness there evidently was, but it was due as often to the weakness of organized religion as to the weakness of women. In the struggle to survive on the mining frontier, many churches also succumbed to worldliness. So Lura Smith explained that she had gone to the theater rather than church, for "it is cheaper to go there occasionally than to hire a seat in a *respectable* church." Whatever the reason, enough women forgot their duty to be noticeable. Wrote Mary Jane Megquier to her mother, "I suppose you will think it very strange when I tell you I have not attended church for one year nor even heard a prayer but I cannot see but every thing goes on as well as when I was at home."

Mary Jane had pointed out several years earlier, "You can do as you please about attending, it is all the same whether you go to church or play monte." Although distinctions between virtue and vice were clearly drawn, there was a certain tolerance for behavior as long as it was not socially dangerous and as long as certain proprieties were observed. Prostitutes might not come to balls or church fairs, but as one Montana woman noted, "We never ask women where they come from or what they did before they came to live in our neck of the woods. If they wore a wedding band and were good wives, mothers, and neighbors that was enough for us to know. A marriage band with us had a way of stopping a lot of silly questions."

"It is so pleasant to have plenty of money, we cannot seem to get a thousand together but if I want ten or twenty it is always ready," Mary Jane commented. Women responded to the materialistic temper of mining society, as ministers had noted, and enjoyed spending easy (or not so easy) money. Their materialism manifested itself in a preoccupation with appearances. Visitors and residents both commented on the interest in female fashion that developed after the hardest days of the early mining frontier had passed. San Francisco papers criticized the luxurious clothing local women preferred which drew its inspiration from France and probably the dress style of the city's prostitutes. If the clothing was impractical and immodest, as papers suggested, women paid no attention. Nor were elaborate clothes confined only to a few women of means. "I have never lived in a place," one woman in Nevada announced, "where people dressed more richly or more extravagantly than in Virginia City. It is not only a few millionaires who indulge in it, but every woman on the Comstock who has a husband earning $4 or $6 a day." What some proponents of woman's place had feared came to pass on the mining frontier. Domesticity had become frivolous.

The quiet domestic vision was also threatened by the variety and stimulation of life on the mining frontier. Not all the excitement was welcome. The wife of a Grass Valley minister who used her iron to fend off an amorous miner who drunkenly confused her with a prostitute named Fanny probably did not relish the incident. But women often enjoyed the drama. "I lead a life of great variety—full of agreeable, and stirring incidents," Martha Hitchcock declared. "I think that I should find any other country very dull after this." Mary Jane Megquier agreed and felt she would "never feel perfectly satisfied with . . . quiet ways again. Here you can step out of your house and see the whole world spread out before you in every shape and form. Your ears are filled with the most delightful music, your eyes are dazzled with every thing that is beautiful, the streets are crowded the whole city are in the street." Not every mining camp was a San Francisco, but every thriving mining town had money, numerous amenities and luxuries, and an atmosphere of excitement which rendered home back East and even the ideal home less attractive to many women.

Those welcoming women and families to the mining West had expected homes to become centers of good influence and many of them were. But it was a sign of the impact of the frontier on women that homes there fostered customs which many moralists saw as scandalous and dangerous. Married women typically entertained married and single men at home. It was a short step for some women, sources show, from entertaining at home to going from home with their men friends and even receiving presents from them. Innocent as such customs might have been initially, moralists believed they allowed young men to insinuate "themselves into the affections of married women." The devil surely lurked behind the custom. "He gives special attention to wives, more particularly the beautiful and young wives . . . He employs a great variety of means for their ruin; wine, flattery, and bribes, in the form of splendid presents," wrote the Reverend Taylor.

Although California and other parts of the mining frontier were not on the brink of a collapse of moral standards as the jeremiads proclaimed, the criticism suggests that sexual mores were less rigid in the new environment. And it was not only the moralists who used the vocabulary of temptation and sin. Sophia Eastman, a woman who had come to the frontier alone, was one who agreed. "I would not let a friend come in the same manner in which I came for unless they had a very strong mind and well formed character they will even before they are aware be led into temptation and at last be ruined."

Court records detailing causes for divorce reveal some aspects of women's sexual activities. A case involving a couple in Union Town, California, in 1853 disclosed that the wife had left her husband, not to live alone, but to share a house with an unmarried male boarder. The community both questioned the propriety of the arrangement and observed it closely. One neighbor said that "it was improper that they should live in the same house together," while another added that "they were greater friends than they ought to be under the circumstances." "Their conduct," he concluded, "would cause people to talk." Yet a third witness revealed for the record how curiosity had gotten the better of him as he passed the house one night. "I heard some low talking . . . I stood there something like ten minutes . . . I was standing as close to the house as one could get to peep in through a crack by the door . . . I saw a light under the door and stooped to look." An aggrieved husband described his wife's adultery in some detail, testifying, "I see a man destitute of clothing save in his shirt come in & get into bed with def[endant]. I shortly got up and went out to the well. I found laying on the outside of the door a pair of pantaloons and shoes." Women proved no more squeamish or less curious than their male observers. Thus, one wife in a 1869 suit told her husband she was off on a neighborly visit. "Instead of going, I returned to the house, and saw this transaction with Mary W. I stopped at the window several moments."

How many women strayed from nineteenth-century norms to commit adultery, to pass themselves as married when they were not, to desert their husbands is, of course, impossible to discover. But they did divorce their husbands. Unreliable as divorce statistics are for this period, they show that the divorce rate for states which were part of the mining frontier were higher than for the United States as a whole (with the exception of certain areas of the South). Critics pointed out that divorce laws and residency requirements on the mining frontier were lax, and they were right. But the stringency or leniency of laws does not seem to be the main factor explaining these high rates, but rather transiency, prosperity, community tolerance, and plenty of opportunity for remarriage. Divorce was an option women on the frontier had and one which they chose.

Mary Jane Megquier's letters spanning 1849–56 illustrate the gradual impact of the mining frontier on one woman. It is true that Mary Jane was by birth middle class, by training literate, and by nature a free spirit. She liked the West, she told her daughter, because there was "not a word about such a thing is not respectable, you know I always detested that." Yet at the same time she was a New Englander, sensitive to her moral responsibilities. She, too, recounted an incident of ejecting a questionable woman from a social affair. Initially, Mary Jane had accompanied her husband to California, expecting, like so many other women, to earn a fortune and return to Winthrop, Massachusetts. And as her early letters show, she worked hard to make the fortune, talked of her old home, and missed her children. At the same time, she noted how much time she spent with men. Gradually her letters described parties and other recreations along with the work, visits to the ice-cream parlor with men friends, her failure to go to church. Her determination to return to the East began to weaken. "A few weeks ago," she wrote, "I could have left without a regret, but we are beginning to live like civilized beings." Finally, she and her husband made the trip to Winthrop; she came back to California without him. Her last surviving letters told her daughter of "Mr. Johnson of whom you often hear me speak . . . my gallant whenever I wish to go," and observed this "is the place to enjoy life."

Certainly not all women experienced the mining frontier as Mary Jane Megquier did, but many seemed to feel there was a freer and more enjoyable life there. As a woman in a silver-mining town characterized her neighbors, "The ladies of Virginia City are always ready for amusement, and I think enjoy it more than any class of people among whom I ever lived."

What, then, did the frontier mean for the women who went there? Women of "honest hearts, have fallen victim to the peculiar seductions [of] the place," one observer mused, but in spite of this, "paradoxical as the statement may sound, it is rigorously true that these women have improved the morals of the community." The comments captured the complexities of female experience on the mining frontier. Many of them tried to live up to the challenge described by Farnham, and others, less worried by role prescriptions, found new enjoyments and freedoms. By their very presence, however, most contributed to the building of a family society and served to remind all of the cluster of ideas associated with nineteenth-century womanhood.

In the end, of course, those hard-core miners who so threatened order, morality, and stability were lured by a new strike and escaped these women altogether. The less adventurous, the towns in decline, the occasional communities which survived boom and bust to achieve some kind of permanence, all felt the impact of women. So, too, did the two great cities, Denver and San Francisco. As the San Francisco *Bulletin* noted, "The time honored anniversary of family reunions, of feasting, fun and frolicking," Christmas, emerged, overshadowing drinking, gambling, and whoring. A victory indeed, but was it more apparent than real?

This was the very question that men and women asked themselves when they tried to understand what the mining frontier had meant to them. As early as the 1850's, William Perkins wondered what time would bring. "Ten years hence, perhaps, the standard of morality will have improved, and something more than a show of respectability will be required, but I question if a jollier *Fandango* than ours, will then be produced." And years later, Eliza Wilson also wondered, as she recalled the old days. "Every lady was overwhelmed with attention," she wrote, also thinking of a dance, "and there was probably more enjoyment that night, on the rough pine floor and under the flickering gleam of tallow candles, than one often finds in our social drawing-rooms, where the rich silks trail over velvet carpets, where the air is heavy with the perfume of exotics, and where the night is turned into a brighter day under the glare of countless gas-jets."

6

"If Polygamy
Is the Lord's Order,
We Must Carry It Out"

Emigrants who passed Mormon wagon trains on the dusty trail
west or who rested in Salt Lake City midway through their journey
observed, often with astonishment, the order, sobriety, and industry
that characterized Mormon society west of the Mississippi. It was,
they realized, an alternative to the less structured pioneering experience encountered on the trail and expected at the trail's end. Yet, if
Mormon society was organized, serious, and industrious, it was not
without a certain gaiety. Dancing, acting, and making music were
integral parts of Mormon life, antidotes to the hardships accompanying the settlement of the frontier. The music itself was good enough
to elicit grudging praise of Mormon musical abilities. However, if the
travelers listened closely, they might find reinforcement for all the
negative stereotypes they had of Mormon life. One song, a favorite
at local festivals, started out, "Now sisters, list to what I say / With
trials this world is rife / You can't expect to miss them all, / Help
husband get a Wife! / Now this advice I freely give, / If exalted you
would be, / Remember that your husband must / Be blessed with
more than thee." The refrain gave further evidence to emigrants of
what was amiss in Utah, for it continued, "Then O, let us say / God
bless the wife that strives / And aids her husband all she can / T'obtain a dozen wives."

The song's lyrics conveyed much about Mormon attitudes to polyg-

147

amy. On the one hand, the chorus gaily urged wives to encourage their husbands to marry, marry, marry for God's abundant blessings but, on the other hand, suggested the tensions of the marriage system with the reference to worldly "trials." To outsiders, the song's attitudes were puzzling, at best, and, to most, scandalous. Polygamy was nothing to sing about. It was a peculiar institution corrupting Mormon society, an institution easily compared to black slavery and open to the same solution: abolition. The analogy and solution were clear in Harriet Beecher Stowe's comment that she trusted the time was right "to loose the bonds of a cruel slavery whose chains have cut into the hearts of thousands of our sisters."

Clearly, the Mormon frontier with its distinctive marriage system and unusual social arrangements disturbed mid-nineteenth-century Americans profoundly. Like black slavery, Mormon "slavery" became the subject of a number of sensational tales purporting to reveal the nature of the Mormon system, especially its impact on women. The novels, of course, further fueled anxiety. Written not by emigrants or travelers who had viewed Mormon society firsthand but by daughters and wives of New England reformers and ministers, the widely read books bore titles like Orvilla Belisle's *The Prophets: or, Mormonism Unveiled*, published in 1855.

Several stock themes appeared time and time again. One centered on a pure and noble heroine who, for one reason or another, became entangled in Mormon life and who then was able to reveal all its horrors and licentiousness. Closely related to this was the escape tale in which the main characters, in a series of thrilling chapters, eluded the avenging and murderous Mormons. A third theme focused on polygamy. The husband in a plural household was characterized as lustful, materialistic, and coarse; for women, polygamy was nothing but a thinly disguised system of prostitution and economic exploitation. In all these treatments Mormon men were villainous, lecherous, and wily. Mormon women were their pitiful victims; the heroines were naturally those women whose intelligence and character led them to resist conversion and reject polygamy. The assumption was that only religious trickery, outright oppression, or female depravity could account for women's acceptance of a religion which encouraged plural marriage.

These novels really revealed more about the concerns of middle-class Americans than they did about life on the Mormon frontier. Harriet Beecher Stowe's description of polygamy as "a slavery which debases and degrades womanhood, motherhood, and family" was typical in its emphasis on the threats Mormonism appeared to pose to women and the family. Polygamy could only be an anathema for a culture which had defined the traditional nuclear family as the source of social stability and the married woman as keeper of morals and culture. Since it was assumed that polygamy destroyed the family and woman's unique place in it and made women unfit for their moral and social responsibilities, social disorder and rampant immorality must inevitably result. Such a view of polygamy reinforced the more general fears that the westward movement might result in the collapse of social order and traditions. Polygamy on the frontier was, thus, a doubly threatening phenomenon.

It was no surprise that much of the anti-Mormon literature was the product of New England women. In the early nineteenth century woman's sphere had been made legitimate and imbued with significance through its identification with home. New England women had been active in propagating this new view of woman's role and subsequently in using it as the basis for a civilizing mission in the West. In less obvious ways, the novels may also have served to release certain tensions resulting from nineteenth-century marriage arrangements. The novels contain a surprising amount of eroticism and violence, suggesting that female writers were, on one level, lashing out against male lust and the double standard and, on another, protesting against norms minimizing sexuality in marriage and female sexuality in general.

Whatever motivations lay beneath the tales of Mormon life, the most explicit message was that the Mormon frontier experiment was to be condemned by all right-minded Americans and eliminated. Thus, Americans were puzzled and shocked by the way in which Mormon women, even those who appeared to be intelligent and virtuous, defended their way of life. Belinda Pratt's letter to her sister in 1854 was typical in the arguments presented in support of polygamy. "Polygamy," Mrs. Pratt wrote, "tends directly to the chastity of women, and the sound health and morals in the constitutions of their offspring." Though the identification of polygamy with chastity was confusing to the outsider, it was a point Mormon women frequently made. Because all women might have husbands, children, and homes, none would be forced by loneliness or poverty to degrade herself by becoming a prostitute. As for men, Mrs. Pratt pointed out, those who were noble were worthy of a hundred wives. Presumably, if they had no legitimate outlets for their "nobility," they would find illegitimate ones. Polygamy, then, kept men virtuous as well as women.

Most nineteenth-century Americans, preferring the message the novels conveyed, rejected the claim that polygamy provided benefits for women out of hand. The truth about polygamy and the Mormon way of life, however, lay somewhere between the defense Mormon women mounted and the exposés the irate female novelists presented. Polygamy was neither so degrading as the Gentiles claimed nor so liberating as the Mormon spokeswomen insisted. With its peculiar tensions and freedoms, polygamy did, of course, shape the Mormon female life on the frontier. Mormon women were different from women on other frontiers in a number of ways which were related to their religion. Yet they also shared with other pioneer women common frontier experiences and even common ideas about woman's place in the world. To be a Mormon woman on the Utah frontier was, therefore, to be both the same as, and different from, pioneer women elsewhere.

Without considering the Mormon settlement of Utah as an experiment in utopia building, however, it would be impossible to understand the Mormon frontier and the experience of women there. For much of the distinctiveness of Mormon society, including plural marriage, resulted from the group's utopian orientation. The settlement of Utah was not merely another chapter in the westward movement but one of the numerous attempts in the middle of the nineteenth century to build a new and more perfect society in the wilderness. Amana in Iowa, Bethel in Missouri, and Aurora in Oregon were other frontier settlements inspired by religious faith; they were committed to building the City of God on earth. Communities like Communia in Iowa differed in having a secular ideological base. It was to be a city of men, but the goal of creating a more perfect society was the same. Of all these frontier experiments, the Mormon undertaking was clearly the largest, the most important, and the most successful.

By withdrawing from what they saw as a corrupt Eastern environment, groups like the Mormons sought to build a new society. Certain assumptions nourished these experiments, which so confidently disregarded conventional social and often economic arrangements. Basic was the conviction that human beings were perfectible. So, too, was the belief that social solidarity and cooperation stemming from a freely given commitment to the group as a whole could replace crass individualism and eliminate the need for social coercion. By its emphasis on the group rather than the individual, the utopian vision implied planning and coordination to ensure material well-being for all and harmonious working arrangements.

Most of these mid-nineteenth-century experiments collapsed in less than sixteen years. As a recent study of ninety-one of these communities suggests, the crucial factors separating the successes from the failures were related to the mechanisms developed to reinforce commitment to the community. Successful utopias created a number of specific techniques to encourage individual identification with the group as a whole. Frequent small group interactions and mutual criticism, modifications of social institutions like marriage, which divided people rather than united them, the sharing of goods, increased the sense of community and often made it difficult for members to leave. Sacrifices like abstinence from liquor reinforced the sense of belonging, as did special rituals. Many of the utopias were guided by charismatic leaders who were able to justify group idiosyncrasies on exalted ideological grounds. Long-term survival, however, depended on a strong organization to carry on after the leader's disappearance. Seen in this context, the survival of the Mormon experiment was due to its success in creating strong individual and group loyalty.

The denomination originally emerged during the period of feverish religious revivals that took root in western New York State in the early nineteenth century; Mormonism was shaped by its inspired leader and self-styled prophet, Joseph Smith. At the age of fourteen, Smith claimed to have had a vision in which God the Father and Christ the Son appeared to him lamenting Christianity's decadence and stressing the importance of recapturing the spirit of the early church. Over the next ten years, Smith's visions continued and resulted in an addition to the Bible, the *Book of Mormon*, and a growing conviction that his personal mission was to reestablish Christ's church. In 1830, Smith organized the Church of Jesus Christ of Latter-day Saints, and the work of conversion began. Smith's prophetic claims were validated in the eyes of his followers by his apparently miraculous powers and his continuing dialogue with the divinity. Rejecting the Calvinist doctrine of original sin and predestination, Smith promised that all believers could be saved and could, indeed, participate at once in creating God's kingdom on earth. Inspired by Smith's vision, the saints, as they referred to themselves, left their homes and headed for the frontier and the new Zion. Settling first in Ohio and Missouri, then in Illinois, where Smith was killed by an angry mob in 1844, and finally escaping to Utah, the saints worked to build a physical kingdom under the close direction of religious leaders whose authority was bolstered by Smith's claim that the priesthood was a restoration of Christ's original one. Commitment to Zion involved sacrifices and suffering. The promised rewards, however, were commensurate with the trials. "As man is, God once was; as God is, man may be."

Early attempts to build the kingdom in the Midwest were also marked by financial hardship, as Zion's location shifted because of violence and persecution. These experiences further strengthened the cohesiveness of the group, now clearly differentiated from the mainstream of American society. Most Americans justified persecution on the grounds that Mormons were theocratic empire builders and, thus, both a political and a religious threat. Mormon religious doctrines seemed both exclusive and excessive, while Smith's revelation that the day should come "when tribulation and desolation are sent forth upon the wicked" was unwelcome news to the wicked. The Mormons' success at building up self-sufficient political units was disturbing, and

Smith's interest in running for the Presidency ominous. Rumors of polygamy, practiced secretly in the eighteen-forties and early fifties, led to charges of immorality. Despite the constitutional guarantee of freedom of worship, Americans had few qualms about driving Mormons out of one settlement after another and eventually a thousand miles away to the desert of Utah.

It was an indication of the cohesiveness of the new Israelites, as the Mormons liked to call themselves, that the group maintained itself in the face of such hostility. Almost twenty years of persecution and suffering created a strong group identity and encouraged Mormons to accept forceful church leadership and planning. United by memorable common experiences, organized by their leaders for common goals, and committed to the new order by peculiar social arrangements as well as by the promise of salvation, the Mormons in 1847 were at last free to claim "the land of promise held in reserve by the hand of God for a resting place for the Saints upon which a portion of the Zion of God will be built." Twenty years later, the dream of creating a utopian society was still strong, as Smith's successor, Brigham Young, made clear. "I have looked upon the community of Latter-day Saints in a vision and beheld them organized as the great family of heaven, each person performing his several duties in his line of industry, working for the good of the whole more than for individual aggrandizement; and in this I have beheld the most beautiful order that the mind of man can contemplate, and the grandest results for the upbuilding of the Kingdom of God and the spread of righteousness upon the earth."

In 1847, however, it took great faith to see Utah as the land of promise. The desert would not become fruitful without tremendous human labor. Church leaders, from the beginning, directed the effort, which was collective and cooperative. Settlers did not scatter to individual homesteads but lived in towns and villages. The church divided and distributed the land around the first settlement at Salt Lake, laid out the community, and directed irrigation programs to reclaim the land and provide water for all the farmers in the community on an equitable basis. In a similar manner, the church sent out groups to colonize other areas, where the same collective approach to settlement, farming, and irrigation followed. The bishop in a new settlement was a key figure, often supervising the digging of canals and ditches and even using the Sunday sermon to inform the congregation of the work schedules for the coming week.

Although these early years were difficult ones, Mormon settlers slowly but confidently conquered their environment. Their faith, freedom from persecution, and memories of the early hardships which so many of them had experienced helped them survive the difficulties of pioneering and reinforced group ties. The church touched every aspect of life. The open support for polygamy after 1852 gave the church influence over the most intimate relationships in addition to influence on general social and economic relations. The sense of identity grew stronger. The careful organization of concentrated settlements contributed to it and undercut the loneliness so common on other frontiers in the early years. Meanwhile, missionary labors, focused in Europe after 1852, mainly in England and Scandinavia, brought in scores of new converts with useful skills and talents and new enthusiasm for the social and religious experiment. The atmosphere which accompanied turning the desert into a garden was characterized by optimism and a strong group consciousness.

The sense of mission and collectivity within a group which was ethnically heterogeneous set the Mormon frontier apart from the typical mining or agricultural frontier. So, too, did its demographic composition. Within a year of the original migration to Utah, there were approximately the same number of women as men. At about the same period in Oregon, only 42 percent of the rural population were women, while under 31 percent of city dwellers were female. Utah's demographic distinctiveness persisted over the next few decades, even as more and more settlers arrived. Immigration from Europe was weighted in favor of women, a remarkable phenomenon in light of the male composition of European immigration as a whole. By 1870, 49.1 percent of Zion's residents were women, while only 41.5 percent of settlers in Oregon were.

What accounted for the numbers of women flocking to Utah and what was the attitude of the church toward them? What kind of a place did the church assign women in frontier society and what kind of a commitment did it require from them? Certainly the converts did not expect the slavery New England novelists described so luridly; nor did they except sexual liberation. Despite the institution of polygamy, the Mormon frontier did not offer women the sexual or familial liberation available in communities like New Harmony, which rejected marriage for free love, or Oneida, with its system of complex marriage. Nor did the emphasis on community usually mean communal living arrangements as far-reaching as those in a settlement like Amana, which freed women from much of the drudgery of housework.

Emigration for many of the women was, in fact, not explicitly linked to liberation from traditional sex roles. Most came with parents or husbands; missionaries carefully concealed or minimized polygamy. Conversion was frequently a family affair, triggered by the promise of heavenly salvation. But religious rewards were paralleled by economic ones, for Zion's kingdom began not in heaven but on earth. New settlers were smoothly integrated into the frontier economy; the opportunities routinely provided seemed especially dazzling when contrasted to the humble background of most converts. Early land policy, for example, provided all settlers with free land, and those with special skills could always be assured of a livelihood. Ann Bringhurst's satisfaction with Zion was materialistic and not surprisingly so. "We have everything arround us we could asks," she wrote to Olivia Wollerton in 1850. "We have the best plase in the world to make money." Then, too, the church made emigration relatively easy. For two decades a significant proportion of church resources went to financing emigration through the Perpetual Emigrating Fund. The fund loaned travel money to converts, while missionaries made the arrangements. Rather than face the trip alone like other emigrants, Mormon converts traveled as a group with leaders. All knew that a livelihood awaited them at the journey's end.

A minority of the women came without families. The recollections of one young Englishwoman show the pattern of conversion and emigration. The woman made initial contact with missionaries in what appeared to be a most unlikely way when she hired a man and his son to paint and paper her house. Hearing that the pair had some strange delusion, she inquired about their peculiar beliefs. The Mormon missionaries were, of course, quick to take advantage of her curiosity and soon provided her with books. As she remembered much later, "I found myself believing! What should I do?" Other women's chance or purposeful encounters with missionaries raised the same question. Because of the group nature of emigration, single women and a surprising number of widows could easily be incorporated into the "gathering," and emigration followed conversion. But if the going was instigated by faith and facilitated by travel arrangements, there were other motives encouraging solitary women to make the trip. General hostility to Mormonism spurred female and male converts to leave their homes. More positive factors encouraging female emigration included recognition of women's individual spiritual gifts, like speaking in tongues or experiencing visions, and the sheer adventure of being able to participate in the creating of God's kingdom on earth. Finally, single converts faced a more promising material future in Utah than they often did at home, where their economic options were limited. Many were in domestic service, probably the most unpleasant of all female employments. Emigration broke the bonds of servitude, and at the journey's end, food, shelter, employment, perhaps even marriage, awaited. In return for these benefits, women would have specific duties and obligations to perform on the frontier.

The official attitude of the church toward women was shaped on the one hand by an evolving theology and on the other hand by a continuing pragmatism. The *Book of Mormon*, which Joseph Smith revealed to the world in 1830, had almost nothing to say about women. The book's virtual neglect of the female sex was buttressed by Smith's theology. Smith taught that Christ's Priesthood had been reinstated in Zion with all believing white males as potential members. Even though hierarchy existed (there were two ranks, the Aaronic or lesser priesthood, and the Melchizedek), every man had important religious duties ranging from conducting worship and instructing others in the faith to healing of the sick. Religious importance translated into social importance. Mormon society was patriarchal, with men's rights well bolstered by theology.

The link connecting women to the priesthood and ultimately salvation was marriage. Only by marrying a man endowed with the priesthood could a woman hope for salvation. The single woman faced the grim prospect of spiritual annihilation. Women were, in one sense, spiritual cripples.

Yet other aspects of Smith's theology partially compensated for women's spiritual inferiority. If a woman married, she and her husband both might acquire salvation, but only a woman could fulfill a crucial part of God's plan for the world. Mormons believed that the universe was filled with souls hungering for human bodies without which salvation was impossible. As Brigham Young pointed out, "It is the duty of every righteous man and every woman to prepare tabernacles for all the spirits they can." Female reproduction was, therefore, the means of releasing souls from a limbolike existence. Ultimately childbearing brought heavenly rewards to both parents, for their position in heaven depended upon the number of their offspring. (Polygamous families had a distinct advantage here.) Since women were so essential to God and men, the church assured them of participation in temple ceremonies.

It is also necessary to appreciate the Mormon church's determination to build a self-contained Zion in Utah in order to understand women's position on the Mormon frontier. In the literal wilderness of the desert, Mormons hoped to create a self-sufficient kingdom to provide a retreat for the faithful and the basis for a new social order. If this vision were to be realized, both sexes would have to work to bring it about. Especially during the early period of settlement (1847–67), women were encouraged to work; laziness was condemned as a major sin. "We do not believe in having any drones in the hive," Mrs. Ezra Benson pointed out. "All are engaged in some useful occupation." Women were full economic partners, performing vital jobs, even those defined as male. So, Mrs. Benson pointed out, "some spin, others weave cloth . . . Some make up the clothing . . . others again make the butter and cheese, and attend to the cows, pigs and poultry." Still others might "plough and harrow the ground, plant the seed, and hoe up the weeds when the time comes. They may also be seen irrigating the crops with water." Women not only had quilting bees but bees to build houses, dig canals, and erect fences. During

the settlement period, in fact, women may have been more than economic partners. With husbands often away on church business, for
years at a time if they were missionaries, women supported themselves
and sometimes helped to support their husbands, all with the church's
encouragement. Women needed to be independent and self-reliant,
Brigham Young pointed out, and mothers should make sure that they
taught these qualities to their daughters. "Mothers in Israel, you
. . . are called upon to bring up your daughters to pursue some useful avocation for a sustenance, that when they shall become the wives
of the elders of Israel, who are frequently called upon missions, or
to devote their time and attention of the things of the kingdom, they
may be able to sustain themselves and their offspring."

The situation of Mormon women was, thus, paradoxical. Despite
the emphasis on patriarchy and male spiritual superiority, economic
sex roles could overlap. And the goals of self-sufficiency and productivity led the church to encourage and praise those women who
became producers, even though they might thereby become less dependent on male support. As one female traveler observed, "They
close no career on a woman in Utah by which she can earn a living."
In his colorful fashion, Brigham Young encouraged women long after
the early years of settlement. "I want young women to learn business," he said. "I want them to be our telegraphers and clerks. Why,
go into a store now for a yard of ribbon, and a great lazy, lubberly
fellow comes rolling up like a hogshead of molasses . . . and cuts
off the ribbon for you. Now that fellow we want out in the fields, up
in the cañon, at work, and we want his and his fellows' places supplied by the young women."

Economic goals, also, worked against the typical definition of femininity, which was, in any case, out of place during the roughest stages
of frontier life. What distinguished the Mormon frontier from other
frontiers, however, was the explicit and constant support given to
productive female behavior and the condemnation (albeit ineffective) of certain aspects of domesticity. Partly because an interest in
appearance and fashion made women consumers of goods from the
outside and partly because of Mormonism's puritanical streak, church
leaders attempted to emphasize some parts of the female image while

minimizing others. So Brigham Young warned against an interest in fashion and recommended that women wear "wooden-bottom shoes" and "use our old pantaloons and make caps out of them." Heber C. Kimball, one of Young's apostles, reminded Mormon women how corsets and petticoats harmed the female body and its reproductive organs. Mormon women were to be mothers, wives, and workers, not frivolous ladies of fashion.

With the emphasis on female productivity and the Mormon emphasis on working toward goals in a collective fashion, it was not at all surprising that the church also encouraged female organizations and gave them important responsibilities. Joseph Smith had presided over the creation of a Female Relief Society in the 1840's, but it had disbanded during the years of persecution, migration, and early settlement in Utah. But by the mid-sixties, Young was urging women to organize "against purchasing goods at the stores." His hope was that women would begin a home-manufacturing program, and a number of women's groups sprang up in response to his suggestions. Two years later, Young was more emphatic. "If the ladies would get up societies by which they could promote the home labor of their sex, they would do what was pleasing in the sight of heaven." Eliza Snow, wife of Joseph Smith and then of Brigham Young, pursued the suggestion and began organizing branches of the Female Relief Society in every Mormon community.

With the church's backing, the Female Relief Society became a permanent fixture of Mormon women's lives, giving them an experience which differed from that of other pioneer women whose organizations often had short and sporadic lives. Although the female president was selected by the priesthood, the society was not initially a male-dominated institution. Rather than using church funds, the society raised its own money and spent it; it even owned property. Early relief activities not only reflected Young's priorities but also focused on matters of special interest to women. Meetings were set aside for encouraging women's spiritual life with Bible readings, prayers, lectures, and discussion. It was this facet of the society's activities which led to the claim that women actually shared a kind of priesthood. Other meetings were devoted to charitable endeavors.

Women sewed, heard reports of their female home visitors who brought goods to the needy and evaluated their situations, and devised ways to help the poor help themselves. "To those who have strength to labor, it is far more charitable to give employment and so direct their energies that they can earn what they need," Young had suggested. The society was, in fact, in the business of running programs to train the poor.

Within a few years after the Relief Society was reestablished in Utah, the Mormon hierarchy gave it new tasks judged essential for the community's survival. As the railroad approached Utah in the late sixties, church leaders fearfully contemplated the possibilities of economic disruption as Gentile goods flowed into the territory. Women were seen as essential to the efforts to meet the expected economic onslaught from the outside. Leaders urged the Relief Society to fight the demand for imports, especially among the young. The women responded by forming "Retrenchment Societies" to teach young women the useful skills of knitting, piecing quilts, and gleaning wheat, while encouraging their cultural aspirations. Later, women became involved in establishing and controlling cooperative stores which sold home manufactures and, then, in the 1870's, with developing home industries like silk manufacturing. In 1876, when Young wished to establish a system of storing grain against future famine or disaster, he once more turned to women. "I have called upon and urged the brethren to lay up grain against a day of want," he explained, but "they do not follow my advice; they excuse themselves by saying their wives and daughters want the proceeds of the grain to buy hats and bonnets." Young's skepticism was evident in the description Emmeline Wells, later president of the Relief Society, provided. "He gave me quite a dissertation on the excuses made by the brethren," she recalled, "and then explained that if the sisters were told to save grain they would not sell it."

The importance of Relief Society operations gave women a power base and a channel of influence with the male power structure. Most of the influence was probably exercised gently behind the scenes; most often the organization cooperated with church directives. Mormon society did not encourage much freedom of thought, and women in the organization generally sympathized with church goals. But occasionally Relief activities led to conflict. As women began their grain operations, for example, the question arose of who was to manage the wheat. When some of the bishops pressed for control, women disagreed and pointed to the terms of their original mission. Young backed them up and instructed bishops to leave the women alone. Women were to raise the wheat, glean it, and lend it to bishops when they needed it for the poor. But the bishops would have to ask. Certainly Young's support strengthened the organization's power, but it is significant that even before his decision women showed their determination to control their own operations. This sense of collective power also translated into individual autonomy. When the silk mission began, for example, local bishops once more were critical. Said one, I don't "like to see the sisters go out into the fields and around and carry bundles of mulberry boughs on their back." Husbands found silkworms in their parlors and unpleasant smells at home. Yet many women disregarded these complaints and pursued their new activity.

As others have pointed out, the Relief Society was far more important than this brief description of its spiritual and economic activities suggests. Since the society was an ongoing institution with significant tasks to perform, it provided an opportunity for Mormon women to develop a strong and positive sense of themselves as women. It was a means, too, of allowing most to pursue socially important tasks and of encouraging some to learn organizational and business techniques. Aided by the Relief Society, a few women became teachers, social workers, and businesswomen. Susanna Cardon of Logan, for example, was an expert silk reeler, who left six children and a year-old baby at home, to train other women to reel silk. The society also instructed women in health care, and supported the first women doctors in Utah. In 1872 society president Eliza Snow asked, "Are there here, now, any sisters who have ambition enough, and who realize the necessity of it, for Zion's sake, to take up this study. There are some who are naturally inclined to be nurses; and such ones would do well to study medicine . . . If they cannot meet their own expenses, we have the means of doing so." Two married women responded and left their families while they attended the Women's Medical College in Philadelphia; they eventually became the first women doctors in Utah.

The position of women on the Mormon frontier was clearly far more complex than the common analogy to slavery would suggest. Mormon women had the support for a responsible and expanded social role which women on other frontiers did not. But when critics of Mormon society spoke of slavery, they did not take into account these facets of female experience. They were speaking of polygamy, which Mormons called the system of plural marriage. Although not all Mormon women were plural wives, a fact which most critics overlooked, plural marriage did color the experience of all women on the Mormon frontier and was central to their identification of themselves as Mormons. Did plural marriage, in fact, enslave women, as critics insisted, or purify them, as supporters argued?

Polygamy had no place in early Mormon theology, and as commentators never tired of pointing out, the *Book of Mormon* condemned the practice in no uncertain terms. Yet Smith may well have begun thinking about polygamy by 1831, and by the early forties, he and other leaders privately began taking plural wives. To Smith, polygamy was a means of removing the evils of instability and individualism that were destroying American society. By linking individuals and families through marriage, he believed, polygamy would strengthen social, familial, and religious ties. The identification which Mormons made between themselves and the Jewish patriarchs provided the needed scriptural reinforcements.

As Smith worked out the theoretical and ritualistic implications of polygamy, he revealed a new and compelling relationship between God and man. There were, Smith came to believe, two kinds of marriage. One was marriage for time, the other for eternity. The first was a marriage limited to earthly existence, while the second, performed in the temple with special rites, was a marriage for eternity. Those married for time could enter only into the lowest order of heaven, but those who chose a marriage for eternity were celestially mobile, eligible for heavenly glory; ultimately they might even become godlike. As a form of celestial marriage, polygamy contributed to heavenly status, for Smith believed that the more celestial wives a man had, and the more children they bore, the more honor he and his wives had in heaven. "We shall not marry . . . or be given in marriage [in heaven] hence it is necessary for us to marry here, and to marry as much as we can, for then in heaven a man will take the wives whom he married on earth, or who have been sealed to him by proxy; they will be his queens, and their children will be his subjects . . . hence we shall ourselves be gods!" Polygamy was a means of social purification and heavenly sanctification, not a means of sexual liberation.

Although members of the Mormon hierarchy practiced polygamy secretly before the migration to Utah, the doctrine and its theological justification were only announced publicly in 1852. Polygamy was openly practiced for the next forty years in Utah, and clandestinely for years after its rejection by Mormon leadership. The acceptance of polygamy was obviously related to the elaborate theological framework, but other factors were also involved. Functionally, polygamy played a major role in committing Mormons to their society, as Smith had thought it would. Asked to give up the marriage form sanctioned by society at large for the sake of their faith, Mormons in plural marriages were at odds with the outside world, which condemned the institution and its practitioners. Few polygamists apostasized. Furthermore, polygamy helped to reinforce group loyalties. In polygamy familial and personal ties extended outward toward the group as a whole rather than inward toward the monogamous family. (It was this dissatisfaction with the privatism of monogamy and the role of women in marriage which led other nineteenth-century utopias like Oneida and New Harmony also to experiment with marital relationships.) Finally, polygamy provided a way to absorb single converts into the social order. When single or widowed women arrived in Utah, the church placed them in various households and hoped for marriage. Since many of these women were somewhat older than the average marriage age (they were usually between twenty-five and thirty-five), they would have been at a disadvantage in a monogamous culture. But polygamy meant that, no matter what their age, they might have husbands and families.

An open rejection of polygamy was equivalent to a rejection of Zion, for criticism from the outside made the doctrine the cutting point of loyalty to the religion and to the place. Over a forty-year period, the hierarchy urged the steadfast to prove their faith in Smith's revelations by adopting polygamy. Yet surprisingly few responded. The actual numbers of those practicing polygamy are unknown, since plural marriages were not recorded in public records. But studies suggest that at the peak, moments of intense religious enthusiasm or periods of serious threats from the outside world, only between 15 and 20 percent of Mormon families were polygamous. At other times, the figure was probably closer to 10 percent. The impact was, however, somewhat greater than these figures suggest. Although only 17 percent of the men in one community practiced polygamy, for example, a quarter of the town's inhabitants belonged to polygamous families. Still, only a minority was involved, and the pattern was not one of steady growth but of sporadic development. Nor did many of the unions resemble those so vividly described by New England novelists. Of a sample of 1,784 polygamous marriages, 66.3 percent involved a husband and only two wives; 21.2 percent of the men took a third wife, but only 6.7 percent a fourth. Fewer than 6 percent of the sample had more than four wives. The statistical picture comes as something of a surprise considering the emphasis on plural marriage on the part of both the hierarchy and the outside world.

Obviously economics was a factor. Few poor Mormons could take on the burden of a large family. Most of the big plural families, in fact, belonged to successful church leaders, who indicated their loyalty to church doctrine by marrying more than once. Then, too, there were controls. Only those Mormons "worthy of participation in the special blessings of the House of the Lord" were eligible for celestial marriage, a decision Brigham Young made himself. Adequate financial resources weighed heavily with Young, and many would-be polygamists were rejected for having insufficient means. But the statistical profile opens the possibility that while many Mormons gave verbal support to the institution and defended it against outside attacks, they rejected it for themselves. Even those who justified it most actively spoke of its heavy burdens and the need for personal sacrifice. As one woman with a monogamous marriage candidly admitted, "When I was told about plural marriage . . . before it was taught publicly, I went into a private room and prayed I might have power given to me that I should never speak against that principle. I knew by the Spirit of God that it was true . . . But have always been afraid of my own weakness and selfishness, but my children know that I have taught them to do right in it." Said another who was a plural wife, "Polygamy was hard to live by, both for the man and the woman."

Even though the women in polygamous marriages on the Mormon frontier were not typical but extraordinary, all women were affected by the institution. Each woman had to confront the possibility of a plural marriage in an uncertain future. Most observed the principle practiced by their neighbors. Almost all defended it when the outside world condemned it as evidence of Mormon women's moral corruption.

Statistical studies suggest what polygamy meant for those few women directly involved in plural marriage. The average polygamous husband married first at twenty-three. His wife was three years his junior, and they lived together as a couple for thirteen years. At that point, the husband, now thirty-six, married a woman eleven years younger than his first wife. Chances were two-to-one that she would be the only new wife to enter the family. But if the husband did marry again, his first wife would be thirty-seven, the second twenty-six, and the third only twenty-two.

All Mormon wives tended to take Brigham Young's message to heart that God required them, "young and old . . . [to] be mothers in Israel." Unlike women on other frontiers, Mormon women apparently used no birth control. There were different fertility patterns among Mormon women, however. Both monogamous and plural wives were prolific. A study of one group of Mormon women revealed, for example, that the monogamous wife had an average of 7.83 children, while polygamous wives had 7.45. But the figures suggest that within polygamous marriages a more complicated situation existed than the averages indicate. The most common polygamous marriage was one with two wives, and in such a union, the fertility of the two women was more than twice that of the average monogamous wife, with the first wife being the most prolific. If a third wife entered the family, the family's total fertility increased by only 25 percent. The first wife, then, bore more children than the other wives, and more children than the average monogamous wife. For all plural wives, however, the spacing between children, after their first, was less than the spacing between births of monogamous women. Whether these figures mean that women in plural marriages had more sex with their husbands than other married women is not clear. What is clear, however, is that polygamy did not lessen the cares of motherhood by decreasing fertility.

Statistics, perhaps, tell a dry story, but story there is. The age and fertility differences between polygamous wives make it clear that the first wife's experience in plural marriage differed in many respects from that of later wives. The most significant aspect of the first wife's marital situation was that she was the only wife for over a decade. Then, perhaps without much preparation, she had to confront the entry of a younger woman into the family and learn to share her husband with the newcomer. "It is the duty of a first wife to regard her husband not with a selfish devotion that would claim the whole of his society, time, and attention, but rather as owing attention to other women also, which they have a right to expect," explained one woman. Although the first wife might have a certain precedence or authority deriving from her longer relationship with her husband and had the only legal marriage, the coming of a younger woman and the arrival of new children to rival her own was a difficult experience. Interviewed in 1880, Mrs. H. D. Richards, first wife of a Mormon elder, confessed, "It was crushing at first but . . . as he was an elder . . . if it was necessary to . . . salvation . . . [to] let another share her pleasures, she would do so." The problem of children was more difficult, for Mrs. Richards admitted "that she should feel like wringing the neck of any other child than hers that should call him papa." Later, as the children arrived, she found that she could take an interest in them, but the interviewer added: "It is not at all the same feeling she has for her own flesh and blood. If his child and hers were drowning and but one could be saved, she should save her own."

The first wife had to accept polygamy, but additional wives chose it. Yet although the choice was theirs, it was not easy to join a relationship of long standing. Some women felt guilty about the disruption they caused. As Annie Tanner, a second wife, reflected, "There is something so sacred about the relationship of husband and wife that a third party in the family is sure to disturb the confidence and security that formerly existed. So far as Aunt Jennie [the first wife] was concerned, I felt like an intruder." Tanner's own mother had been a second wife and had faced another common difficulty. Her husband's first wife enjoyed a preferred status; her home was her husband's headquarters and she had charge of handing out household supplies. Her mother's inferior position and dependency on the first wife was, at times, humiliating. Nor did a second wife's youth always turn out to be an advantage, for it could make it more difficult to relate to the older woman. Some ended their isolation by becoming close friends of the first wife's children, but not all had this option. Finally, a second and later marriage had no legal standing.

Women's experience in polygamy also differed according to the period in which they married. The first polygamous wives coming out of a monogamous culture faced the painful task of rejecting strong cultural taboos. "When the principle of polygamy was first taught," Phoebe Woodruff recalled, "I thought it the most wicked thing I ever heard of; consequently I opposed it to the best of my ability, until I became sick and wretched." Prayer and the belief in Joseph Smith's prophetic powers eventually helped many women accept their husbands' desire to take additional wives. Some eased their anxieties by convincing themselves, as did Mrs. Richards, that "his love was not lustful; he married simply because his religion demanded it." The belief in a husband's pure motives was a common way of coping with the situation. Whatever the psychological burdens were, the early plural wives also faced difficult and primitive conditions; poverty, as most Mormons agreed, increased the tensions inherent in polygamy. Later, material conditions were far better, and it was possible to work out more elaborate living arrangements than during early pioneer days. By that time, there were also some general cultural supports for polygamy. But even as support for polygamy emerged, the persecution of polygamous families by federal authorities increased. Many second and third wives lived an underground existence, even delivering their own babies.

There is much evidence to suggest that Mormons found plural marriage difficult at all times. The song favored at local festivals indicated that it was a "trial." Memoirs and journals echoed the same belief. Why, then, did women choose to enter into such marriages? Certainly not for romantic love. This Martha Cox acknowledged: "It was not a marriage of love . . . [my family] claimed and in saying so they struck me a blow for I could not say that I had really loved the man as lovers love."

Some women, of course, never chose. Although husbands were supposed to consult their wives before marrying again, they did not always do so. Some, in fact, took additional wives over the vigorous protests of the first wife. So Mary Ann Hafen described the conditions of her marriage, noting, "Susette was opposed to his marrying again, but the authorities advised him to do so anyway, saying that she would be reconciled. I did not like to marry him under those circumstances, but being urged on by him and my parents, I consented." (It was hardly surprising that Mary Ann cried all the way to her wedding.)

Most women who recorded their thoughts about their marriages emphasized how seriously they took religious imperatives. "I knew the principle . . . to be correct," Martha Cox explained, for it was "the highest, holiest order of marriage." Eternal happiness depended on a husband's wives and their children. While this belief motivated most women, it had great impact on infertile wives. Annie Tanner was told by her future husband's first wife that although she had an aversion for polygamy, she had failed to conceive after five years of marriage. So she concluded, "I can't deprive Marion of a family, and of all the girls I know, you are my choice." Another motive is suggested by a study of polygamous families revealing that 31.2 percent of the marriages included at least two sisters. Women used plural marriages as a means of incorporating female relatives into their own families.

Younger wives were additionally drawn to polygamy because the attentions of an older man flattered them, while polygamy seemed to offer social and economic status and perhaps emotional security. The latter attracted Martha Cox, who lived with a polygamous family as an unmarried woman and discovered "perfect order prevailed . . . and did much to soften the prejudice I had formed in my mind against the principle of plural marriage. I learned here to pay respects to ordinances of the gospel which before I had treated lightly." Jane Woolsey, on the other hand, proposed to a fifty-five-year-old man while in her teens, saying, "A home is what I want & a kind Friend to protect me. You are the man of my choice & can furnish me with the home I want." Yet older women also had pragmatic reasons for accepting new wives in their homes. "I thank the Lord every day that now I am infirm," one woman explained, that "Brother Samuel has her at his side to watch over him, and see that his health and comfort are attended to as he is growing old." The emphasis on the household help younger women might provide is supported by the number of women who entered a household as servants and ended as wives.

To generalize about how Mormon women felt about their own polygamous situations is difficult, for their reactions differed. Some, for example, believing polygamy to be a religious obligation or at least likely, urged husbands to take wives. In promoting matches they may have been trying to screen the candidates. Some found they could live harmoniously with new wives, but others could not. Especially when women still thought of the marriage as an exclusive relationship, polygamy, all too often, resulted in rivalry, jealousy, and competition.

Part of the women's problem with polygamy resulted from the institution's place in Mormon culture. Although theologically polygamy had firm roots and was defended warmly against outside attacks, the statistics suggest that the new social patterns were never thoroughly embedded in the culture. Monogamy remained the preferred choice of the majority. In addition, there were never clearly defined standards or norms to guide those heeding the church's injunctions. Husbands, for example, were urged to be evenhanded with their money and time, but general principles never resulted in specific guidelines. Nor was the status of different wives ever formalized. Even the crucial procedures and rules for selecting a new wife were uncertain. Although men were supposed to discuss marriage plans with their wives, church leaders themselves, as Mary Ann Hafen's case indicates, complicated the process by taking sides. As one scholar has pointed out, polygamous societies normally develop distinctive housing patterns, for living arrangements are fundamental to the ultimate success of the institution. In Utah, however, housing for plural families varied widely, according to the individuals involved, their ideas and resources. Some husbands chose to live with all their wives in a common house, although the women had their own rooms. Others established wives in separate houses, sometimes in the same community, sometimes in widely scattered locations. Some men rotated between houses, others used one house as a headquarters. Much evidence suggests that polygamy worked best in Utah when wives had their own homes and their husbands visited them, yet such an arrangement was never standardized. The uncertain place polygamy occupied in the culture and the variety of arrangements make generalization difficult.

Most sources, however, point to the painful adjustments polygamy demanded. Even Joseph Smith had trouble at home, since his first wife, Emma, opposed the principle. She was never to know how many women he actually married. Brigham Young urged polygamous families to try harder and so revealed the troubles polygamy brought. "It is frequently happening," he said, "that women say they are unhappy. Men will say, 'My wife, though a most excellent woman, has not seen a happy day since I took my second wife'; 'No, not a happy day for a year,' says one; and another has not seen a happy day for five years. It is said that women are tied down and abused: that they are misused and have not the liberty they ought to have; that many of them are wading through a perfect flood of tears because of the conduct of some men, together with their own folly." Young challenged the women to leave Zion or to adjust: "In their hearts that they will embrace the Gospel—the whole of it." In fact, there was another alternative beyond Young's take-it-or-leave-it approach, divorce. Although the church disapproved of it, the tensions of the system of plural marriage made divorce a necessary solution. Significantly, it was easier for wives to win divorces than their husbands.

The divorce system suggests that polygamy was most difficult for women who had to share their husband's affection, time, and resources with other women and their children. Without a commonly accepted way of allocating any of these, women were forced to depend on their husband's sense of fair play and generosity. Some women solved their financial dependency by learning to support themselves, while others tried to win their husbands by proficient housekeeping. Good housekeeping became a favored means of strengthening marital affection and achieving stability, because polygamous wives could adopt more forthright tactics only at some risk. Nagging, for example, could easily backfire by driving a husband to another wife. "The wife whom he leaves behind is, of course, broken-hearted," a Mormon plural wife explained. "She would frequently blame herself and resolve never to have that experience repeated."

Burdens of child rearing and decision-making fell heavily on polygamous wives. For "in polygamy, the man's interests are scattered," one woman explained. "He may be influenced by members of his other family, or families. He would need to be almost a superhuman man to help each wife *equally* with the problems of rearing a family, and to resist the biased influence of other family members." Nor could these women necessarily look forward to assistance or security in their later years. Since only the first marriage was recognized by law, plural wives were not assured of sharing their husband's estate nor were their "illegitimate" children. Only if husbands gave wives (and/or children) property before their death or specifically mentioned their plural families in their wills would wives and their children be provided for.

The strain was not solely on the women, however. The economic burdens were real, and so were the emotional ones. As one father told his daughter, who was contemplating becoming a second wife, it was easy to win the affections of a girl, "but it is not, in polygamy, an easy task to keep her affections." It was, of course, more difficult to develop good relationships with several wives than with one, and it was necessary to try, at least, to appear impartial and fair with them all. Above all, men had to try to avoid giving cause for jealousy, for jealousy was the bane of polygamy and could make the marriage miserable for everyone. Thus, courtships were to be brief and to the point. Once married, the wise avoided showing any special affection to one wife over another. The strains on both men and women in plural marriage and the need to avoid giving cause for envy, in fact, led to a minimization of romantic love before and after marriage. Young's insistence that Mormon women dress simply and unfashionably, his comment that he was "ashamed to see the tight clothes—to see the shape of the ladies," had more than an economic rationale behind it. Physical attractions and romantic passions were antithetical to the smooth workings of the marriage system, and each sex was wise to keep a certain emotional distance from the other. Describing the ideal marital relationship, one wife said that she should be "pleased to see [her husband] . . . when he came in as she was pleased to see any friend." Women counseled one another to take such a detached view. Thus, an older friend encouraged Mrs. Richards "to make herself happy whether her husband was here or not; not to think about it; where he was or who he was with, and that She would outgrow all the troubles she met at the outset."

If there were stresses and strains, however, there were also high stakes to make plural marriages work. How could men who failed to manage their earthly families successfully expect heaven's highest honors? Women, too, focused on religious rewards. "I want to be assured of *my position in God's estimation*," one plural wife revealed. "If polygamy is the Lord's order, we must carry it out." Such determination could make plural marriage succeed. One admittedly small study of polygamous families found over half of the marriages were very successful or reasonably successful. About a quarter of them reported some difficulty but were considered moderately successful nonetheless, while the other quarter reported real, serious problems.

It is inconceivable that so many of those involved would see their marriages as reasonably successful, however, if the only rewards were heavenly ones. Clearly women would not defend the institution so

heatedly unless, at least occasionally, they derived some earthly benefits from it. Women in polygamous marriages represented an ideal
and gained prestige thereby. Their religious status often also signified
high social and economic position, since church leaders and potential
leaders were more likely to be polygamous than the population at
large. Moreover, the glorification of motherhood helped to compensate for some of the difficulties of being a plural wife. "Are you tor-
menting yourselves by thinking that your husbands do not love you?"
Brigham Young asked Mormon wives. "I would not care whether
they loved you a particle or not; but I would cry out, like one of the
old, in the joy of my heart, 'I have got a man from the Lord!'
'Halleluya! I am a mother—I have borne an image of God!'" The
ideological support for motherhood (rather than wifehood) was
matched on another level by the rewards of motherhood. Because
fathers could not oversee the children of their various wives as closely
as they could in monogamous marriages, wives often ended up by
taking charge of the children. Though the responsibility could be, at
times, a strain, many women enjoyed rearing their children and
identified with them rather than with their husbands. Certainly they
felt great pride in their children. "My children, their life and health,
was an attainment," one wife reported, which no one "could take
from me."

Occasionally, polygamous wives also formed close and satisfying
ties with one another. Sometimes ties of affection or blood drew
women into a plural household in the first place. Whatever the original bonds, female friendships could become more intimate and
affectionate than relationships between friends or relatives separated
by circumstance. "We three . . . loved each other more than sisters,"
one wife movingly testified, and will "go hand in hand together down
till eternity." The very real practical advantages which polygamy
could provide for women equaled the emotional satisfactions. When
polygamous wives got along, they often made a division of labor
which freed each from some female chores. Mary Ann Bentley
sketched the division of labor in her family. One wife, without children of her own, became the family business head and general manager, while the second wife spent most of her time weaving. It was

the third wife who was responsible for cleaning, cooking, and dishwashing. The family operation worked smoothly and amicably.

As polygamy could result in a certain freedom from domestic chores and responsibilities, so, too, could it lead to an independence from men themselves. Despite the church's emphasis on patriarchy, plural wives were more likely to be household heads than monogamous wives, and this status suggested the possibility for autonomy. Since both polygamy and the church made great demands on men's time, many plural wives soon learned to make decisions and to handle routine details of management. They were also likely to share certain powers with their husbands. One study of polygamous marriages revealed, for example, that men and women in plural marriages more often shared financial responsibilities than husbands and wives in monogamous marriages, where men wielded more power than women. When husbands were away on missionary trips or located their families in remote communities, women learned how to fend for themselves and to take pride in their ability to face life alone. "I had the attitude of many Mormon women in polygamy," one wife pointed out. "I felt the responsibility of my family; and I developed an independence that women in monogamy never know . . . [for the plural wife] becomes conscious of her own power to make decisions. She learns that it takes more than the authority of the leader in a patriarchal marriage to make a successful home." In the end, many women felt they had achieved a psychic independence, that they had worked out "individual character as separate from . . . their husband['s]." Certainly, their activities belied the conventional stereotype of nineteenth-century woman as passive and economically dependent on her husband.

When all the pluses and minuses of polygamy are balanced, one must remember that although it was the approved standard, many Mormon settlers quietly rejected it for themselves. Most of those in polygamous marriages accepted its trials and rewards. The home non-Mormon women opened to receive women "escaping" from polygamy had only a few residents. But passive resistance there was. The majority of men and women refused to enter into plural marriage. Opposition may have been centralized in certain localities, and future research may well reveal interesting patterns. But certain parts of the pattern are suggested by reminiscences. Martha Cox, for example, grew up in a monogamous family and openly admitted to being prejudiced against polygamy. When she changed her mind and decided to enter a plural household, her family vigorously opposed her. Her friends criticized her decision and pointed to the poverty of the family she had chosen to join. Female friends argued that she was demeaning herself by accepting a married man's proposal. Martha's only strong support came from "the good kind women whom I had chosen to share the burdens of life."

The support for monogamy, the criticism young women faced who chose plural marriage, the economic and emotional burdens polygamy entailed, must have kept many Mormons from entering into it. Yet, if there was passive resistance within Mormon society, few in the outside world knew of it. Because the attack on polygamy was so clearly an attack on Mormon society as a whole, Mormons rose to defend it. Women were particularly vocal defenders, and over the years, their arguments served to strengthen their sense of collective identity just as much as they served to answer outside criticism. The *Woman's Exponent,* a publication established in 1872 and run largely by women for women, helped to create a sense of who Mormon women were. Certainly they were not enslaved, nor were they unfit to carry out their moral and domestic obligations. Indeed, Mormon women took these responsibilities just as earnestly as American women did everywhere. Far from being degraded by their religion, the writers insisted, Mormon women were made stronger, more useful, and contented.

The issue of polygamy and the efforts of the United States government to wipe it out furthered the sense of female collective identity by drawing women into organized protest. Female mass meetings, involving many women in monogamous marriages, as well as those who practiced polygamy, petitions and resolutions against national anti-polygamy legislation, all testified to women's growing political awareness and to the evolution of an image of Mormon women as persecuted but justified in their beliefs. Female vindications of polygamy resembled those developed by their society as a whole, but women claimed that polygamy was a pragmatic institution benefitting women. Polygamy, women argued, created a more acceptable life for women than the one available to their counterparts in the outside world. For polygamy controlled men and their appetites. In Gentile society lustful men exploited female prostitutes and innocent wives suffered. In Mormon society, however, the option of polygamy eliminated the drive that led to prostitution and infidelity. Every woman could enjoy marriage, home, family, and a security ensured by the elimination of infidelity and the double standard. Furthermore, the institution provided plural wives with more time for themselves and offered more opportunities for independence than monogamy could.

Through their defense of polygamy, then, Mormon women were politicized, learned to evaluate their role in settling Utah, and gained a perspective on themselves as women, rather than merely as isolated individuals on the frontier. The utopian nature of the frontier experience and the organization of frontier life had also contributed to a heightened female self-consciousness. Mormon leaders, planning for Utah's self-sufficiency, urged women to help achieve their goals, supported them in their departures from conventional roles, and praised them for their social and religious contributions. Female organizations brought women together to work for a variety of objectives and reinforced their sense of their sex's usefulness. For a few individual women, participation in the Mormon experiment also meant unexpected support for radically new social roles. The first women doctors in Utah were such women.

Of course, if the Mormon frontier experience did, in some ways, contribute to women's consciousness and helped to create a strong collective identity, there were costs and limitations. There was little place in Mormon society for the woman who could not accept the utopian vision or who openly challenged the goals and directives of the priesthood. Social experiments like polygamy created stress and demanded sacrifices from many of the individuals involved. The recollections of one of the first women doctors gives some sense of the personal suffering departure from conventional social roles might entail. Responding to the call church leaders put out, Romania Bunnell Pratt decided to study medicine in Philadelphia. Romania convinced her husband she had made the right decision, sold both her house and her piano to help finance her studies, and left five of her seven children with her mother. When she returned, she found her home "still, quiet and empty, but hearing voices in the orchard I wandered back and found my dear faithful mother and two youngest children gathering fruit. My heart was pierced with sorrow when my little ones opened wide their eyes in wonder and with no token of recognition of their mother. I wept bitterly that I had been forgotten by my babes." Because of the Mormon emphasis on the family, the acceptance of new roles could produce conflict and personal unhappiness. Romania herself ended by divorcing her husband of twenty years.

In the 1890's, when persecution by the federal government finally led the leadership to abandon polygamy, Utah gave up its attempt to maintain self-sufficiency and separation from the outside world and began its long process of integrating into American society. Even before that time, there were signs that the pattern of female experience on the Mormon frontier might ultimately resemble that of pioneer women elsewhere. Usefulness did not necessarily mean the rejection of domesticity. Indeed, Brigham Young's exhortations to Mormon women to be productive members of society suggested that women were already fully immersed in domesticity and needed to be reminded that important tasks existed outside their homes. And his attempts to persuade women to dress plainly in homemade garments testified to their interest in the female world of gentility and fashion. Bolts of cloth from the East topped the list of imports to Utah and were transformed into clothes which differed little from Eastern fashions.

There are many indications, in fact, that Mormon women, like women on other parts of the frontier, wished to re-create a female sphere. During the earliest years, the need to survive conflicted with this goal, as it did on most frontiers. But as soon as they could, Mormon women shaped their female world. Census collectors in 1870 and 1880 noted that most women were "keeping house," rather than teaching, practicing medicine, or working in stores, despite the church's encouragement. Women's organizations, though exposing members to new skills and providing them with socially valued work, did not usually mean the neglect of home and family. Even individual and collective identities worked out in opposition to criticism during the first decades of settlement could not be so sharp and clear once outside criticism ceased. And with the church's accommodation to the Gentile world, the leadership no longer had the same requests to make of Mormon women and no longer furnished the same support for expanded female roles. In fact, during the twentieth century, Mormon women lost respect and power, rather than acquired them. Even their organizations ceased to play the independent role they once had. By the mid-twentieth century, indeed, Mormon women had become the bulwarks of social and sexual conservatism.

What the Mormon frontier experiment did show, more clearly than other frontiers, was the power of domestic ideology. Despite frontier conditions and despite unique religious and social conditions, once again women found that domesticity gave their lives meaning. Since the lower-class background of Mormon emigrants is well established, the Mormon frontier gives plain evidence that ideology about woman's place had impact on the lower ranks of society as well as on the middle levels. As Eliza Dilworth wrote to her brother in 1856, "Virtue is my motto and all my children are honnorabel." She was a true woman of her times.

7

"Will She Not Overstep the Bounds of Propriety If She Ventures into the Arena of Action?"

Phoebe Judson's reminiscences, entitled *A Pioneer's Search for an Ideal Home*, were shaped by her conviction that her life's meaning came from her quest for a perfect home. Her narrative catalogued all her temporary stopping places on the frontier, until finally she described the family's comfortable homestead, "remote from the world, surrounded by the beauties and bounties of nature." It was this lovely spot that was the right location for the home she had so long desired. As time passed, however, the place became less remote, and the beauties and bounties of nature began to fade. In short, Phoebe Judson's narrative shows a community growing up around her home, a forest despoiled, all in the name of progress. Yet the changes, far from marring her home, only improved it, Phoebe thought. When a church with a bell was erected, Phoebe recalled she had "realized that my 'ideal home' was one more step nearer completion."

Phoebe Judson's comments highlight the pioneer determination to turn wilderness into civilization and to accept the costs involved in the transformation. Men and women like the Judsons were modernizers, believing in the necessity of progress, which they defined as re-creating communities and institutions in the West. But though the goal was widely accepted, the process of community building itself was not smooth; along with cooperation came dissension. Indeed, the transiency of frontier society, the different regional, cultural, reli-

179

gious, and political loyalties found in a new community, the economic uncertainties of early frontier life, all suggest unavoidable clashes as communities were established and grew. Although the struggles were rarely acknowledged in early community histories, recently historians have looked behind the boosterism of local chronicles to discover the economic, political, and social battles for power which accompanied growth and modernization.

The new awareness of conflict, however, tends to focus on dissension in the male world, with only passing attention to the sexual struggles implicit in community building. Yet Phoebe Judson's reminiscences are filled with clues about the encounters between the sexes which occurred. There was, she pointed out, initially no gambling den, no saloon, no drugstore "to cast its debasing gloom over . . . [the] captivating landscape" of the young town. Eventually, "a dark cloud" appeared in the form of two strangers who applied for a saloon license. "With hearts all aflame with love for husbands, sons and fathers," she recalled, the women "rallied to the rescue," only to find that rescue was not desired. "We visited by ones and twos, and in companies, the different members of the city council, and pleaded for the safety of our loved ones; but all in vain—our pleadings, prayers and entreaties—greed of gold carried the day."

Although the incident Phoebe described gave little indication of the women's anger and frustration at their defeat, the incident was typical of the kinds of encounters which routinely occurred with growth. For men and women often held different visions of community. Men sought a community marked by outward order, but it was to be a place where individuals had freedom to pursue their fortunes and their pleasures. The vision could allow compromises with strict morality as the frontier habit of doing business on the Sabbath and condoning prostitution testified. Indeed, nineteenth-century norms, in a sense, legitimated such compromises, for men were not really responsible for the moral order; women were. Many women, probably middle class in background, saw the ideal community in a different light; it was to be a place of real, rather than apparent, order, a place without disruptive threats to family unity and purity. If domestic ideology encouraged women to visualize the community in these terms, ironically it could involve them in organizational activities which contributed to the very social disorganization they deplored. Like Phoebe Judson and her friends, numerous Western women would cause trouble by assaulting the male world and its standards and attacking the entrepreneurial ethic, that "greed of gold" which Phoebe identified as the root of all evil. A few would even go on to wish for the vote, rather than, as Phoebe put it, "bear the disgrace, poverty and heartrending sorrow in silent tears, without protest" when they saw the land "we have so dearly purchased and help to make blossom like the rose" sullied.

An examination of some of the organized activities of frontier women, then, shows how their organizations moved from community building to a sometimes disrupting reformism and attack on the male sphere. It also shows, however, that while frontier conditions may have sharpened sexual conflict, the pattern of Western organizational activities resembled that in the East. The issues arousing women's groups in the West, the rationale used to justify their actions, and the outcome of their efforts paralleled Eastern experience. In both places organizational activities gained strength from and tended to reinforce the traditional sexual division of society. Far from providing a setting in which women liberated themselves from conventional views of sex relations, the frontier was an environment calling for a reaffirmation of woman's nature. Even suffrage and coeducation, supposedly two badges of frontier freedom, suggest how the new society failed to reinterpret woman's place in society.

Of all their organized activities on the frontier, female charitable organizations seem, on the surface, to have had little potential for social disruption. As mothers, women were responsible for caring for the weak, the sick, the disabled. It was a short step from these domestic cares into charitable work, and for many a frontier woman, the Civil War provided the incentive for such a step. Numerous Sanitary Aid Societies and Ladies Aid Societies were formed nationwide to help with the war effort. Society projects appeared both harmless and helpful, but even on the frontier the propriety of public charitable efforts had to be discussed. Elizabeth Thurston brought up the question before the Oregon Sanitary Aid Society in 1863. "What can women do? Will she not overstep the bounds of propriety if she ventures into the arena of action?" she asked. The answer was, in her opinion, negative; "Thanks to the Sanitary Commission . . . all honor to the noble minds who projected it." Not all agreed, however, as the McMinnville Ladies Sanitary Aid Society in Oregon discovered. So careful were the ladies not to give unnecessary offense that their discussion of a July 4 celebration in 1865 led to the conclusion "that it was not best for us as a Society to do any thing about it, but to use our influence to induce the gentlemen of our village to get up a celebration." But despite their caution, their pious project of buying pocket Bibles for soldiers, and despite their decorous meetings, "always . . . opened by reading the Scriptures and prayer and generally characterized by unity of feeling and harmony of deliberation," there were critics who saw the women as disruptive. As one woman reflected, "Discouragements were not lacking, and many were the criticisms of those who 'went not with us.' "

Buying Bibles, supporting soldiers' families, raising money seemed harmless enough, even though some might object to these activities as unseemly. Certainly the charitable endeavors held little criticism of the male world unless it was that men were so busy fighting the war they did not have time to care for its casualties. But other equally benevolent efforts suggested a far less flattering assessment of the male world, even if the assessment was implicit. The San Francisco Ladies' Protection and Relief Society, established in 1853, was one such organization. Its inspiration came from Mrs. A. B. Eaton, who opened her cottage door one day to find a young woman asking for assistance. Her brother, the woman said, had planned to meet her at the steamer but had never arrived, leaving her with nowhere to stay and no one to whom to turn for help. Realizing the plight of women in this kind of a position, Mrs. Eaton called together her friends to form an organization to "render protection and assistance to strangers, to sick and dependent women and children." Within a year the group had decided to open a home for "all respectable women in want of protection, employment in families or as needlewomen." The decision to open the home was accompanied by a bitter debate, and some officers resigned.

Although the reason for the disagreement is not clear, it could be that the cynical evaluation of men as sexual predators which underlay the scheme struck some of the women as shocking. But shocking or not, many female charitable organizations which cared for destitute and homeless women and children had this evaluation as a basic premise. Certainly, many women felt it was up to them to protect other women and children, and that most men could not be trusted.

At times seemingly innocent charitable activities resulted in open criticism of the male order. The activities of the Wichita Ladies Aid Society show women moving to an explicit condemnation of the male community. During the 1870's, the agricultural frontier of Kansas was struck by calamities as locusts followed drought to destroy the unpromising harvests of pioneer farmers. As winter came on, it was the women of Wichita who organized to cope with what promised to be widespread rural destitution. The women, however, faced male opposition from town boosters and property owners who rejected the "whining" cries for aid. Fearing either to acknowledge the extent of the disaster or to accept out-of-state aid, men minimized the situation because, as the newspaper concluded, the truth "will retard immigration . . . they do not want the true condition of the 'Great Arkansas Valley' known, for they say that 'this valley has been advertised to the world as one of the best agricultural countries in existence, and if we go east to solicit aid to keep body and soul together, how can we ask people to immigrate here?" As winter wore on, the situation of farming families became increasingly desperate. Women struggled to relieve suffering and finally attacked townsmen in an open letter in the newspaper. "It is *absolutely true*," they wrote, "that there are families in the country whose only safety from starvation lies in the charity of the people . . . that women and children have no shoes and stockings . . . that many cabins have no floors, and their inmates at this inclement season place their beds upon the ground. To those who, like doubting Thomas will not believe, we propose to furnish transportation into the country and let them see for themselves . . . As far as the injury to the country is concerned by the circulating of the truth, will it hurt the country as much to help these people in their need, as to let one man or woman die of cold or starvation?" The doubting Thomases were, of course, men.

The impassioned letter proved persuasive, and the women obtained supplies of food, clothing, and cash to distribute to destitute families. When it phased out operations late in the spring, the society had some pithy comments for the male community, which had for so long allowed its entrepreneurial and speculative vision to hinder relief efforts. "We have pursued our way, in regard to 'aid,' for the last eight months, not without any hindrances and much criticism."

Female campaigns against gambling, prostitution, and drinking more explicitly pitted women and their allies against the male world than did their charitable endeavors. The virulence of some women's response to gambling and prostitution in the West has already been suggested in earlier chapters. Here the emphasis is on women's greatest organizational effort on the frontier, the attempt to control the use of liquor. Female efforts to bring prohibition to the frontier represented the epitome of their struggle with barbarism in the new society and with male tolerance of vice, either because of its profit or its pleasure, or both.

In general, Western prohibition campaigns paralleled Eastern ones. As an organized movement, prohibition was a nineteenth-century response to a nineteenth-century problem. Alcoholic overindulgence was, of course, not new, but in the seventeenth and eighteenth centuries drunkenness had been surrounded by traditional restraints and customs. These were, however, breaking down as America changed from an agricultural society to a commercial, urbanized, industrialized society and as continual migration west undercut the force of tradition. At the same time, because of new distilling techniques and the reduction or elimination of government taxes on spirits, hard liquor was increasingly available. Beer and ale drinking declined in the first decades of the nineteenth century, while the consumption of hard liquor increased. Possibly new cultural distinctions made between the male and the female sphere also encouraged male drinking either as an affirmation of masculinity or as a means of relieving tensions concerning it. In any case, by the early nineteenth century drunkenness was endemic and was beginning to be seen by some as a serious social problem demanding an organized response. New means of controlling the consumption of liquor had to be devised to protect families and society at large.

In the West, drinking seemed to be especially troublesome. There, the weakness of institutionalized restraints and the drudgery of so much of frontier life may well have fostered excessive private drinking. Certainly the frontier saloons and whiskey tents encouraged public drunkenness with free lunches, the custom of allowing the drinkers to fill their own glasses (the price being the same whether or not the glass was filled to the brim), and the encouragement of treating. Frontier accounts give ample evidence of long drinking bouts, especially in those communities on the mining, cattle, or urban frontier, where there were large transient male populations. As these communities matured, the signs of other male vices faded; gambling disappeared, and prostitution became discreet. But drinking did not. The number of saloons, in fact, increased with growth, and so, too, did their trade. California was the leader in this respect; by 1888, it was estimated that the state had a saloon for every sixteen voters. San Francisco boasted thirty-one times as many saloons as churches and had more than twice as many saloons in relation to its population as New York or Chicago and nine times as many as either Boston or Philadelphia. Other Western communities had less depressing statistics, but the problem was the same. Drinking was a threat to social stability and social values.

Since drinking was primarily a male phenomenon, early-nineteenth-century temperance groups had been restricted to men. The roots of drunkenness, it was supposed, lay in the moral weakness of the individual drinker. By persuading drinkers (and nondrinkers) to take the pledge of abstinence, and then by providing them with fellowship, it was hoped that they would abandon the evil habit. Early Western temperance activities followed this pattern of moral persuasion. In the first year of the gold rush, for example, a San Francisco temperance meeting resulted in eighteen pledges and the prompt formation of the Washingtonian Society of San Francisco. Women, though not members of the society, lent their support to its efforts. Other early activities on the frontier resulted from the fear of liquor-crazed Indians. Oregon's 1844 legislation forbidding the introduction or sale of liquor in the territory was probably passed by the assembly with the Indian in mind.

With the passage of the "Maine law" at mid-century, the direction of national and Western temperance activity changed. The law, which prohibited the production and distribution of drink, was aimed less at the moral reform of the individual drinker than at the legal restriction of liquor producers and distributors. Copied in a number of states including Iowa and Nebraska, the legislation was significant because it brought the liquor question directly into politics. Although the legislation was eventually declared unconstitutional in most of the states where it had passed, the new approach seemed promising if unlikely to produce immediate results, since the Civil War consumed Americans' attention. A more serious drawback was prohibition's unpopularity with the men who would determine the outcome of any legal approach to the liquor problem.

When women entered the prohibition movement after the Civil War to become its main support, the strength of their male opposition was evident. An attempt to establish the right of local option failed to win even 30 percent of an 1887 vote in Washington Territory, for example. Though often defeated, the tactics women used in their prohibition campaigns in the West reveal the sharp edge of their criticism of the male world as well as its limitations.

Tactics used first in the Middle West inspired Western prohibition activities in the 1870's. After a Christmas Eve church service in 1873, seventy irate women placed themselves in front of a local saloon in Hillsboro, Ohio, to sing and pray that the saloon stop serving and the drinkers stop drinking. This was not just a Christmas Eve stand; the women returned for months to harass the owners and drinkers. News of this extraordinary female behavior spread and inspired a women's crusade against saloons both in the East and the West.

Although visitations of the Ohio sort occurred in California, the women's crusade there adopted different techniques. California women had a special opportunity because the legislature had passed a local option law. The law stated that if a quarter of the voters in a township or incorporated city or town petitioned the proper authorities, an election could be held to decide whether to close down saloons (in effect) by forbidding the sale of liquor in quantities of under five gallons. Women's Temperance Alliances were formed all over the state to get the liquor question to the voters. Strengthened by daily prayer meetings, the women sought signatures for the petitions needed for local option elections and then canvassed the voters themselves. Although early campaigns were quiet, they became, with time, more aggressive and openly hostile to men, as women individually and collectively challenged men with explosive results. Efforts in San Jose revealed the rising tempers of both sexes. While some of the town's clergy criticized their efforts, and hecklers caused trouble, the women resolutely set up a temperance tent for their daily meetings. Election day approached, and tension grew. Determined to bring out as many helpers as they could, the activist women appealed to their stay-at-home sisters through a letter to the newspaper which was marked by militant vocabulary. "Young ladies, throw away all timidity," they urged, "and come out to help us fight the hard battle on Saturday . . . If you are too bashful to talk, go with those that can, thus lending aid by merely your presence . . . Think not what people will say, but come boldly to the front and God will reward you." The letter makes clear that the temperance workers were encouraging women to be aggressive, even unfeminine. The modification of behavior was suitable in the struggle with evil.

On Election Day women, sure of their righteousness, walked the streets in groups, giving speeches, arguing and persuading men to support their cause. Fifty children were taken around to the different polling places to sing, "Father, dear father, come home with me now." Female tactics, despite some sweet smiles and the presence of little children, were correctly perceived as a challenge, and the mood became bitter. During the afternoon one of the women, Sallie Hart, was heckled and booed so vociferously that the police were forced to hurry her away. The crowds became drunk and disorderly. When the votes were counted, the drinkers had won, 1,430 to 918. The next week in Alameda the women's cause fared no better; a drunken mob chased the women into their temperance tent and further amused itself by holding a mock funeral for the intrepid but hated Sallie Hart. Despite the law, beer flowed freely during the election and certainly contributed to the day's violent and ugly tone, but the disorder had been triggered by the women themselves who had approached men to urge them to forsake the pleasures and profits of drink and to accept a female vision of the ideal community.

In Portland, Oregon, women borrowed tactics of their Ohio counterparts. Like California workers, they challenged masculine habits and fomented disorder. Female activities got off to a slow start as news of Ohio events reached Oregon in the winter of 1874. Though there was no defined plan of action, some Portland women, interested in the liquor problem, began to meet together. In March, their enthusiasm and involvement grew, as did their numbers when they began to "exchange experiences" of their confrontations with drunken husbands, fathers, and sons. An energetic new organization, the Women's Temperance Prayer League, with meetings twice a day, grew out of the emotional exchanges. Soon the league was involved in a campaign to collect abstinence pledges, and as if this was not enough, openly exhorted saloonkeepers to close down their businesses. Even these activities did not satisfy the majority of the women. Although a few league members refused to adopt more militant tactics, most agreed to attack the saloons directly. First, the women haunted the saloons, soliciting pledges. Drinking men disliked being disturbed at the bar, but they didn't like it much more when the women began to pray and sing in front of the Webfoot Saloon, which became the symbol of THE SALOON. The situation became increasingly explosive as women appeared day after day with their prayers and songs. Some days saw only curious crowds and hoopla, others antagonistic mobs. The women were in and out of jail, but they always came back. They supported temperance candidates and petitioned city councils.

However, their campaign, like the efforts of their California counterparts, fizzled out. A scurrilous little broadside, purportedly the work of the league, but actually the work of league opponents, caused an uproar and damaged the women's reputation as moral arbiters. Support, already weakened by female militance, evaporated. The weakhearted returned home, and the saloon was safe for the time being in Portland.

The Western prohibition campaigns of the seventies, like earlier efforts in the West, came to nothing. California's local option law was finally declared unconstitutional by the state supreme court, and temperance work flagged there, as it did in Oregon. The WCTU, established in 1879 in California and in 1881 in Oregon, had a slow beginning in both places. The importance of female reform was not, therefore, that it succeeded, for it most obviously did not. Its importance was that it illustrated the different views of community held by frontier men and women and showed that, at times, women could be outspoken in their criticism of the male version. Men clearly perceived the threat female reform posed and often reacted fiercely, only to make women more certain than ever that theirs was a righteous cause.

From one perspective, reformism radicalized women at least temporarily as they took to the streets, made speeches, and went to jail. But it is significant that Western women, in the end, retired to their homes. Since their reform activities were not rooted in a new conception of their sex but in an expansive vision of themselves as community moral arbiters, most in the long run were reluctant to move far beyond this vision. The hint of sexuality in the Portland broadside sent them swiftly home. Later workers in the WCTU avoided confrontation tactics and utilized a less threatening version of domesticity. Running a coffee house or sponsoring writing contests in schools was not difficult for women, or even for many men, to accept. In the long run, the WCTU also raised female consciousness but brought about no thoroughgoing reformulation of the female role.

The Western prohibition movement, inspired by Eastern experience, did not make most Western women radicals. Nor do there seem to have been many facets of the frontier experience encouraging women to break with prevailing concepts of the sexual order. It is true that there were a few outstanding women like Abigail Scott Duniway whose frontier life encouraged her to question woman's place. "To bear two children in two and a half years from my marriage day, to make thousands of pounds of butter every year for market . . . to sew and cook, and wash and iron; to bake and clean and stew and fry; to be in short a general pioneer drudge . . . was not a pleasant business." But Abigail Scott Duniway seems the exception, not the rule, and even she admitted that her business experience was the catalyst "that brought me before the world as an evangel of Equal Rights For Women."

It is important to stress this point, because much has been made of the argument that women enjoyed "freedom" in the West. The implication of such a statement is that there was something about the frontier that liberated women from conventional sex roles and made them nearly equal to men. As evidence for such an analysis, historians usually emphasize early territorial suffrage in Wyoming and Utah and point out that ten of the eleven Western states gave women the vote by 1914, when only one Eastern state had emancipated women. Additional evidence is drawn from the popularity of coeducation in Western colleges and universities. Yet just as women's participation in reform suggests that Western women were no more emancipated from social norms than their Eastern sisters, the evidence used to support the case for the West as a liberating environment, upon closer examination, proves weak.

The general connection of the political emancipation of women with social and sexual emancipation is one which historians have recently questioned. Although the implications of suffrage were radical, victory in the twentieth century did not bring about a revolution in society's attitudes toward women or in women's understanding of themselves. Certainly an investigation of Western suffrage "triumphs" suggest that they were not related. A careful study of the two territories granting suffrage to women in 1869 and 1870 reveals, first of all, that the vote was offered to women, not because women thought to ask for it, but because it suited a minority of men to give it and, second, that the arguments made in favor of granting women the suffrage were conservative. Women were to vote not because they were the same as or equal to men but because they were different from men. The domestic conception of women provided the basis for the suffrage defense.

In Utah, granting suffrage to women was part of the attempt to maintain Mormon society and plural marriage. The suffrage issue came to the surface the very year that the transcontinental railroad pulled Utah into closer contact with the rest of the country and the very year that broad antipolygamy legislation was introduced in Congress. Mobilizing Mormon women as voters would serve several purposes. It would balance and perhaps neutralize the potential political power of Gentiles, who could now so easily come to Utah; it would prove to the rest of the country that Mormon women were not, in fact, slaves or prostitutes but were highly regarded members of their community. There was little interest, however, in making any argument that women were to be men's equals. It was expected that they would keep their place and vote as they were told. The San Francisco *Chronicle* quoted a Mormon bishop as saying, "Our vote is solid and will always remain so. It will be thrown where the most good will be accomplished for the church. The women of Utah vote, and they never desert the colors of the church; they vote for the tried friends of the church. You can imagine the results which wisdom may bring about, with the assistance of a church organization like ours." Whether or not the bishop actually said what the paper claimed, election statistics suggest the accuracy of the comments. Mormon women voted solidly with their men.

The reasons for granting women the vote in Wyoming differed in details, but the same conservative impulse existed. In 1869 and 1870 the territory had only a small permanent population and all too many transient lawless elements connected with building the railroad. By granting women suffrage, legislators hoped that they might attract stable and responsible settlers to the territory. They wanted not a new society but a tamed society. Recollections of the debate in the legislature stressed this point. *"The favorite argument . . . and by far the most effective was this:* it would prove a great advertisement, would make a great deal of talk, and attract attention to the legislature, and the territory, more effectually than anything else." These hopes were vain but, once granted the vote, Wyoming women did introduce a small measure of propriety into Wyoming frontier life. At election time, they seem to have been treated courteously because men saw them as symbols of civilization and home. But their attempts to wield powers connected with their status as voters showed just how little Wyoming men thought to grant full political, let alone social, equality. It is true that one woman was appointed justice of the peace, while a few others served on petit and grand juries, once granted voting rights. But the woman after judging thirty or forty cases was not nominated to run for regular election as a judge. And when a grand jury composed of six women and nine men in Laramie indicted all the saloons for not observing Sunday closings, the days of women on juries were limited. In 1870 the practice was ended on the grounds that jury duty had no connection with the suffrage. It was 1950 before women served on Wyoming juries again.

These early Western triumphs for women suffrage were exceptional. After 1867, seventeen referenda on the issue of granting women the vote were held in eleven states. Of the eleven, eight were, it is true, west of the Mississippi but there were only two victories. Perhaps there was more sympathy for voting on the question in the West, but there was also more interest in turning it down. In Oregon, for example, the question came to the vote six times after 1859, and despite all the energy and time devoted to the campaign, suffrage did not come until 1911. A letter printed in the *Iowa State Weekly Register* in 1871 reflected the sentiments of much of the male community in the West when it came to the suffrage issue. If "all the principles that suffragists are promulgating to take firm root in society, become the law of our land," the writer pointed out, "our choicest treasures, the dear little daughters of to-day, will before the close of the next decade become a prey to the licentious libertine."

In other Western states and territories the question came up before the legislature, always an easier route than putting it before the male electorate. But results were the same. Whatever freedoms the West gave to women, it had not changed the thinking of their men enough to make the majority of legislators favor granting full political rights to women. In the territory of Washington, for example, a legislator originally from Maine introduced a female suffrage bill in the first session of 1854. It was defeated, and the body ignored the issue until 1869, when a supporter once more introduced a suffrage bill. The debate was bitter and the measure attracted only five favorable votes. Two years later, the legislature rejected yet another bill, and since a few ardent women had insisted on trying to vote on the grounds that the 1866 election code defined voters as *"all* white citizens," it went on to respond to the women clearly. The act they devised warned all settlers that "hereafter no female shall have the right of ballot or vote at any poll or election precinct in this Territory, until the Congress of the United States of America shall, by direct legislation upon the same, declare the same to be the supreme law of the land." Ultimately the Washington legislature was converted and granted suffrage. But when women began to exercise their political rights with some of the same moral fervor of the early Wyoming women, the state's supreme court voided the act. Another suffrage bill met the same fate. Finally, difficulties involved with suffrage led the constitutional convention to decide not to include female emancipation in the proposed 1889 state constitution but to allow voters to decide on that issue and prohibition separately; 40,152 men voted for the constitution, 19,546 for prohibition, but only 16,527 favored emancipation. It would be another twenty-one years before Washington women voted, and those few who had worked for the cause lost heart and gave up the fight.

If men seemed reluctant to offer women political rights, only a small number of women challenged them. The leaders of the campaign to bring suffrage to the Western states were few, and they openly acknowledged that their support from other women was limited. Although a number of states in the seventies and eighties allowed women some voting privileges on the local level, there was little pressure from women to expand those rights. Some of the suffrage leaders reasoned that far from fostering interest in political equality, frontier conditions explained female apathy. Women were scattered in the country and therefore hard to reach and slow to develop bonds with other women. There was some truth in this analysis, but the underlying factor was female disinterest in political rights. Despite the inconvenience of frontier conditions, women organized for religious and charitable purposes, and they joined temperance organizations far more readily than they supported suffrage. Indeed, some women even organized against the woman suffrage movement. And in a similar fashion, when a registry board in Clarinda, Iowa, decided in 1871 that women might vote, the newspaper observed, "Several gentlemen got on their ear about it and erased their wives' names. Several ladies got their precious backs up also, and erased their own names. None but the sons of Adam, however, offered to vote, and Clarinda is now as peaceable as Mary's little lamb."

Those women who pressed for political rights were atypical. Some of them, like Abigail Scott Duniway, came into suffrage work partly because of their experiences on the frontier. Lacking sufficient biographical information on early leaders, it is impossible to know whether the new environment was a crucial factor in bringing them into the struggle or not. A profile of the leaders of the California suffrage movement between 1897 and 1911 does exist, and, while it is dangerous to use this profile to characterize the leadership of an earlier period, the profile has some interesting suggestions. Of the 1,911 leaders for whom sufficient information existed, 65 percent were born before 1861, during the early frontier period. But the majority of the women came from New England or the Midwest, rather than from California. They were well educated, prosperous, Protestant, and married. Some of the women were obviously seeking sexual independence and harbored angry feelings against men, but others still saw themselves as true women, selfless and sacrificing. Their reasons for participating in the suffrage movement varied. The older women (born before the Civil War) tended to see the suffrage issue in humanitarian terms, while younger women were influenced by the new arguments that the vote was a means of attacking other problems of society. There was little typically frontier about the group or its motivations.

The arguments such women developed to attract support from timid sisters and to disarm male opposition were similar to those current elsewhere. Rarely did they urge their listeners or readers to think about developing themselves as individuals or to examine conventional norms shaping their lives. Nor did they mention job discrimination. Rather they argued that women should vote because their moral perspective and domestic responsibilities allied them with those anxious to ameliorate the problems of an increasingly complex world. The later victories of suffrage in the West stemmed from the conservatism of these arguments buttressed by Western experience. Those few states which had emancipated women early found little sign that their vote unleashed social or sexual revolution.

Superficially, the evidence concerning coeducation buttressing the analysis of the West as a place fostering great freedom for women seems as convincing as the political argument. In 1872, for example, there were ninety-seven major private and public coeducational institutions in the country, and the majority of them, sixty-seven, were located in the West. The assumptions behind citing the popularity of coeducation in the West and the relative absence of it in the East are that coeducation meant equal education and a belief in the equality of women's and men's intellectual capacities. More relevant, but rarely considered, is the question of whether the coeducational experience affected the way in which women viewed themselves.

Certain frontier conditions and attitudes explained the popularity of coeducation in the West. The founding of new colleges and universities was part of the frontier experience. Fears that the new society would sink into barbarism stimulated missionaries to establish colleges as an "important part in Christian strategy," while bustling new communities intent on making boasts of a dazzling future come true contributed to the proliferation of colleges. Indeed, communities often vied for proposed institutions by donating sites and cash to the would-be founders. With the passage of the Morrill Act in 1862, which provided federal lands to initiate a system of public higher education, the community competition for educational institutions increased.

The enthusiasm for founding colleges and universities was premature. Since most frontier states had few public secondary schools, there were not enough qualified students of either sex to give substance to the college title. Most early colleges were in fact high schools. The year after the University of Kansas was so ambitiously started, though "somewhat embryonic" in form, there were only two students in the college course, but sixty-eight pupils enrolled in the preparatory department. The number of institutions and the limited pool of students led colleges to compete for students both to justify their existence and to gain operating funds. Most private colleges were financially shaky, since they were established long before frontier communities or religious denominations were able to support them on a steady basis. Nor did the land grants which provided the impetus to public education provide a steady revenue; state legislators were usually niggardly in helping out fledgling public institutions. All these factors meant that any and all students were welcome on any and all levels. Of the two college students at the University of Kansas, both were women.

The instability of these early institutions fostered coeducation even if separation of the sexes was the initial goal. The 1864 charter for the University of Kansas called for male and female branches, with the woman's branch separate and taught by women. Lack of funds prevented realizing such a plan, however. Coeducation was a financial necessity and one whose wisdom was highlighted during the Civil War. During those years, as men left school for the war, it was only the presence of women students that allowed many schools to stay open. And, as time passed, private colleges faced increasing competition from state schools. Coeducation offered a means of survival for many private all-male institutions.

Certainly much of the education provided for women in these early days reflected conventional cultural assumptions about women. The status of women in the land-grant schools, devoted to teaching the agricultural and mechanical arts, is a case in point. Though some of the impetus behind the schools was the belief in equal education, the objective was seldom realized. The work requirement predictably put women in the most traditional places, the laundry, the dining room, and, of course, the kitchen. Eventually experience with the work requirement led some of the schools to develop courses in "domestic economy," which further differentiated the women students from the men. In Iowa Agricultural College, for example, the president's wife was responsible for lecturing on cooking to the women working in the college kitchen. Her teaching inspired her to develop a department of "cookery and the household arts" for the women students, and, by 1875, she had established the first experimental kitchen in the United States. By 1890, similar departments existed in Kansas, Oregon, and South Dakota. But this preparation was aimed not at training women for a career but rather at preparing them for marriage. Land-grant colleges primarily instructed women to be teachers first and wives later.

The land-grant colleges often had special "ladies' courses" for the female student body. Nor was the practice confined to the land-grant colleges. When the University of Washington was established in the 1860's newspaper ads announced female courses on the college and preparatory level. Readers were informed that "MISS. MAY W. THAYER, formerly a Teacher in the University, has been engaged as assistant, and in addition to the branches usually taught, will give particular instruction in Etiquette, Conversation, Needlework, &c." As time passed, two separate college tracks appeared, the classical one for men and the science course, often only three years in length, for women, who substituted music, painting, drawing, and modern languages for the more difficult classics and higher mathematics. Not until the end of the century did women in many Western colleges study the male curriculum. Similar reservations about women in higher education were revealed in the treatment of female faculty. At the University of Oregon, for example, professional women early on taught in the prep department but were replaced by male college graduates who wished a few terms in the classroom before beginning another profession.

Although coeducation became an accepted practice in the West, women were not seen as intellectually equal to men nor were they treated in the same way as men. Stereotypes of women as weak in body and intellect were still current despite the experience of the frontier. Special facilities protected "frail" women in some schools; at the University of Washington the women lived in the president's house under the watchful eye of his wife, rather than in the dormitory. Women were excluded from certain campus activities. College campuses, in fact, provided many symbolic statements of women's true status, and few women missed the message. At Grinnell, for example, the female literary society invited a prominent woman to speak at commencement in 1869 and caused a controversy on the campus. The faculty was up in arms and pressed the trustees to write a letter to the speaker's husband informing her that "the Faculty and

Trustees of the College are not yet prepared to allow a woman to occupy the college platform at commencement." It was hardly surprising that little thought was given to the future of the coeds, for it was clear that the future of the educated women was a teaching job, perhaps, but most probably marriage.

Nor, of course, was a college education of any kind the typical experience for women in the West or elsewhere. The earliest comprehensive statistics collected by the U.S. Commissioner of Education revealed that only a quarter as many women as men received any post-secondary education and that most of them attended either normal schools or seminaries and academies which did not offer a college degree. Furthermore, coeducation was not an early frontier commitment. In 1870, most of the women students in colleges and universities still were found in women's colleges rather than in coeducational institutions. This would shift in the following ten years, but to look at the Western educational system as a badge of woman's freedom in the West seems inappropriate.

The myth that frontier women had a more egalitarian status in the new society was perpetuated by women like Abigail Scott Duniway, who spent most of her life working unsuccessfully for woman suffrage. "Nowhere else, upon this planet, are the inalienable rights of women as much appreciated as on the newly settled borders of these United States," she announced. "Men have had opportunities, in our remote countries, to see the worth of the civilized women, who came with them, or among them, to new settlements after the Indian woman's day." Duniway's image making was, no doubt, an attempt to push men on the issue of female rights, but it neither described the reality of Western female experience nor did it achieve her tactical goals. Certainly, frontier social and sometimes political arrangements stood in contrast to those in the East. But this was hardly because men appreciated the "inalienable rights of women." Women valued themselves and were valued for their traditional qualities. When women collided with the male world, it was often precisely because they believed in their traditional role and sought to live up to it. The collisions could be bitter, for the realities of frontier life and male priorities often made it so. But few responded by casting off convention. The behavior of a suffrage group in Walla Walla, Washington, in the 1880's is instructive. After seeing the men of their territory defeat the suffrage question, the women quietly retired, never bothering to meet together again, either to make future plans or even to preside over their organization's demise.

Epilogue

The emigrant bride who traveled the overland route at mid-century was not yet seventy when historian Frederick Jackson Turner announced in 1893 that America's frontier era had ended. In her lifetime, she and others like her had left their Eastern homes to confront the many hardships of frontier life. But by their mature years, the circle had come full turn. The wilderness was transformed, and, as emigrant guidebooks had promised, the West could brag of "all the enjoyments and luxuries of civilized life." Women who had left family homes with tears in their eyes returned years later, traveling east by train. As they headed back to the West, they sped over the plains and prairies and thought of the months spent in lurching, jolting wagons many years before. "It seems very strange now that we ever had the patience to travel so slowly," one woman mused. She was not the only one to wonder at the transformations she had witnessed or to try to make sense of them. If only to answer the never-ending questions "Did I come around the Horn, cross the Isthmus, or come across the plains? Was I not afraid of the Indians and much more?" women began to write down their life stories. Pioneer reunions, with parades, dinners, and visits, also highlighted addresses which attempted to set the frontier experience in some perspective. If not all agreed on what the frontier had meant, all were convinced that they had made history. Looking back over long lives, men and women compressed most

201

of it in order to elaborate on their pioneer years. That time was, for some of them, "more real than the present."

None could overlook the contrast between the moment of writing and the past about which they wrote. For some the present suffered in the comparison. Because of the relationship between emigration and age, the pioneer experience had coincided for most of them with young adulthood, when bodies were strong and dreams still possible. Nostalgia for lost youth colored their recollections, and the pioneer period became a golden age marked by youthful simplicity, virtue, and happiness. As writers contemplated the present, they noted subtle signs of decline. First of all, their ranks were thinning. Every pioneer reunion mourned the passing of some of their number, while those who remained felt increasingly the burdens of old age. Although all acknowledged the material advances which had transformed the frontier, they pointed to the social complexity and the loss of character which seemed to have accompanied progress. Pioneer women noted the pretentiousness of the present and the lamentable spinelessness and artificiality of the young, although they were always careful to exclude their own children from such generalizations.

As women reflected on their early frontier experiences, it was evident that their own past behavior contrasted dramatically with that of the new generation. Had they not known it before, these women realized now how strong and successful they had been in meeting the challenges of frontier life. Of course, many had had little choice but to meet the challenges. They did not stress their lack of options but their heroism. As one writer described a woman giving birth on the overland trail, she typically concluded, "Think of the women now who have a doctor, a trained nurse and a girl in the kitchen and then do not do as well."

Even if the past seemed golden, it was impossible to reject the present altogether. For had not women helped to create it? Those who refused to romanticize the past looked back with surprise at their life so many years before. "It all seems like a far away dream to me now," one wrote. "I don't know how I stood it and how I was satisfied. I suppose it was because I was young and we lived almost altogether in the future. It never came home to me till afterward how poor and desolate our home was." These recollections emphasized the hardships and privations of frontier life. Had they known what lay in store, some admitted, they would not have set out so lightheartedly so many years before. Although they remembered the pioneer period with distaste, these women also described themselves as courageous and brave. They had been not weak but strong; they had been not passive but active. They had triumphed over frontier conditions heroically. "The true pioneer combines every element of the hero," announced a speaker at an Iowa Pioneer Reunion in 1885. His listeners agreed. Whether the past had been the best time of all or the worst, women knew that they had been at their best.

Although some of the women felt ambivalent about the nature of the society they had worked to create, and the social changes which they saw around them, the blame was not theirs. None thought to reject the civilizing mission they assumed they had consciously performed. Women's recollections highlighted their efforts to establish orderly family life in the wilderness and expanded on their contributions to early community life. Women, an address to Iowa pioneers pointed out, had "helped to make the settlement a success. They brought the bible with them and organized the Sunday school. They were superintendent and teacher, and with their women's work assisted in building the school houses and the churches, and in laying the foundations of civilized society. And they laid the foundations of society better than they knew."

If women insisted on their strength and heroism, then, it was not because strength and heroism had inspired them to carve out new goals but because they had helped women to complete their given mission. If the present was different from what they had expected, they were still proud. Despite the references to decadence, recollections often end by describing a thriving and changing community and the progress of husband, children, and grandchildren. If proof were needed of pioneer women's accomplishments, it was available. Phoebe Judson's reminiscences made the point which so many others echo. "After all the trials and hardships that have been our lot while journeying through the wilderness, I would not exchange my 'buried' life, as it has been called, for the 'wear and tear' of the fashionable society woman who must fulfill her social obligations, with no fruit to show as the result of her hard labor."

Bibliography

A good deal of the time spent in researching this book was devoted to studying pioneer women's documents. Many of their journals, reminiscences, and letters are still unpublished; some were printed in limited quantities and are now rare items. It is, therefore, especially difficult to do without footnotes. Since this book is intended for the general reader rather than the scholar, however, I will merely enumerate the most important published works which I consulted and cite the locations of the collections which proved most helpful in my work. Those who are interested in exploring women's experience on the frontier will be able to start with the published works mentioned here and will find a wealth of material in the following repositories.

The Western collection at the Bancroft Library, University of California at Berkeley, is justifiably famous. There are large numbers of overland trail diaries deposited there and interesting transcriptions of interviews with pioneer women done late in the nineteenth century. The Henry E. Huntington Library collections in Pasadena, California, were useful, although at the time I used them, they were poorly catalogued for anyone interested in women's history. Manuscript and rare-book holdings at the Beinecke Library, Yale University; the Schlesinger Library, Radcliffe College; the Milton Eisenhower Library, Johns Hopkins University; Stanford University; and at the Library of Congress proved valuable, as did the Western collections at the Newberry Library in Chicago. The archives at the University of Oregon in Eugene were particularly rich, and the archivist, Martin Schmitt, unfailingly courteous. The University of Washington's manuscript collection, while hardly as extensive as that at the University of Oregon, yielded additional information about the pioneer period in the Pacific Northwest. I also consulted records at the Society of California Pioneers, which proved to be disappointingly skimpy on women pioneers. The California Historical Society, the Oregon Historical Society, and the State Historical Society of Iowa yielded a wealth of information. The Iowa state archivist has done a superb job of cataloguing women's manuscripts, and it was a pleasure to work there. I also went to the Connecticut Historical Society to read the records of the Board of National Popular Education.

A general introduction to Western history, which makes little mention of women, however, is Ray Allen Billington's *American Frontier Heritage* (New York: Holt, Rinehart & Winston, 1966). Billington's account is influenced by Turner's thesis and stresses change on the frontier. His pamphlet *The American Frontier Thesis: Attack and Defense* (Washington: American Historical Association, 1971 ed.) gives a helpful summary of Turner's thought and the controversies it generated. Robert F. Berkhofer, Jr.'s "Space, Time, Culture and the New Frontier," *Agricultural History*, 38 (January 1964), pp. 21–30, deals with the issue of culture and persistence, as does Earl Pomeroy's article "Toward a Reorientation of Western History: Continuity and Environment," *Mississippi Valley Historical Review*, 40 (March 1955), pp. 579–600. Pomeroy's longer work, *The Pacific Slope: A History of California, Oregon, Washington, Idaho, Utah, and Nevada* (New York: Alfred A. Knopf, 1965) emphasizes the conservative nature of the westward movement. *The New Country: A Social History of the American Frontier, 1776–1890* (New York: Oxford University Press, 1974) by Richard A. Bartlett is a recent overview which makes a token, but not very important, effort to include women. Paula A. Treckel's "An Historiographical Essay: Women on the American Frontier," *The Old Northwest*, 1 (December 1975), pp. 339–404, summarizes the treatment pioneer women have received at the hands of historians. Lillian Schlissel's "Women's Diaries on the Western Frontier," *American Studies*, 18 (Spring 1977), pp. 87–100, Christine Stansell's "Women on the Great Plains 1865–1890," *Women's Studies*, 4 (1976), pp. 87–98, and Michael Fellman's "Julia

Louisa Lovejoy Goes West," *Western Humanities Review*, 39 (Summer 1977), pp. 227–42, begin to provide a corrective for the general omission of women's experience on the frontier and have proved helpful, although my interpretation differs in many respects from theirs.

Chapter 1

Mary P. Ryan's somewhat rambling but rich *Womanhood in America from Colonial Times to the Present* (New York: New Viewpoints, 1975) and Ann D. Gordon, Marie Jo Buhle, and Nancy E. Schrom, "Women in American Society: An Historical Contribution," *Radical America*, 5 (July–August 1971), pp. 3–66, give a broad view of American women's historical experience, while John Demos's "The American Family in Past Time," *American Scholar*, 43 (Summer 1974), pp. 422–46, focuses on the family. Studies of the status of women in the early nineteenth century include Nancy F. Cott's excellent book *The Bonds of Womanhood: "Woman's Sphere" in New England, 1780–1835* (New Haven: Yale University Press, 1977) and Nancy Osterud's "Sarah Josepha Hale: A Study in the History of Women in 19th-Century America" (Radcliffe College, unpublished honors thesis, 1971). Caroll Smith-Rosenberg has written an important article on the close emotional relationships women routinely formed with one another, "The Female World of Love and Ritual: Relations Between Women in 19th-Century America," *Signs*, 1 (Fall 1975), pp. 1–29. Anne Firor Scott in *The Southern Lady: From Pedestal to Politics, 1830–1930* (Chicago: University of Chicago Press, 1970) illustrates the power of domestic ideology in the South. Other stimulating work on women in the first half of the nineteenth century includes Ronald W. Hogeland, " 'The Female Appendage': Feminine Life-Styles in America, 1820–1861," *Civil War History*, 17 (June 1971), pp. 101–14; Barbara Welter, "Anti-Intellectualism and the American Woman: 1800–1860," *Mid-America*, 48 (October 1966), pp. 258–70; John C. Ruoff, "Frivolity to Consumption: Or Southern Women in Antebellum Literature," *Civil War History*, 18 (September 1972), pp. 213–29; Glenda Gates Riley, "The Subtle Subversion: Changes in the Traditionalist Image of the American Woman," *Historian*, 32 (February 1970), pp. 210–27; and Charles E. Rosenberg, "Sexuality, Class and Role in 19th-Century America,"

American Quarterly, 25 (May 1973), pp. 131–53. Keith Melder discusses women's voluntary organizations in "Ladies Bountiful: Organized Women's Benevolence in Early 19th-Century America," *New York History*, 48 (July 1967), pp. 231–54. Kathryn Kish Sklar's fine biography of Catherine Beecher, *Catherine Beecher: A Study in American Domesticity* (New Haven: Yale University Press, 1973), is essential not only for an understanding of this remarkable woman but also for an understanding of the ideology about woman's place which emerged in the first half of the nineteenth century. Joan N. Burstyn's "Catherine Beecher and the Education of American Women," *New England Quarterly*, 47 (September 1974), pp. 386–403, supplements Sklar's work. Ruth Miller Elson's *Guardians of Tradition: American Schoolbooks of the 19th Century* (Lincoln: University of Nebraska Press, 1964) suggests how widespread views of woman's place were while B. M. Stearns, "Early Western Magazines for Ladies," *Mississippi Valley Historical Review*, 18 (December 1931), pp. 319–30, and David Donald and Frederick A. Palmer, "Towards a Western Literature, 1820–1860," *Mississippi Valley Historical Review*, 35 (December 1948), pp. 413–28, show how quickly the publishing industry followed the move west.

Richard Slotkin's *Regeneration Through Violence: The Mythology of the American Frontier, 1600–1860* (Middletown: Wesleyan University Press, 1973) treats the Boone legend in detail. Helen B. Kroll's "The Books That Enlightened the Emigrants," *Oregon Historical Quarterly*, 45 (June 1944), pp. 103–23, describes emigrant guidebooks. Some of these, like Lansford Hastings, *The Emigrants' Guide to Oregon and California* (New York: Da Capo Press, 1969), and Joseph E. Ware, *The Emigrants' Guide to California* (Princeton: Princeton University Press, 1932), have been reprinted and are available in many libraries. Roy Harvey Pearce, "The Signs of the Captivity Narrative," *American Literature*, 19 (March 1947), pp. 1–20, and David T. Haberly, "Women and the Indians: *The Last of the Mohicans* and the Captivity Tradition," *American Quarterly*, 28 (Fall 1976), pp. 431–43, explore the captivity tales. Stories written by and for women about Western life are sprinkled through the pages of *Godey's Lady's Book*. Caroline M. Kirkland's accounts of Western life, including *A New Home—Who'll Follow? Or Glimpses of Western Life* (New York: L. S. Frarars, 1830) and Lydia H. Sigourney's *The Western Home and Other Poems* (Philadelphia: Parry & McMillan,

1854) are also good primary sources. Secondary sources include Randal V. Mills's "Emerson Bennett's Two Oregon Novels," *Oregon Historical Quarterly*, 41 (December 1940), pp. 367–81, and Mary Kelley's "The Unconscious Rebel: Studies in Feminine Fiction, 1820–1880" (University of Iowa, unpublished Ph.D. thesis, 1974).

Chapter 2

Historians have recently begun to study and analyze women over-land emigrants. John Faraghar and Christine Stansell's article "Women and Their Families on the Overland Trail to California and Oregon, 1842–1867," *Feminist Studies*, 2 (1975), pp. 150–66, pro-vides a valuable introduction to women's experience but offers a different interpretation than the one presented here. Also useful are Robert L. Munkres, "Wives, Mothers, Daughters: Women's Life on the Road West," *Annals of Wyoming*, 42 (October 1970), pp. 191–224; Ruth Barnes Moynihan, "Children and Young People on the Overland Trail," *Western Historical Quarterly*, 6 (July 1975), pp. 279–94; and Georgia Willis Read, "Women and Children on the Oregon-Trail in the Gold-Rush Years," *Missouri Historical Review*, 39 (October 1944), pp. 1–23. Unpublished, but available on micro-film, are John Faraghar's "Midwestern Families in Motion: Women and Men on the Overland Trail to Oregon and California, 1843–1870 (Yale University, unpublished Ph.D. thesis, 1977); Michael B. Hus-band's "To Oregon in 1843: The Backgrounds and Organization of the 'Great Migration'" (University of New Mexico, unpublished Ph.D. thesis, 1970); and John D. Unruh, "The Plains Across: The Overland Emigrants and the Trans-Mississippi West, 1840–1860 (University of Kansas, unpublished Ph.D. thesis, 1975). Unpublished materials by Amy Kesselman (available at the Oregon Historical So-ciety), John Faraghar, and Howard Lamar were provocative and helpful.

There are a number of women's trail diaries and reminiscences in print. Not all the unpublished material is as vivid as the following accounts: Lavinia Honeyman Porter, *By Ox Team to California: A Narrative of Crossing the Plains in 1860* (Oakland: Oakland Enquirer Publishing Co., 1910); Mary Jane Hayden, *Pioneer Days* (San Jose: Murgotten's Press, 1915); Lodisa Frizzell, *Across the Plains to Cali-fornia in 1852* (New York: New York Public Library, 1915); Margaret M. Hecox, *California Caravan: The 1845 Overland Trail Memoir of Margaret M. Hecox* (San Jose: Harlan-Young Press, 1966); Agnes Ruth Sengstacken, *Destination: West!* (Portland: Binsfords & Mort, Pubs., 1942); Phoebe Goodell Judson, *A Pioneer's Search for an Ideal Home* (Tacoma: Washington State Historical Society, 1966); Mary Ringo, *The Journal of Mrs. Mary Ringo* (Santa Ana: privately printed, 1956); Harriet Scott Palmer, *Crossing Over the Great Plains by Ox-Wagons* (no place, no publisher, no date); Miriam Davis Colt, *A Heroine of the Frontier* (Cedar Rapids: privately printed, 1941); Lucy Rutledge Cooke, *Crossing the Plains in 1852* (Modesto: privately printed, 1923); Julia Archibald Holmes, *A Bloomer Girl on Pike's Peak* (Denver: Denver Public Library, 1949); Sarah J. Cummins, *Autobiography and Reminiscences* (La Grande: La Grande Printing Co., 1914); Elizabeth Lord, *Reminiscences of Eastern Oregon* (Portland: Irwin-Hudson Co., 1903); Luzena Stanley Wilson, *Luzena Stanley Wilson: '49er* (Mills College: Eucalyptus Press, 1937); Emma Shepard Hill, *A Dangerous Crossing and What Happened on the Other Side* (Denver: Smith-Brooks, 1914); and Mary E. Ackley, *Crossing the Plains and Early Days in California's Golden Age* (San Francisco: privately printed, 1928). Still other primary sources can be found in journals: "Diary of Mrs. Elizabeth Dixon Smith Geer," *Oregon Pioneer Association Transactions*, 35 (1907), pp. 153–79; "Diary of Mrs. Amelia Stewart Knight, An Oregon Pioneer of 1853," *Oregon Pioneer Association Transactions*, 56 (1928), pp. 38–53; "Diary of Asahel Munger and Wife," *Oregon Historical Quarterly*, 8 (December 1907), pp. 387–405; "Diary of a Trip Across the Plains in 1863," *Oregon Pioneer Association Transactions*, 47 (1919), pp. 178–226; "Diary of Maria Parsons Belshaw, 1853," *Oregon Historical Quarterly*, 33 (December 1932), pp. 318–33; "Diary of Celina E. Hines," *Oregon Pioneer Association Transactions*, 46 (1918), pp. 69–125; "Overland by Ox-train in 1870: The Diary of Maria Hargrave Shrode," *Quarterly of Historical Society of Southern California*, 26 (March 1944), pp. 9–37; "Diary of Mrs. Cornelia A. Sharp: Crossing the Plains from Missouri to Oregon in 1852," *Oregon Pioneer Association Transactions*, 30 (1902), pp. 171–88; "From Ithaca to Clatsop Plains: Miss. Ketcham's Journal of Travel," *Oregon Historical Quarterly*, 62 (September, December 1961), pp. 237–87, 337–402; "Iowa to California in 1862; The Journal of Jane Holbrook Gould," *Annals of Iowa*, 37,

38 (Fall 1964 and Winter, Spring, and Summer 1965), pp. 460–76, 544–59, 623–40, 68–75; "Crossing the Plains in 1852, Mrs. Cecilia Emily McMillen Adams," *Oregon Pioneer Association Transactions*, 32 (1904), pp. 288–329.

Those interested in emigration songs might look at John Anthony Scott, *The Ballads of America: The History of the United States in Song and Story* (New York: Bantam Books, Inc., 1966); Harold W. Thompson, *A Pioneer Songster: Texts from the Stevens-Douglass Manuscript of Western New York 1841–1856* (Ithaca: Cornell University Press, 1958); and John A. Stone *et al.*, *The Pacific Song Book: Containing All the Songs of the Pacific Coast and California* (San Francisco: D. E. Appleton, 1861).

Katheryn Kish Sklar's *Catherine Beecher*, cited earlier, gives an account of Beecher's efforts to send young teachers to the West. Missionary wives have been virtually neglected, although their husbands have had better luck. Background material may be gleaned from Colin Brummitt Goodykoontz's *Home Missions on the American Frontier with Particular Reference to the American Home Mission Society* (Caldwell: The Caxton Printers, Ltd., 1939). R. Pierce Beaver's *All Loves Excelling* (Grand Rapids: William B. Eerdmans Pub. Co., 1968) focuses on women going to foreign missions, but the motivation of home missionaries was similar. Worth looking at is Janice Cessna Clarke's "Women of the Oregon Missions" (Reed College, unpublished seminar paper, 1963).

Chapter 3

Early life on the agricultural frontier is comprehensively treated in Gilbert C. Fite's *The Farmers' Frontier 1865–1900* (New York: Holt, Rinehart & Winston, 1966). Useful demographic profiles of frontier areas include George M. Blackburn and Sherman L. Richards, "A Demographic History of the West: Nueces County, Texas, 1850," *Prologue*, 4 (Spring 1972), pp. 3–20; William Bowen, "The Oregon Frontiersman: A Demographic View," in Thomas Vaughan (ed.), *The Western Shore: Oregon Country Essays Honoring the American Revolution* (Portland: Durham & Downey, 1975), pp. 181–97; David J. Wishart, "Age and Sex Composition of the Population of the Nebraska Frontier, 1860–1880," *Nebraska History*, 54 (Spring 1973), pp. 106–19; and Mary Anne Norman Smallwood, "Childhood on the

Southern Plains Frontier, 1870–1910" (Texas Tech., unpublished Ph.D. thesis, 1975). Rapid settlement patterns are discussed by David J. Wishart in "The Changing Position and Nature of the Frontier of Settlement on the Eastern Margins of the Central and Northern Great Plains 1854–1920" (University of Nebraska, Lincoln, unpublished Ph.D. thesis, 1968), and by Milton E. Holtz in "Early Settlement in Eastern Nebraska: A Case Study of Cass County" (University of Nebraska, Lincoln, unpublished M.A. thesis, 1964).

Wilson H. Grabill, Clyde V. Kiser, and Pascal K. Whelpton give an introduction to family size in *The Fertility of American Women* (New York: John Wiley & Sons, 1958). Linda Gordon's book, *Woman's Body, Woman's Right: A Social History of Birth Control in America* (New York: Grossman Publishers, 1976), is a must. Fertility patterns on the Midwestern frontier are the subject of John Modell's "Family Fertility on the Indiana Frontier, 1820," *American Quarterly*, 23 (December 1971), pp. 615–34, and James Edward Davis's "Demographic Characteristics of the American Frontier, 1800–1840" (University of Michigan, unpublished Ph.D. thesis, 1971). For case studies of the trans-Mississippi West, refer to Mildred Throne, "A Population Study of an Iowa County in 1850," *Iowa Journal of History*, 45 (October 1959), pp. 305–30; Seymour V. Connor, "A Statistical Review of the Settlement of the Peters Colony, 1841–1848," *Southwest Historical Quarterly*, 57 (July 1953), pp. 38–64; Blaine T. Williams, "The Frontier Family: Demographic Fact and Historical Myth," in Harold M. Hollingsworth and Sandra L. Myres (eds.), *Essays on the American West* (Arlington: University of Texas Press, 1969), pp. 40–65. Also important are Maris A. Vinovskis's "Socioeconomic Determinants of Interstate Fertility Differentials in the United States in 1850 and 1860," *Journal of Interdisciplinary History*, 6 (Winter 1976), pp. 375–96; and Richard A. Easterlin, "Factors in the Decline of Farm Family Fertility in the United States: Some Preliminary Research Results," *Journal of American History*, 63 (December 1964), pp. 600–14.

Earl Pomeroy discusses the different regional backgrounds of emigrants in *The Pacific Slope*, already cited. Raymond D. Gastil's "The Pacific Northwest as a Cultural Region," *Pacific Northwest Quarterly*, 64 (October 1974), pp. 147–56, is also helpful.

Nancy Wilson Ross gave vignettes of a few important women's lives on the frontier in *Westward the Women* (New York: Alfred A.

Knopf, 1945). Plains frontierswomen are the subject of Una M. Brooks's "The Influence of the Pioneer Women Toward a Settled Social Life in the Llano Estacado" (West Texas State Teachers College, unpublished M.A. thesis, 1942). Among recent collections of primary sources are P. Richard Metcalf (ed.), *The American People on the Western Frontier* (West Haven: Pendulum Press, Inc., 1973); Christiane Fischer, *Let Them Speak for Themselves: Women in the American West, 1849–1900* (Hamden, Conn.: The Shoestring Press Inc., 1977); and C. Richard King (ed.), *Victorian Lady on the Texas Frontier: The Journal of Ann Raney Coleman* (Norman: University of Oklahoma Press, 1971).

Individual women's accounts of the early settlement period include the volumes by Sengstacken and Judson already cited; Mollie Sanford's lively journal, *Mollie: The Journal of Mollie Dorsey Sanford in Nebraska and Colorado Territories 1857–1866* (Lincoln: University of Nebraska, 1959); Mary Bennett Ritter, *More Than Gold in California, 1899–1933* (Berkeley: The Professional Press, 1933); Polly Jane Purcell, *Autobiography and Reminiscences of a Pioneer* (no place, no publisher, no date); Sarah Brewer-Bonebright, *Reminiscences of Newcastle, Iowa, 1848: A History of the Founding of Webster City, Iowa* (Des Moines: Historical Dept. of Iowa, 1921); and Elise Dubrich Isley, *Sunbonnet Days* (Caldwell: Caxton Printers Ltd., 1935). The two-volume collection of letters of Ephraim Adams and his wife, Elisabeth, provides material on many phases of Iowa frontier life, *A Collection of Letters* (Berkeley: Copy Centers of Berkeley, 1973, 1974).

The following primary sources have been published in various journals and are worth consulting: Maria Cable Cutting, "After Thoughts," *Oregon Historical Quarterly*, 63 (June–September 1962), pp. 237–41; "A Nebraska Homesteading Story—1872," *Nebraska History*, 12 (October–December 1929), pp. 377–98; "The Letters of Charles and Helen Wooster: The Problems of Settlement," *Nebraska History*, 46 (June 1965), pp. 121–37; "Mrs. Butler's 1853 Diary of Rogue River Valley," *Oregon Historical Quarterly*, 41 (December 1940), pp. 337–66; "Letters of John and Sarah Everett, 1854–1864: Miami County Pioneers," *Kansas Historical Quarterly*, 8 (February, May, August, November 1939), pp. 3–34, 143–74, 279–310, 350–83; "Diary of Col. and Mrs. I. N. Ebey," *Washington Historical Quarterly*, 7, 8 (July, October 1916, January 1917), pp. 239–46, 307–21,

40–62; "An Autobiography and a Reminiscence," *Annals of Iowa*, 37 (Spring 1964), pp. 241–60; "Pioneer Life in Palo Alto County, Memoirs of E. May Lacey Crowder," *Iowa Journal of History and Politics*, 46 (April 1948), pp. 156–98; "Private Journal of Mary Ann Owen Sims," *Arkansas Historical Quarterly*, 35 (Summer and Fall 1976), pp. 142–87, 261–91; "Two Letters by a Pioneer from Arkansas," *Oregon Historical Quarterly*, 45 (September 1944), pp. 228–37; "The Letters of Roselle Putnam," *Oregon Historical Quarterly*, 29 (September 1928), pp. 242–62; "The Reminiscences of Mrs. Dilue Harris," *Quarterly of the Texas State Historical Association*, 4, 7 (October and January 1901, January 1904), pp. 85–127, 155–89, 214–22. "The Letters of Ed Donnell, Nebraska Pioneer," *Nebraska History*, 41 (June 1960), pp. 123–52, give his candid views of marriage and married life while Rufus Rittenhouse tells of childhood in *Boyhood Life in Iowa Fifty Years Ago* (Dubuque: Charles B. Door, 1880). A midwife's experience is covered in "19th Century Midwife, Some Recollections," *Oregon Historical Quarterly*, 70 (March 1969), pp. 39–49.

Chapter 4

In addition to works dealing with frontier settlements cited in the section on chapter 3, the reader might refer to Frederick A. Shannon's *The Farmers' Frontier 1865–1900* (New York: Holt, Rinehart & Winston, 1966). The path-breaking book on the urban frontier is Richard Wade's *The Urban Frontier: The Rise of Western Cities, 1790–1830* (Cambridge: Harvard University Press, 1959). Gunther Barth deals with the rapid pace of urbanization on the frontier in *Instant Cities: Urbanization and the Rise of San Francisco and Denver* (New York: Oxford University Press, 1975). Studies of individual cities include Kenneth W. Wheeler's *To Wear a City's Crown: The Beginnings of Urban Growth in Texas, 1836–1865* (Cambridge: Harvard University Press, 1968), A. Theodore Brown's *Frontier Community: Kansas City to 1870* (Columbia, Mo.: University of Missouri Press, 1963). An overview is provided by Lawrence H. Larsen, *The Urban West at the End of the Frontier* (Lawrence: Regents Press of Kansas, 1978).

Rural mobility patterns are discussed in Throne's work and others mentioned in the bibliography for chapter 3 and in William L.

Bowers's "Crawford Township, 1850–1870: A Population Study of a Pioneer Community," *Iowa Journal of History*, 58 (January 1960), pp. 1–30. Social and economic inequalities are the subjects of Paul W. Gates's "Frontier Estate Builders and Farm Laborers," in Walker D. Wyman and Clifton B. Kroeber (eds.), *The Frontier in Perspective* (Madison: University of Wisconsin Press, 1957), pp. 143–63. Herbert T. Hoover gives a graphic picture of the poorer sort of pioneers and gives selections of letters in "John Milton Leeper: Pioneer Farmer," *Nebraska History*, 52 (Spring 1971), pp. 32–44.

Urban inequality and transiency are the subjects of William Grover Robbins's "The Far Western Frontier: Economic Opportunity and Social Democracy in Early Roseburg, Oregon" (University of Oregon, unpublished Ph.D. thesis, 1969) and the theme of two articles, "Community Conflict in Roseburg, Oregon, 1870–1885," *Journal of the West*, 12 (October 1973), pp. 618–32, and "Opportunity and Persistence in the Pacific Northwest: A Quantitative Study of Early Roseburg, Oregon," *Pacific Historical Review*, 39 (August 1970), pp. 279–96. Susan Jackson has treated Houston in "Movin' On: Mobility Through Houston in the 1850's," *Southwestern Historical Quarterly*, 81 (January 1978), pp. 251–82. For comparisons with the East, see Stephan Thernstrom, *The Other Bostonians: Poverty and Progress in the American Metropolis 1880–1970* (Cambridge: Harvard University Press, 1973). Mary C. Wright provides valuable information on women in Portland, Oregon, in "The World of Women: Portland, Oregon, 1860–1880" (Portland State University, unpublished M.A. thesis, 1973).

The part women played in establishing and staffing community institutions can be discovered in their reminiscences, letters, and journals. In addition, Wallace D. Farnham provides suggestive information on women's cultural role in "Religion as an Influence in Life and Thought: Jackson County, Oregon, 1860–1890" (University of Oregon, unpublished Ph.D. thesis, 1955). Richard M. Bernard and Maris A. Vinovskis examine Eastern teachers and establish the proportion of Massachusetts women who taught in "The Female School Teacher in Ante-Bellum Massachusetts," *Journal of Social History*, 10 (March 1977), pp. 332–45. It may be that the proportion of Western women teaching was similar to that in the East. Ruth A. Gallaher gives information on frontier wage discrimination in *The Legal and Political Status of Women in Iowa: An Historical Account of the*

Rights of Women in Iowa from 1838–1918 (Iowa City: State Historical Society of Iowa, 1918). See also Keith E. Melder, "Woman's High Calling: The Teaching Profession in America, 1830–1860," *American Studies*, 13 (Fall 1972), pp. 19–32; Wayne E. Fuller, "Country Schoolteaching on the Sod-House Frontier," *Arizona and the West*, 17 (Summer 1975), pp. 121–40; David Tyack, "The Tribe and the Common School: The District School in Ashland, Oregon in the 1860s," *Call Number* (Spring 1966), pp. 13–23; Barbara J. Finkelstein, "The Moral Dimensions of Pedagogy: Teaching Behavior in Popular Primary Schools in Nineteenth-Century America," *American Studies*, 15 (Fall 1974), pp. 79–89; and Joseph F. Kett, *Rites of Passage: Adolescence in America 1790 to the Present* (New York: Basic Books, Inc., 1977). Lillian Schlissel is studying working women in the West, and it is to be hoped that some of her conclusions will soon be in print.

Little has been done on women's role in the churches. Important background studies include T. Scott Miyakawa, *Protestants and Pioneers: Individualism and Conformity on the American Frontier* (Chicago: University of Chicago, 1964); Timothy L. Smith, *Revivalism and Social Reform in Mid-19th-Century America* (Nashville: Abingdon Press, 1957). Barbara Welter discusses women's growing importance in Protestantism in "The Feminization of American Religion, 1800–1860," in William L. O'Neill (ed.), *Insights and Parallels, Problems and Issues of American Social History* (Minneapolis: Burgess Publishing Co., 1973). Among primary sources written by women are "Ketturah Belknap's Chronicle of the Bellfountain Settlement," *Oregon Historical Quarterly*, 38 (September 1937), pp. 265–99; Mary W. Gaylord, *Life and Labors of Rev. Reuben Gaylord* (Omaha: Rees Printing Co., 1889); Mary M. Boardman, *Life and Labours of the Rev. W. E. Boardman* (New York: D. Appleton & Co., 1887); Lois L. Murray, *Incidents of Frontier Life* (Goshen, Indiana: Evangelical Methodist United Mennonite Publishing House, 1880); A. J. Marshall, *The Autobiography of Mrs. A. J. Marshall, Age 84 Years* (Pine Bluff, Arkansas: Adams-Wilson Printing Co., 1897); Ruth McKee (ed.), *Mary Richardson Walker; Her Book* (Caldwell: The Caxton Printers, Ltd., 1945); and "A Missionary's Wife Looks at Missouri: Letters of Julia Barbard Strong," *Missouri Historical Review*, 47 (July 1953), pp. 329–46. Ministers' letters and reminiscences also provide insights into women's work in the churches. See Ephraim Adams, *The Iowa Band* (Boston: Congregational Pub. Soc., 1870) ; John L. Dyer, *The Snow-Shoe Itinerant: An Autobiography of the Rev. John L. Dyer* (Cincinnati: Cranston & Stowe, 1890) ; Myron Eells, *Father Eells or the Results of Fifty-five Years of Missionary Labors in Washington and Oregon: A Biography of Rev. Cushing Eells* (Boston: Congregational Sunday-School and Pub. Soc., 1894) ; "Establishing a Church on the Kansas Frontier: The Letters of Rev. O. I. Woodford and His Sister Henrietta, 1857–1859," *Kansas Historical Review*, 37 (Summer 1971), pp. 153–91; "Diary of George H. Atkinson, DD.," *Oregon Historical Quarterly* (March–December 1939, March–June 1940), pp. 52–63, 168–87, 265–82, 341–61, 416–33, 288–304; "Correspondence of the Rev. Ezra Fisher," *Oregon Historical Quarterly*, 16, 17 (March, December 1915; March, December 1916), pp. 65–104, 277–310, 379–413, 55–76, 147–76, 267–339, 431–80; "American Home Missionary Society Letters from Iowa," *Annals of Iowa*, 37 (Summer and Fall 1963), pp. 45–76, 95–120. Unpublished letters from missionaries to the American Home Missionary Society are available on microfilm. A good analysis of the pattern of missionary careers is Peter French's "The Home Missionary in Oregon: Individual Failure and Organizational Success" (Reed College, unpublished B.A. thesis, 1968).

Church discipline is treated by Robert Norton Peters, "From Sect to Church: A Study in the Permutation of Methodism on the Oregon Frontier" (University of Washington, unpublished Ph.D. thesis, 1973). For an example of church records, see "Minutes West Union Baptist Church," *Oregon Historical Quarterly*, 36 (September, December 1935), pp. 247–62, 365–79.

Richard S. Alcorn points out the cultural influence of the small but permanent groups but in another location, in his article, "Leadership and Stability in Mid-19th-Century America: A Case Study of an Illinois Town," *Journal of American History*, 61 (December 1974), pp. 685–702. As for like-minded later settlers, see James C. Malin, "Kansas: Some Reflections on Culture Inheritance and Originality," *Midcontinental American Studies Journal*, 2 (Fall 1961), pp. 3–19, and Dorothy O. Johansen, "A Working Hypothesis for the Study of Migrations," *Pacific Historical Review*, 36 (February 1967), pp. 1–12. Don Harrison Doyle's "Social Theory and New Communities in 19th-Century America," *Western Historical Quarterly*, 8 (April 1977), pp. 151–65, emphasizes the tension between disintegrating and stabil-

izing factors in early communities while his article, "The Social Functions of Voluntary Associations in a 19th-Century Town," *Social
Science History*, 1 (Spring 1977), pp. 333–55, shows how voluntary
associations helped to tie communities together.

Beverly J. Stoeltje describes images of women on the frontier in
" 'A Helpmate for Man Indeed,' The Image of the Frontier Woman,"
Journal of American Folklore, 88 (January–March 1975), pp. 25–41.

Chapter 5

The dramatic events of the gold rush and subsequent mining
frontiers have produced a rich historical literature, and only a few
of the works can be mentioned here. Among helpful general studies
of the mining frontier and the life which flourished are Rodman Wilson Paul, *Mining Frontiers of the Far West* (New York: Holt, Rinehart & Winston, 1963) ; John Walton Caughey, *Gold Is the Corner-
stone* (Berkeley and Los Angeles: University of California Press,
1948) ; W. Turrentine Jackson, *Treasure Hill: Portrait of a Silver
Mining Camp* (Tucson: The University of Arizona Press, 1963) ;
Duane A. Smith, *Rocky Mountain Mining Camps: The Urban
Frontier* (Bloomington: Indiana University Press, 1967) ; and Vardis
Fisher and Opal Laurel Holmes, *Gold Rushes and Mining Camps of
the Early American West* (Caldwell: Caxton Printers Ltd., 1968).
Two broad studies which assess the impact of the gold rush on Cali-
fornia's development are David Lavender, *California: Land of New
Beginnings* (New York: Harper & Row, 1972), and Kevin Starr,
Americans and the California Dream, 1850–1915 (New York: Oxford
University Press, 1973). Examinations of specific aspects of frontier
life include Ralph Emerson Mann's important dissertation "The
Social and Political Structure of Two California Mining Towns,
1850–1870" (Stanford University, unpublished Ph.D. thesis, 1971),
as well as his short article, "The Decade After the Gold Rush: Social
Structure in Grass Valley and Nevada City, California, 1850–1860,"
Pacific Historical Review, 41 (November 1972), pp. 484–504, Lyle
Allen Schwarz's "Theater on the Gold Frontier: A Cultural Study
of Five Northwest Mining Towns, 1860–1870" (Washington State
University, unpublished Ph.D. thesis, 1975), Georges Sabagh's "A
Critical Analysis of California Population Statistics with Special Ref-
erence to Census Data: 1850–1870" (University of California, Berke-

ley, unpublished M.A. thesis, 1941); William Francis Hanchett's "Religion and the Gold Rush, 1849–1854: The Christian Churches in the California Mines" (University of California, unpublished Ph.D. thesis, 1952); his article, "The Question of Religion and the Taming of California, 1849–1854," *California Historical Quarterly*, 32 (March, June 1953), pp. 49–56, 119–44; Alice Cowan Cochran's "Miners, Merchants, and Missionaries: The Role of Missionaries and Pioneer Churches in the Colorado Gold Rush and Its Aftermath, 1858–1870" (Southern Methodist University, unpublished Ph.D. thesis, 1975); and Lynn I. Perrigo's "Law and Order in Early Colorado Mining Camps," *Journal of American History*, 28 (June 1941), pp. 41–62. A very good study of San Francisco which considers early female residents is Roger W. Lotchin's *San Francisco 1846–1856: From Hamlet to City* (New York: Oxford University Press, 1974).

Eliza W. Farnham raised the question of how women would fare in California in *California, Indoors and Out; Or How We Farm, Mine, and Live Generally in the Golden State* (New York: Dix, Edwards & Co., 1856). Elisabeth Margo answered Farnham's question and provided a useful analysis for this study in her *Taming the Forty-Niner* (New York: Rinehart & Co., 1955). The primary sources for the mining frontier are rich, and many of them have been published. Luzena Wilson's recollections, cited earlier, give a vivid picture of her early life in California. Louise Amelia Knapp Clappe's *The Shirley Letters from the California Mines, 1851–1852* (New York: Alfred A. Knopf, 1949); Anna Lee Marston's (ed.) *Records of a California Family: Journals and Letters of Lewis C. Gunn and Elizabeth Le Breton Gunn* (San Diego: no publisher, 1928); Mary Jane Megquier's *Apron Full of Gold: The Letters of Mary Jane Megquier from San Francisco, 1849–1856* (San Marino: The Huntington Library, 1949); Mary M. Mathews's *Ten Years in Nevada: Or Life on the Pacific Coast* (Buffalo: Baker, Jones & Co., 1880); Sarah Royce's *A Frontier Lady: Recollections of the Gold Rush and Early California* (New Haven: Yale University Press, 1932) record the impressions of some women, mostly from New England, of mining life, as does "A Literate Woman in the Mines: The Diary of Rachel Haskell," *Journal of American History*, 31 (June 1944), pp. 81–98. Other useful primary collections include Bianca Morse Frederico and Myrtle Brown (eds.), *Gold Rush: The Letters of Joel and Ann Brown, 1852,*

1854–1855 (no place, privately printed, 1972); Dale L. Morgan and James R. Scobie (eds.), *Three Years in California: William Perkins' Journal of Life at Sonora, 1849–1852* (Berkeley and Los Angeles: University of California Press, 1964); *Gideon Lee Knapp and Augusta Murray Spring His Wife: Extracts from Letters and Journal* (New York: no publisher, 1909); Ledyard Frink (ed.), *Journal of the Adventures of a Party of California Gold-seekers* (Oakland: no publisher, 1897); Joseph Schafer (ed.), *California Letters of Lucius Fairchild* (Madison: State Historical Society of Wisconsin, 1931); Anthony and Allison Sirna (eds.), *The Wanderings of Edward Ely: A Mid-Nineteenth Century Seafarer's Diary* (New York: Hastings House, 1954); and Walker D. Wyman, *California Emigrant Letters* (New York: Bookman Assoc., Pubs., 1952).

Ministers have left vivid pictures of their battles on the mining frontier. D. S. Tuttle, *Reminiscences of a Missionary Bishop* (New York: Thomas Whittaker, 1906); William Taylor, *Seven Years' Street Preaching in San Francisco, California: Embracing Incidents, Triumphant Death Scenes, etc.* (New York: Carlton & Porter, 1857); S. H. Willey, *Thirty Years in California: A Contribution to the History of the State, from 1849 to 1879* (San Francisco: A. L. Bancroft & Co., 1879); and "Selected Letters of Osgood Church Wheeler," *California Historical Quarterly*, 27 (March, June, September, December 1948), pp. 9–18, 123–31, 229–36, 301–09, suggest that Protestant ministers, no matter what their denomination, viewed the mining frontier as a major challenge to morality and Christianity. The target of much of their anger, prostitution, has not yet received the kind of historical attention which it deserves. Jacqueline Baker Bernhart stresses the economic aspects of prostitution in "Working Women: Prostitution in San Francisco from the Gold Rush to 1900" (University of California, Santa Cruz, unpublished Ph.D. thesis, 1976), while Anne M. Butler highlights the hazards of the profession in "The Frontier Press and Prostitution: A Study of San Antonio, Tombstone, and Cheyenne" (University of Maryland, unpublished M.A. thesis, 1975). W. N. Davis, Jr.'s article points to the rich material on prostitution (and other aspects of mining society) contained in court records in "Research Uses of County Court Records, 1850–1879: An Incidental of Intimate Glimpses of California Life and Society," *California Historical Quarterly*, 52 (Fall and Winter 1973), pp. 241–66, 338–65.

The divorce question is treated by Nelson Manfred Blake in *The Road to Reno: A History of Divorce in the United States* (New York: Macmillan Co., 1962), by J. P. Lichtenberger in *Divorce: A Social Interpretation* (New York: McGraw-Hill Book Co., 1931), by William L. O'Neill in *Divorce in the Progressive Era* (New Haven: Yale University Press, 1967), and by Walter Francis Willcox in "The Divorce Problem: A Study in Statistics," *Studies in History, Economics and Public Law*, 1 (1891), pp. 9–89.

Chapter 6

The Mormon frontier is best understood in relation to other nineteenth-century utopian experiments. Rosabeth Moss Kanter's *Commitment and Community: Communes and Utopias in Sociological Perspective* (Cambridge: Harvard University Press, 1972) gives an excellent analysis of factors distinguishing successful attempts to establish a new and more perfect society. Raymond Lee Muncy's *Sex and Marriage in Utopian Communities: 19th Century America* (Bloomington: University of Indiana Press, 1973) provides little analysis but detailed descriptions of sexual arrangements in a number of nineteenth-century utopian settlements. Mark Holloway gives another overview in *Heavens on Earth: Utopian Communities in America, 1680–1880* (New York: Dover Pubs., Inc., 1966), as does Robert V. Hine in *California's Utopian Colonies* (San Marino: The Huntington Library, 1953). William Lawrence Foster's study "Between Two Worlds: The Origins of Shaker Celibacy, Oneida Community Complex Marriage, and Mormon Polygamy" (University of Chicago, unpublished Ph.D. thesis, 1976) suggests some of the linkages between the sexual arrangements of three different communities and is a provocative work. Studies of other utopian components of Mormon life include Ephraim Edward Ericksen, *The Psychological and Ethical Aspects of Mormon Group Life* (Salt Lake City: University of Utah Press, 1975); Gustive O. Larson, *Prelude to the Kingdom: Mormon Desert Conquest, a Chapter in American Cooperative Experience* (Francestown: Marshall Jones Co., 1947); William J. McNiff, *Heaven on Earth: A Planned Mormon Society* (Oxford: The Mississippi Valley Press, 1940); Edward J. Allen, *The Second United Order Among the Mormons* (New York: Columbia University Press, 1936); Leonard J. Arrington, "Orderville, Utah: A Pioneer Mormon

Experiment in Economic Organization," *Utah State Agricultural College Monograph Series*, 2 (March 1954), pp. 5–44; Hamilton Gardner, "Cooperation Among the Mormons," *Quarterly Journal of Economics*, 32 (May 1917), pp. 461–99; his "Communism Among the Mormons," *Quarterly Journal of Economics*, 37 (November 1933), pp. 134–74, and Joel Edward Ricks, "Forms and Methods of Early Mormon Settlement in Utah and the Surrounding Region, 1847–1877," *Utah State University Press Monograph Series*, 11 (January 1964), pp. 2–141. Also useful are Mario S. De Pillis's "The Quest for Religious Authority and the Rise of Mormonism," *Dialogue*, 1 (Spring 1966), pp. 68–88, and L. H. Kirkpatrick, "When a Bishop Was a Shepherd of His Flock," *Western Humanities Review*, 19 (Fall 1956), pp. 386–88.

Thomas F. O'Dea's *The Mormons* (Chicago: University of Chicago Press, 1957) sets the Mormon experience in religious perspective. Robert Bruce Flanders discusses early Mormon history in *Nauvoo: Kingdom on the Mississippi* (Urbana: University of Illinois Press, 1965). The story is continued in Stanley P. Hirshson's *The Lion of the Lord: A Biography of Brigham Young* (New York: Alfred A. Knopf, 1969); in Wallace Stegner's *The Gathering of Zion: The Story of the Mormon Trail* (New York: McGraw-Hill Book Co., 1964); in William Mulder's *Homeward to Zion: The Mormon Migration from Scandinavia* (Minneapolis: University of Minnesota Press, 1957); in Nels Anderson's *Desert Saints: The Mormon Frontier in Utah* (Chicago: University of Chicago Press, 1942); in Norman F. Furniss's *The Mormon Conflict 1850–1859* (New Haven: Yale University Press, 1960); in F. Mark McKiernan, Alma R. Blair, and Paul M. Edwards (eds.), *The Restoration Movement: Essays in Mormon History* (Lawrence: Coronado Press, 1973); and in Gustive O. Larson's *The "Americanization" of Utah for Statehood* (San Marino: The Huntington Library, 1971).

The bad press Mormons routinely received in the nineteenth century is treated by Leonard J. Arrington and Jon Haupt in "Intolerable Zion: The Image of Mormons in Nineteenth Century American Literature," *Western Humanities Review*, 22 (Summer 1968), pp. 243–60; Charles A. Cannon in "The Awesome Power of Sex: The Polemical Campaign Against Mormon Polygamy," *Pacific Historical Review*, 43 (February 1974), pp. 61–82; and Richard Olsen Cowan in "Mormonism in National Periodicals" (Stanford University, unpublished Ph.D. thesis, 1961). A few firsthand views of the Mormons are "A Lady's View of Utah and the Mormons, 1858: A Letter from the Governor's Wife," *Western Humanities Review*, 10 (Winter 1955–56), pp. 27–35; Elizabeth Wood Kane, *Twelve Mormon Visits in Succession on a Journey Through Utah to Arizona* (Salt Lake City: University of Utah Library, 1974); and Richard F. Burton, *The City of the Saints and Across the Rocky Mountains to California* (New York: Alfred A. Knopf, 1963).

The part women played on the Mormon frontier and the ways in which their religion affected the experience there have received some study. Leonard J. Arrington gives a general introduction in "Women as a Force in the History of Utah," *Utah Historical Quarterly*, 38 (Winter 1970), pp. 3–6, and "The Economic Role of Pioneer Mormon Women," *Western Humanities Review*, 9 (Spring 1955), pp. 145–64. Maureen Ursenbach Beecher has written two insightful but as yet unpublished papers, "Pioneer Women of the Mormon Frontier" and "Women's Work on the Mormon Frontier." Claudia Bushman (ed.), *Mormon Sisters: Women in Early Utah* (Cambridge: Emmeline Press Ltd., 1976), has some useful essays. Studies of two important women reveal a good deal of information about the pioneer period: Juanita Brooks, *Emma Lee* (Logan: Utah State Press, 1975) and Jill C. Mulvay, "The Liberal Shall Be Blessed: Sarah M. Kimball," *Utah Historical Quarterly*, 44 (Summer 1976), pp. 205–21. Lucile Johnson focuses on the Ladies Relief Society in "A Social Analysis of the L.D.S. Relief Society" (Utah State Agricultural College, unpublished M.S. thesis, 1950), while Keith Calvin Terry looks at medical women in "The Contribution of Medical Women During the First Fifty Years in Utah" (Brigham Young University, unpublished M.A. thesis, 1964).

Kimball Young's *Isn't One Wife Enough?* (New York: Henry Holt & Co., 1954) provides a lively introduction to polygamy and contains information collected from family and friends. The demographic impact of polygamy receives attention in James E. Smith and Phillip R. Kunz, "Polygyny and Fertility in Nineteenth-Century America," *Population Studies*, 30 (November 1976), pp. 465–80; Stanley S. Ivins, "Notes on Mormon Polygamy," *Western Humanities Review*, 10 (Summer 1956), pp. 229–39; and Dean L. May, "People on the Mormon Frontier: Kanab's Families of 1874," *Journal of Family History*, 1 (Winter 1976), pp. 169–92. An early tract on polygamy is the subject of Lawrence Foster's "A Little-Known Defense of Polygamy from the Mormon Press in 1842," *Dialogue*, 9 (1974), pp. 21–34. Studies which give some sense of women's experience in polygamy include Herbert Ray Larsen, " 'Familism' in Mormon Social Structure" (University of Utah, unpublished Ph.D. thesis, 1954); J. E. Hulett Jr., "Social Role and Personal Security in Mormon Polygamy," *American Journal of Sociology*, 45 (January 1940), pp. 542–53; Juanita Brooks, "A Close-Up of Polygamy," *Harpers Magazine*, 168 (February 1934), pp. 299–307; Mary Ann Hafen, *Recollections of a Handcart Pioneer of 1860* (Denver: privately printed, 1938); and Annie Clark Tanner, *A Mormon Mother: An Autobiography* (Salt Lake City: University of Utah Press, 1969). Gustive O. Larson points out that attempts to "liberate" Mormon women failed in "An Industrial Home for Polygamous Wives," *Utah Historical Quarterly*, 38 (Summer 1970), pp. 263–75.

The ways in which Mormonism contributed to women's self-awareness are apparent in Gail Farr Casterline's " 'In The Toils' or 'Onward for Zion': Images of the Mormon Woman, 1852–1890" (Utah State University, M.A. thesis, 1974) and Sherilyn Cox Bennion's "The *Woman's Exponent:* Forty-two Years of Speaking for Women," *Utah Historical Quarterly* (Summer 1967), pp. 222–39. Kathleen Marquis assesses the impact of traditional ideas of woman's sphere in " 'Diamond Cut Diamond': Mormon Women and the Cult of Domesticity in the 19th Century," *University of Michigan Papers in Women's Studies*, 2 (1974), pp. 105–23.

Chapter 7

The struggles involved in community growth are suggested by Don Harrison Doyle's "Social Theory and New Communities in 19th-Century America," *Western Historical Quarterly*, 8 (April 1977), pp. 151–65. Not much attention has been paid to women's charitable endeavors on the frontier, but Robert R. Dykstra's *The Cattle Towns* (New York: Alfred A. Knopf, 1968) is suggestive of the disruptive nature of some of these activities. Rowena Beams's *"Inasmuch . . .":* *The One Hundred Year History of the San Francisco Ladies' Protection and Relief Society 1853–1953* (San Francisco: James J. Gillick & Co., 1953) tells the story of one organization. Women's work in the temperance movement has attracted more interest than their charitable efforts. Ronald G. Walters in *American Reformers 1815–1860* (New York: Hill & Wang, 1978) devotes a chapter to the early nineteenth-century temperance movement, while Norman H. Clark in *Deliver Us from Evil: An Interpretation of American Prohibition* (New York: W. W. Norton & Co., 1976) gives a good overview of national efforts during the century. Studies of Western temperance activities at the state level include Gilman M. Ostrander, *The Prohibition Movement in California, 1848–1933* (Berkeley and Los Angeles: University of California Press, 1957); Norman H. Clark, *The Dry Years: Prohibition and Social Change in Washington* (Seattle: University of Washington Press, 1965); John E. Caswell, "The Prohibition Movement in Oregon, 1836–1904," *Oregon Historical Quarterly*, 39 (September 1938), pp. 235–61; and Malcolm H. Clark, Jr., "The War on Webfoot Saloon," *Oregon Historical Quarterly*, 58 (March 1957), pp. 48–62. Ross Evans Paulson's *Women's Suffrage and Prohibition: A Comparative Study of Equality and Social Control* (Glenview: Scott, Foresman & Co., 1973) sets the prohibition and suffrage movements in a comparative framework.

Abigail Scott Duniway tells a vivid if incomplete story of her suffrage battles in *Path Breaking: An Autobiographical History of the Equal Suffrage Movement in Pacific Coast States* (New York: Schocken Books, 1971). Eleanor Flexner's *Century of Struggle: The Women's Rights Movement in the United States* (Cambridge: Belknap Press, 1975) was one of the first studies of women's fight for the vote and is well worth reading. David Morgan gives a good overview of suffrage activities in *Suffragists and Democrats: The Politics of Woman Suffrage in America* (Michigan State University Press, 1972). Alan P. Grimes in *The Puritan Ethic and Woman Suffrage* (New York: Oxford University Press, 1967) emphasizes the conservatism of Western suffrage victories but should be balanced by Ellen Carol Du Bois's argument that suffrage had radical implications in *Feminism and Suffrage: The Emergence of an Independent Women's Movement in America: 1848–1869*. Studies of state battles include Dennis Anthony Fus, "Persuasion on the Plains: The Woman Suffrage Movement in Nebraska" (Indiana University, unpublished Ph.D. thesis, 1972); the following articles by T. A. Larson, "Dolls, Vassals, and Drudges—Pioneer Women in the West," *Western Historical Quarterly*, 3 (January 1972), pp. 5–16; "Women Suffrage in Wyoming," *Pacific Northwest Quarterly*, 56 (April 1965), pp. 57–

66; "The Woman's Rights Movement in Idaho," *Idaho Yesterdays*, 16 (Spring 1972), pp. 2–19; "The Woman Suffrage Movement in Washington," *Pacific Northwest Quarterly*, 67 (April 1976), pp. 49–62; "Montana Women and the Battle for the Ballot," *Montana, the Magazine of Western History*, 23 (January 1973), pp. 24–41; A. Elizabeth Taylor, "The Woman Suffrage Movement in Texas," *Journal of Southern History*, 17 (May 1951), pp. 194–215; her "The Woman Suffrage Movement in Arkansas," *Arkansas Historical Quarterly*, 15 (Spring 1956), pp. 17–52; Gordon Morris Bakken, "Voting Patterns in the Wyoming Constitutional Convention of 1889," *Annals of Wyoming*, 42 (October 1970), pp. 224–42; Billie Barnes Jensen, "Colorado Woman Suffrage Campaigns of the 1870's," *Journal of the West*, 12 (April 1973), pp. 254–71; and Nelson A. Ault, "The Earnest Ladies: The Walla Walla Woman's Club and the Equal Suffrage League of 1886–1889," *Pacific Northwest Quarterly*, 42 (April 1951), pp. 123–37. Ronald Schaffer gives an interesting profile of suffrage leaders in "The Problem of Consciousness in the Woman Suffrage Movement: A California Perspective," *Pacific Historical Review*, 45 (November 1976), pp. 469–94.

What Western educational opportunities meant for women has hardly been studied. Jill K. Conway raises some of the significant questions in "Perspectives in the History of Women's Education in the United States," *History of Education Quarterly*, 14 (Spring 1974), pp. 1–12. Ronald W. Hogeland points out that coeducation did not necessarily mean equal education in "Coeducation of the Sexes at Oberlin College," *Journal of Social History*, 6 (1972–73), pp. 160–76. A detailed but unfocused account of women's educational opportunities is provided by Thomas Woody in *A History of Women's Education in the United States* (New York: The Science Press, 1929). More analytical and concise is Mabel Newcomer's *A Century of Higher Education for American Women* (New York: Harper & Bros. Pubs., 1959).

Daniel Boorstin describes the local boosterism which led to the proliferation of colleges in the West in *The Americans: The National Experience* (New York: Random House, 1966). The religious impulse is the subject of Donald G. Tewksbury's *The Founding of American Colleges and Universities Before the Civil War with Particular Reference to the Religious Influences Bearing Upon the Col-*

lege Movement (New York: Teachers College, 1932); Bernard J. Kohlbrenner, "Religion and Higher Education: An Historical Perspective," *History of Education Quarterly*, 1 (June 1961), pp. 45–56; Natalie Naylor, "The Ante-Bellum College Movement: A Reappraisal of Tewksbury's Founding of American Colleges and Universities," *History of Education Quarterly*, 13 (Fall 1973), pp. 261–74; James Findlay, "The SPCTEW and Western Colleges: Religion and Higher Education in Mid-Nineteenth Century America," *History of Education Quarterly*, 17 (Spring 1977), pp. 31–62.

Other views of institutional growth and change are Frederick Rudolph, *The American College and University* (New York: Alfred A. Knopf, 1962); John S. Brubacher and Willis Rudy, *Higher Education in Transition: A History of American Colleges and Universities, 1630–1976* (New York: Harper & Row, 1976); Earle D. Ross, *Democracy's College: The Land-Grant Movement in the Formative State* (Ames: The Iowa State College Press, 1942); and Edward Danforth Eddy, Jr., *Colleges for Our Land and Time: The Land-Grant Idea in American Education* (New York: Harper and Bros., 1956). Although few of the following studies focus on women, their experience in coeducational environments can be extracted from William Warren Ferrier, *Ninety Years of Education in California, 1846–1936: A Presentation of Educational Movements and Their Outcomes in Education Today* (Oakland: West Coast Printing Co., 1937); Roy W. Cloud, *Education in California: Leaders, Organizations, and Accomplishments of the First Hundred Years* (Stanford: Stanford University Press, 1952); Michael McGiffert, *The Higher Learning in Colorado: An Historical Study, 1860–1940* (Denver: Sage Books, 1964); John Scholte Nollen, *Grinnell College* (Iowa City: The State Historical Society of Iowa, 1953); Robert E. Belding, "Iowa's Brave Model for Women's Education," *Annals of Iowa*, 43 (Summer 1976), pp. 342–48; Louise Molde Lex, "Mary Newbury Adams, Feminist Forerunner from Iowa," *Annals of Iowa*, 43 (Summer 1976), pp. 323–41; Clifford S. Griffen, *The University of Kansas: A History* (Lawrence: University Press of Kansas, 1974); Charles M. Gates, *The First Century at the University of Washington, 1861–1961* (Seattle: University of Washington Press, 1961); Edmond S. Meany, "Early Records of the University," *Washington Historical Quarterly*, 8 (April 1917), pp. 114–23; James Rood

Robertson, "Origin of Pacific University," *Oregon Historical Quarterly*, 6 (June 1905), pp. 109–46; and Henry D. Sheldon, *History of University of Oregon* (Portland: Binfords & Mort, Pubs., 1940).

Epilogue

In addition to the sources already listed, the following works were helpful in assessing how women evaluated their pioneer years: *Reports of Annual Reunions of the Old Settlers of Johnson County, 1866–1897* (no place, no publisher, no date); *Reminiscences of Oregon Pioneers* (Pendleton: East Oregonian Pub. Co., 1937); Abner Sylvester Baker, "The Oregon Pioneer Tradition in the 19th Century: A Study of Recollection and Self-Definition" (University of Oregon, unpublished Ph.D. thesis, 1968); and Valeda Katharine Wood, "The Life of the Pioneer Woman on the Kansas-Nebraska Frontier" (University of Nebraska, Lincoln, unpublished M.A. thesis, 1940).

INDEX

abortion, *see* birth control
activities, centers of, 80–1;
  leisure, 82–4; organizational,
  of women, 181–4, 186–9, 193;
  see also associations, female
  and politics
Adair, Mary Ann, 74
Adams, Elisabeth, 74, 86
Adams, Ellen Tompkins, 39, 42
Adams, Ephraim, 98
adultery, 143–4
agricultural frontier, xiv, 110;
  settlement of, 51–7, 59; women
  and, 59, 94, 114, 128, 140,
  183–4; growth of, 79–81, 85;
  social distinctions on, 80, 82;
  transient population of, 81–4;
  characteristics of, 82–3; *vs.*
  other frontiers, 82, 84, 111–12,
  154; background of inhabitants
  of, 111; locusts on, 183–4; *see*
  also farmers *and under items*
  throughout
Alameda, and drinking, 187–8
Allan, Augusta, 35
Allyn, Henry, 34

Alta, 116–17
Amana, Iowa, 150–1, 155
American Home Missionary
  Society, 130
American Lyceum, 12
Applegate, Rachel, 105
associations, female, 10–11, 13,
  79, 87, 159–61, 176–8; *see also*
  institutions *and* activities,
  organizational
Atkinson, Reverend, 98, 100, 104
Atwater, Maria, 92
Aurora, Oregon, 150–1

Ballou, Mary, 126
Beam, Almira, 69, 75
"Beauty Out West . . . ," 23
Beecher, Catherine, 5, 12–13, 34,
  79, 89–90
Belisle, Orvilla, 148
Belknap, Ketturah, 99
Belknap, Wilda, 70
Benson, Mrs. Ezra, 157
Bentley, Mary Ann, 173
Bethel, Missouri, 150–1

229